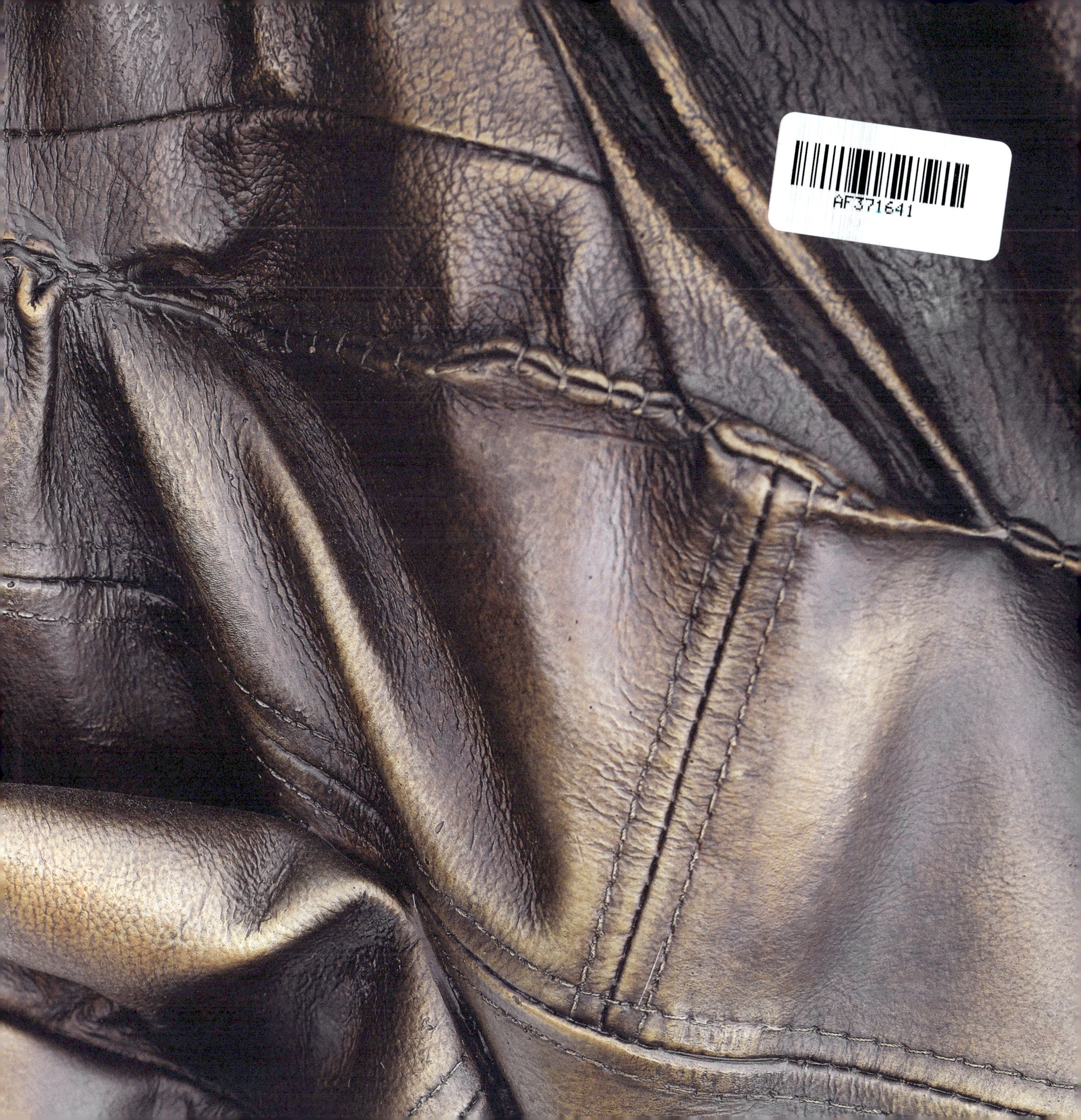

AF371641

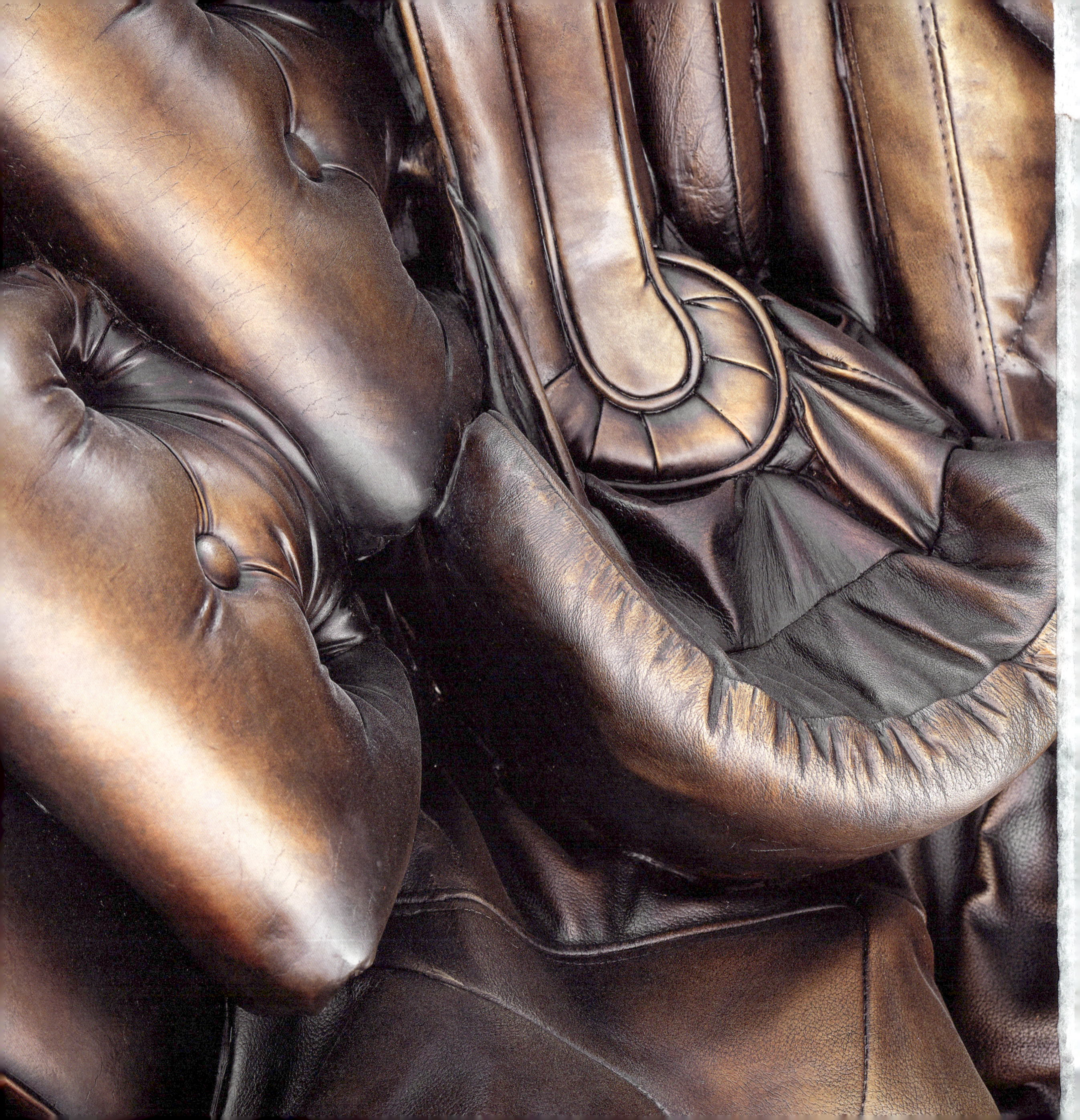

COUCH MONSTER:

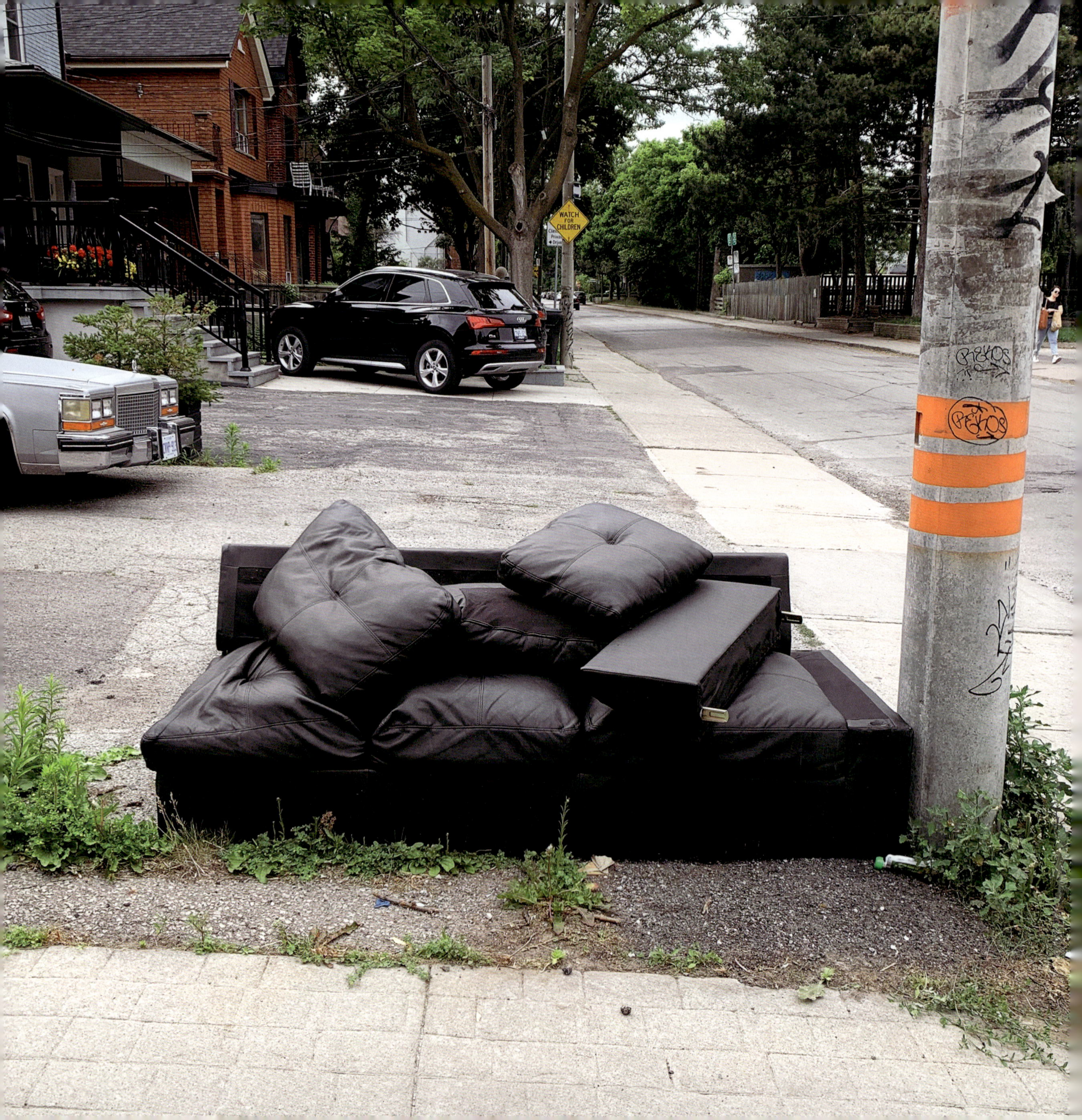

WATCH
FOR
CHILDREN

SADZĚ?
YAAGHĘHCH'ILL

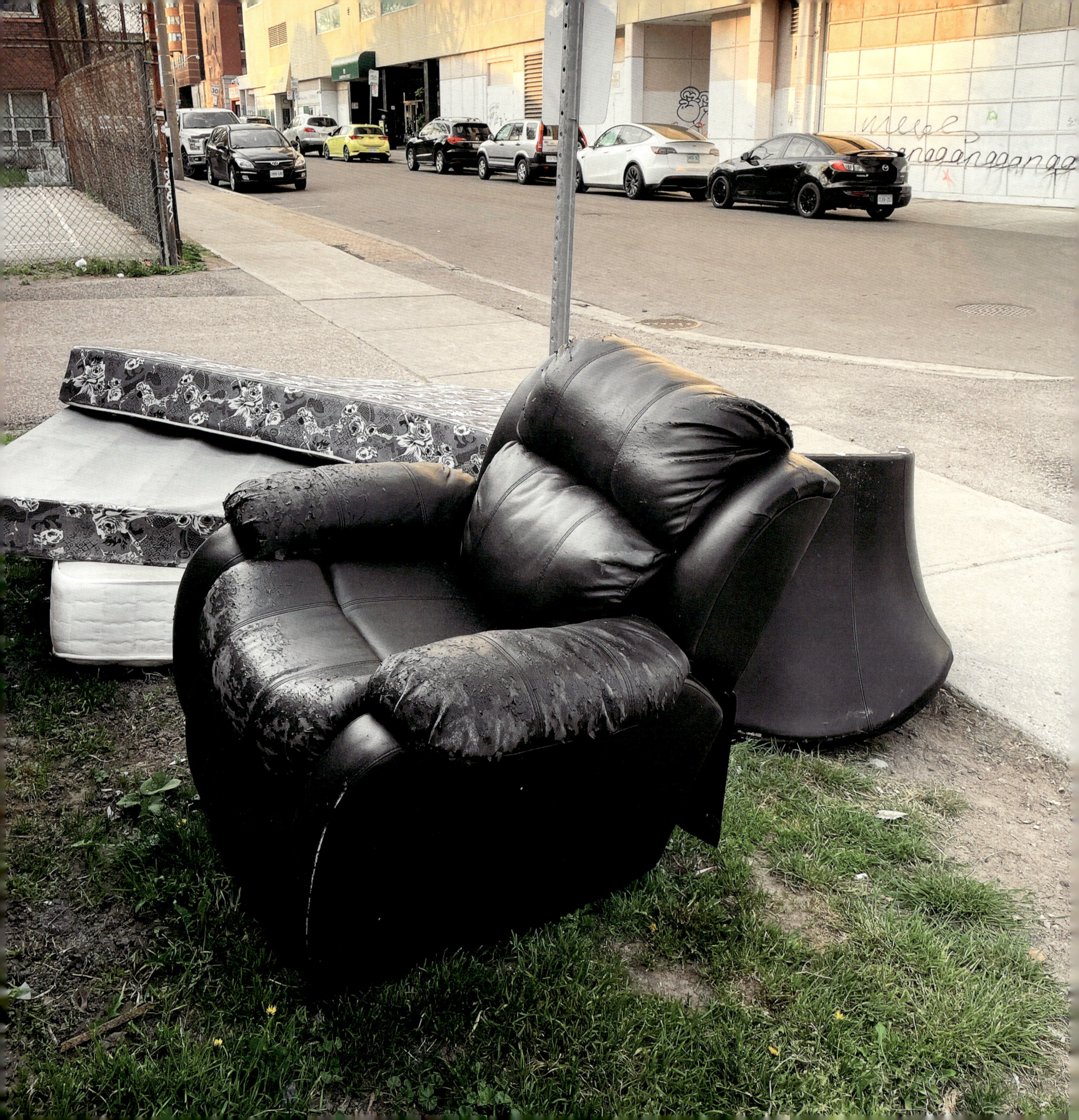

BRIAN JUNGEN

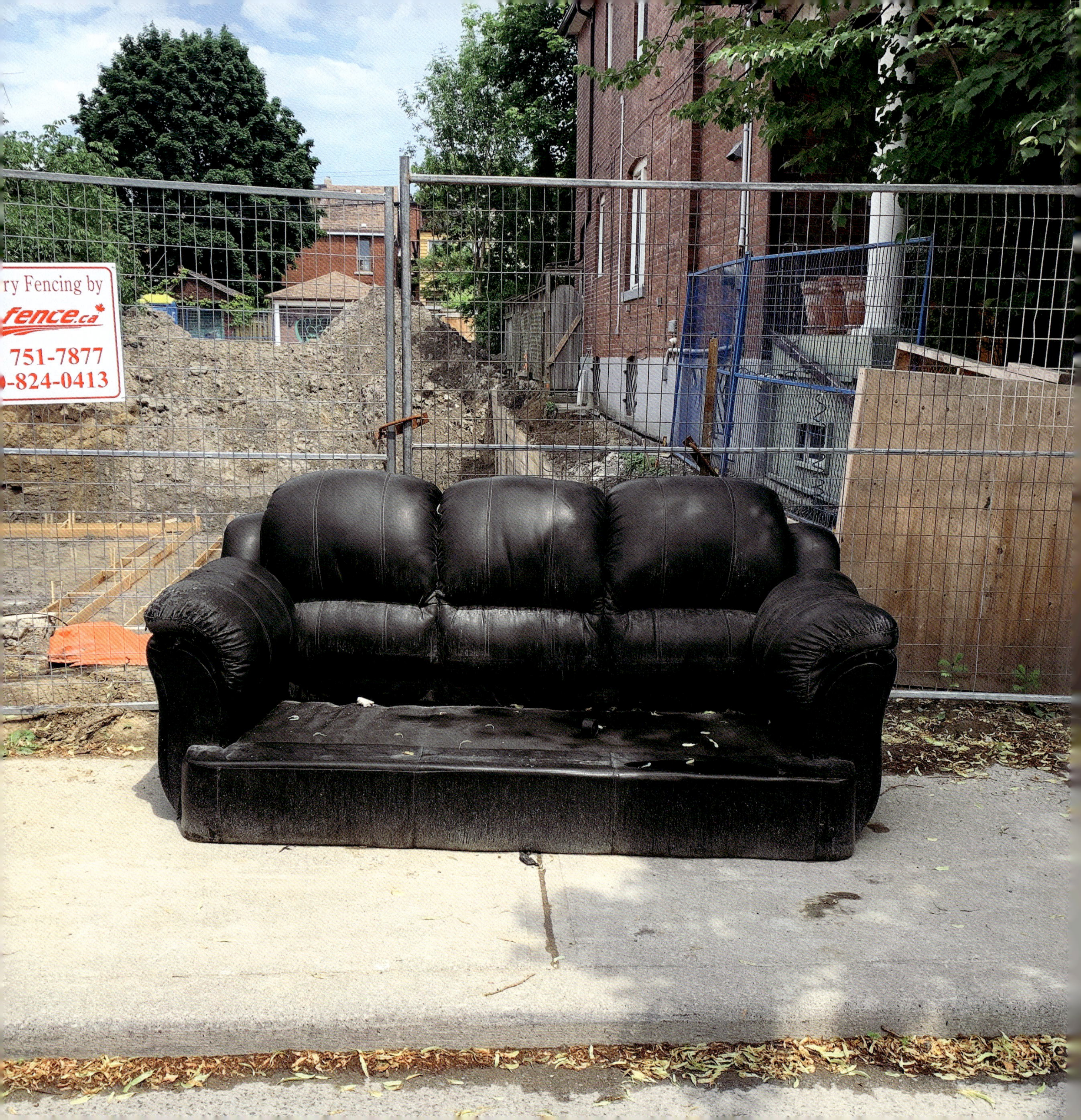
ry Fencing by
fence.ca
751-7877
0-824-0413

COUCH MONSTER: SADZĚ? YAAGHĘHCH'ILL

BRIAN JUNGEN

ART GALLERY OF ONTARIO
DELMONICO BOOKS • D.A.P. NEW YORK

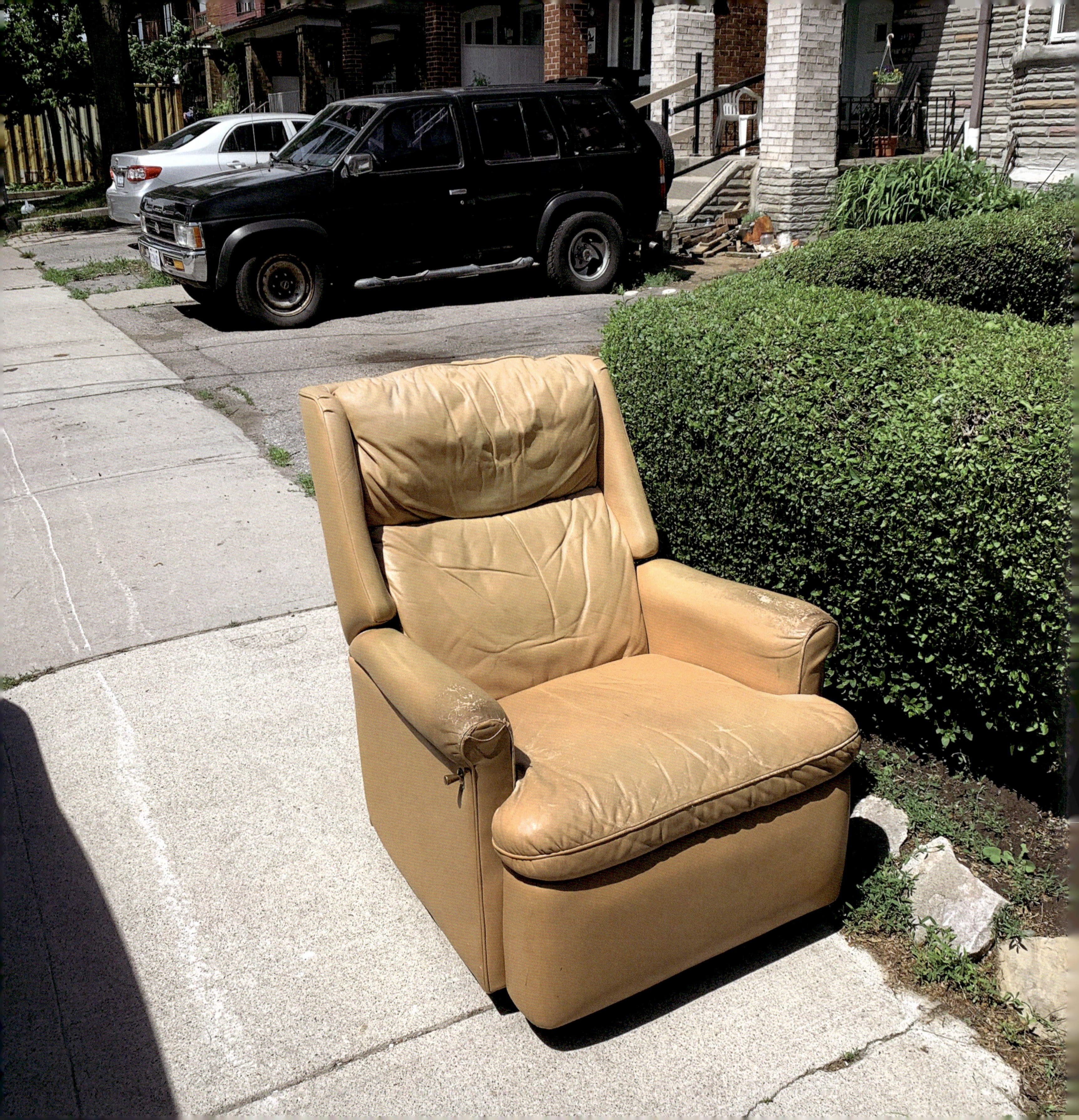

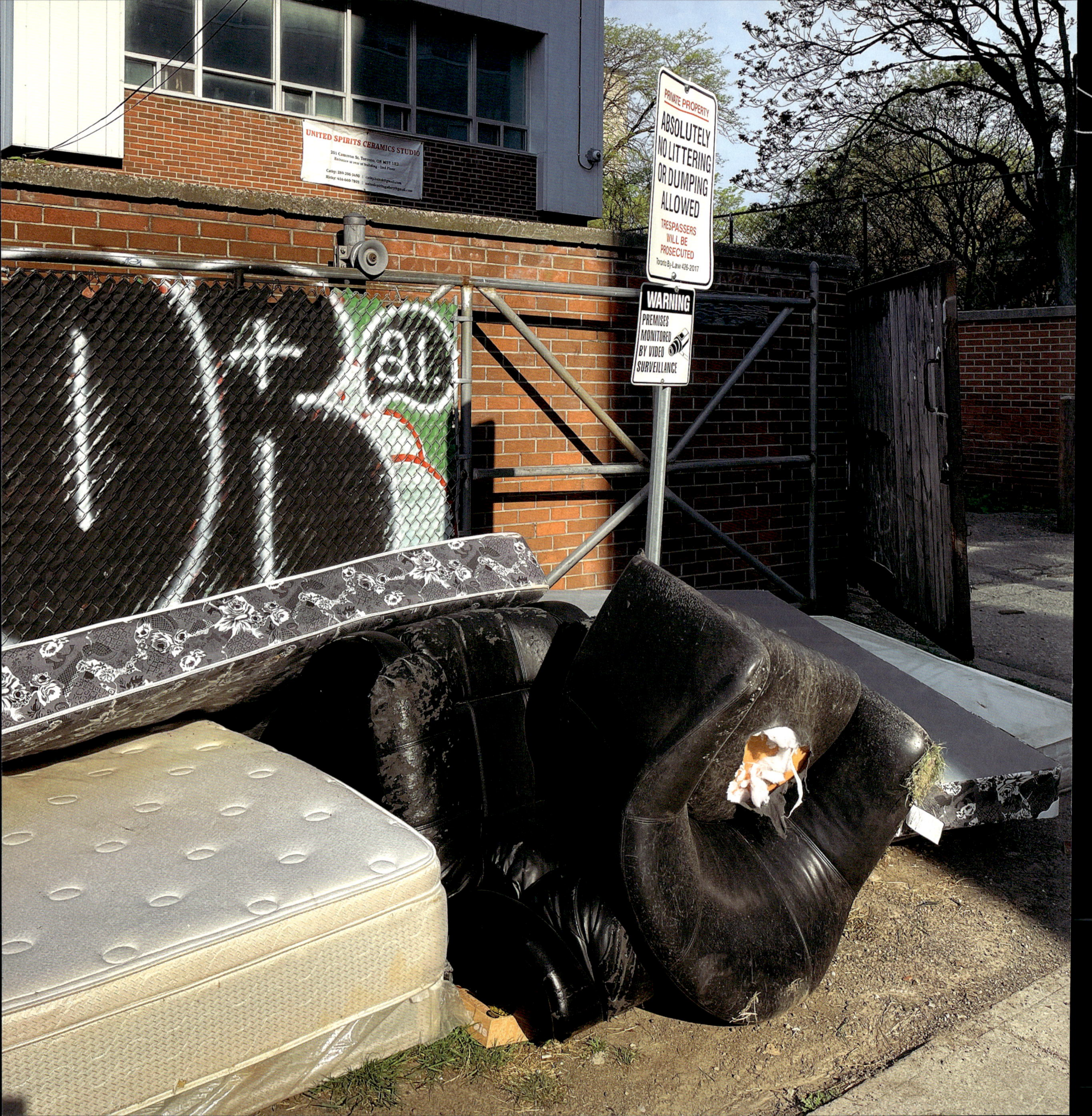

UNITED SPIRITS CERAMICS STUDIO
201 Cameron St. Toronto, ON M5T 1E2
Entrance at rear of building 2nd Floor
Cathy: 289-200-3450
Ricky: 416-660-7893
PRIVATE PROPERTY
ABSOLUTELY NO LITTERING OR DUMPING ALLOWED
TRESPASSERS WILL BE PROSECUTED
Toronto By-Law 426-2017
WARNING
PREMISES MONITORED BY VIDEO SURVEILLANCE

CONTENTS

Director's Foreword

On June 20, 2022, we were delighted to unveil the Art Gallery of Ontario's first-ever public art commission, a bronze sculpture by the contemporary artist Brian Jungen titled *Couch Monster: Sadzě? yaaghęhch'ill*. An ambitious collaboration several years in the making, the work now stands in front of the Gallery at the corner of Dundas and McCaul streets, taking over the space where Henry Moore's *Large Two Forms* held court between 1974 and 2016. (The Moore sculpture was relocated to Grange Park in June 2016, on the south side of the Gallery.) This large-scale piece began as a studio prototype made by piecing together carved-up leather couches; the bronze elephant is not only a fitting tribute to Moore, whose work Jungen has long admired, but also a feat of technical mastery in which the artist creates the illusion of the original model's plump leather cushions and textured folds.

When we began brainstorming ideas for the space, it was imperative that the commission meet three criteria: be conceived by a Canadian artist, be an extraordinary piece of art, and have instant recognizability for people passing the Gallery on foot or by streetcar. Kitty Scott, the AGO's former Carol and Morton Rapp Curator of Contemporary Art, chose Jungen and initiated the project. I am proud to say we met all three of those requirements. The commission was announced to the public during the closing days of *Brian Jungen: Friendship Centre*, the artist's momentous solo show in the AGO's Sam and Ayala Zacks Pavilion, in the summer of 2019.

Couch Monster: Sadzě? yaaghęhch'ill was inspired by the story of Jumbo, a circus elephant who was killed by a train in St. Thomas, Ontario, in 1885. For Jungen, who is of Swiss and Dane-zaa heritage, the title evokes the broken spirit of animals held captive for human entertainment; the Dane-zaa subtitle can be understood as "my heart is ripping." After finishing work on the sculpture at his property near Vernon, British Columbia, Jungen shipped it off to the Walla Walla Foundry in Washington State for bronze casting and final waxing in March 2020—though these plans were subject to significant change due to the challenges of the COVID-19 pandemic. We are extremely grateful to the staff at the Walla Walla Foundry, including President Jonathan Follett, Project Manager Matt Ryle, Project Coordinator Hannah Bartman, and the 105 technicians, who made truly Herculean efforts to realize Jungen's artistic vision and facilitate this remarkable venture under such unprecedented circumstances.

The AGO gratefully acknowledges the following funders for their exemplary support in bringing this commission to life: The Renette and David Berman Family Foundation, Charles Brindamour & Josée Letarte, Canada Council for the Arts's New Chapter program, Bob Dorrance & Gail Drummond, Angela &

David Feldman, the Government of Canada through the Federal Economic Development Agency for Southern Ontario (FedDev Ontario), Hal Jackman Foundation, Phil Lind & Ellen Roland, T.R. Meighen Family Foundation, Partners in Art, Paul & Jan Sabourin, and an anonymous donor. We are also grateful for the additional support of the Henry Moore Foundation. The AGO could not have accomplished this feat without all of our supporters' generous financial aid and belief in this ambitious vision. In addition, all of our exceptional public talks related to the commission are presented as part of ArtworxTO.

An undertaking of this scale would also not have been possible without the passionate stewardship and direction of the AGO's Deputy Director & Chief Curator, Julian Cox, who brought this complicated endeavour to fruition. Tremendous thanks as well to Adelina Vlas, the AGO's former Associate Curator of Contemporary Art, for pushing the project forward, along with Laura Comerford, Associate Director of Exhibitions, who oversaw the myriad details of production and installation. We are indebted to Jessica Bright, Chief, Exhibitions, Collections, & Conservation, and Iain Hoadley, General Manager, Logistics and Art Services, for their invaluable contributions to the scope of this endeavour (and to Total Transport Solutions for managing the extraordinary logistical demands), as well as to Project Manager Sarah Yaffe, Research Assistant Yasmin Nurming-Por, Curatorial Coordinator Debbie Johnsen, and Production Manager Malene Hjørngaard and her team. We also give massive thanks to Jim Shedden, Manager of Publishing, and his team, as well as designer Lauren Wickware, for this beautiful catalogue, which features great insights from Cox and Jungen. And we are profoundly grateful to our Development team, who demonstrated exceptional creativity and determination in generating support for this project.

The circumstances surrounding the creation of this sculpture meant that Jungen was separated from the work for more than two years, making its completion during the pandemic and grand unveiling in Toronto that much more meaningful. The commission speaks to the artist's desire to make his work accessible to everyone, and it is a great privilege to welcome visitors to our front door with such a powerful visual experience. At the end of the day, public art is for the public. We are honoured to be able to share this work.

Stephan Jost
Michael and Sonja Koerner Director, and CEO
Art Gallery of Ontario

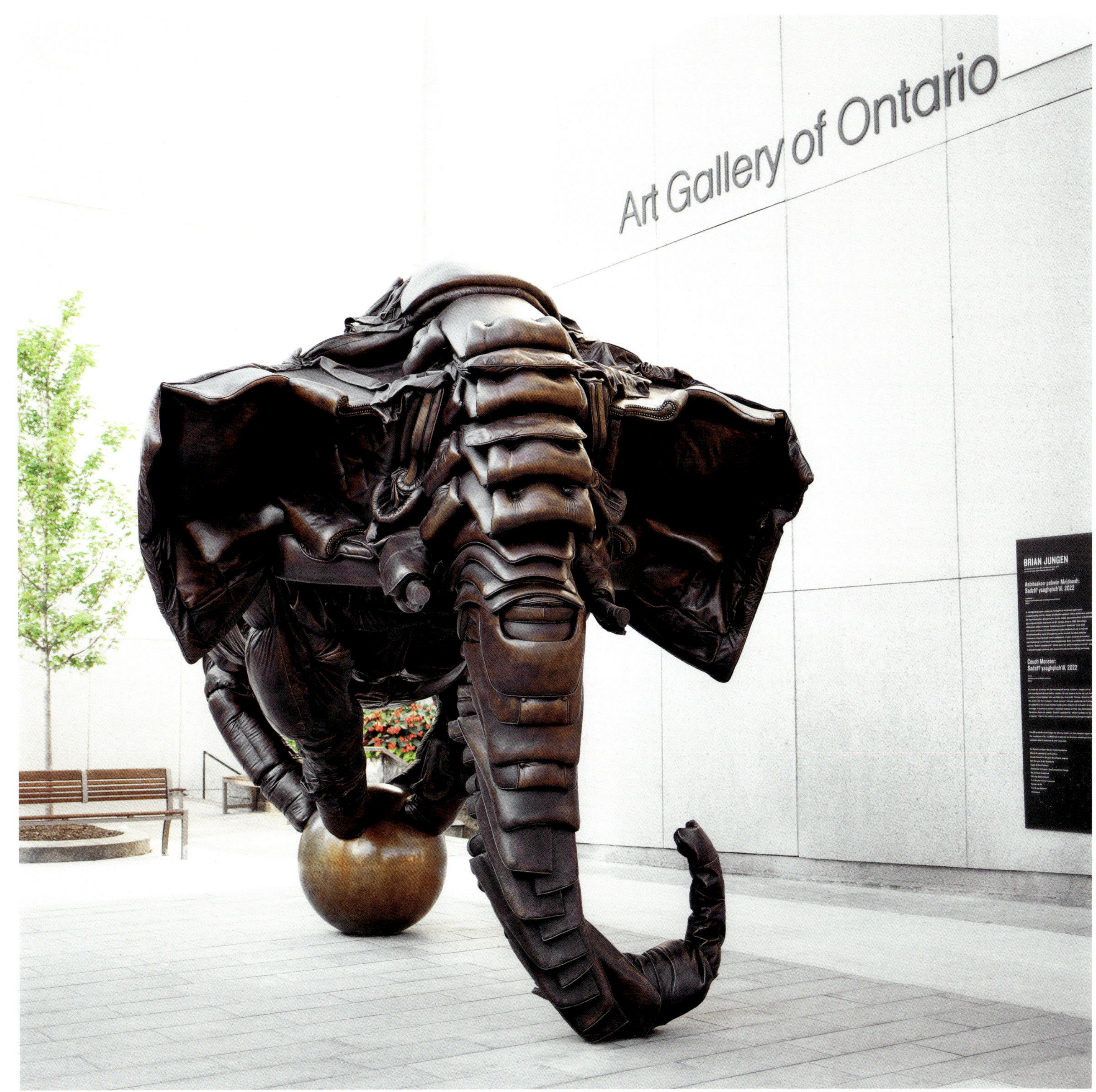

Art Gallery of Ontario
BRIAN JUNGEN
Couch Monster:

Couch Monster
A conversation with Brian Jungen

Julian Cox

The following is based on a conversation that took place between Brian Jungen and Julian Cox on May 19, 2022. This exchange has been edited for length and clarity.

JULIAN COX It's great to hear from you about the making of this work of art, Brian, and exciting to share a peek behind the curtain at the moment of the sculpture's birth. I'd like to start by asking where you are, exactly.

BRIAN JUNGEN I'm at the Walla Walla Foundry in Walla Walla, Washington, and I'm in the patina room, which is a fairly large space, and I am standing next to my sculpture, which they have been working on intensively for the last two years. We're just finishing up with the patina and the waxing of the piece.

JC This isn't just any foundry. The Walla Walla Foundry is one of the largest contemporary fine art foundries in the world, specializing in the production of extraordinary large-scale works. Can you describe what it's been like to collaborate with them on this project?

BJ It's been fantastic. I started working with the Foundry a few years ago on another smaller project, and that went very well, and then we decided to work together on this project. It's been a bit of a learning experience for everybody. What we were going after with this piece, trying to capture the texture of the leather—I think they have done an outstanding job. I had never done anything like this, and his was something new for them, too, so we walked through this together, in the middle of a pandemic. That it turned out so … perfect, really, is remarkable. And I have such a sense of relief. [laughs]

JC Yes, it has been an unusual and challenging project on so many levels. I want to bring us back to the point of origin for this commission, which is the corner right outside the AGO in the city of Toronto, where Dundas Street meets McCaul. A beautiful Henry Moore sculpture, *Large Two Forms,* was installed at that location for almost forty years until it was moved to its new home in Grange Park on June 6, 2016 (page 18). What are your thoughts about that location at the east end of the AGO, and about the work of Henry Moore, which is so integral to our sculpture collection and such a significant part of our identity as a museum? I know you've been thinking very deeply about this over the last few years.

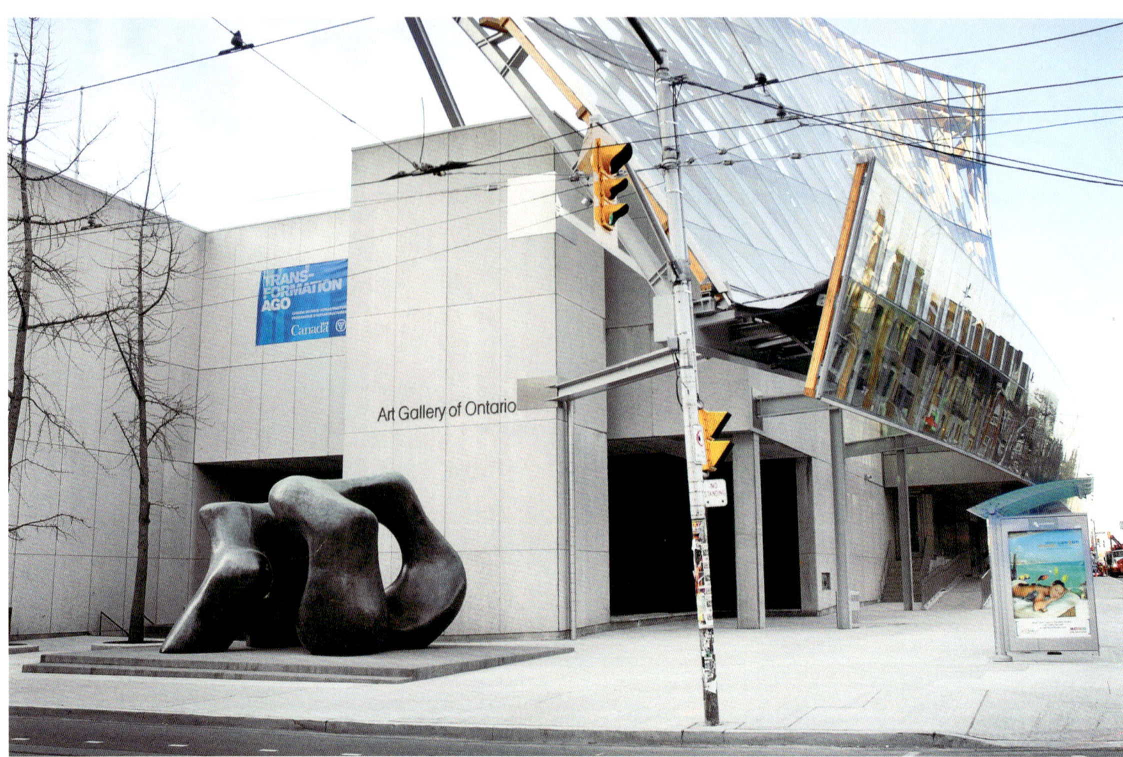

top: Henry Moore's *Large Two Forms* (1966–1969) at the southwest corner of Dundas and McCaul streets by the Art Gallery of Ontario, 2008.

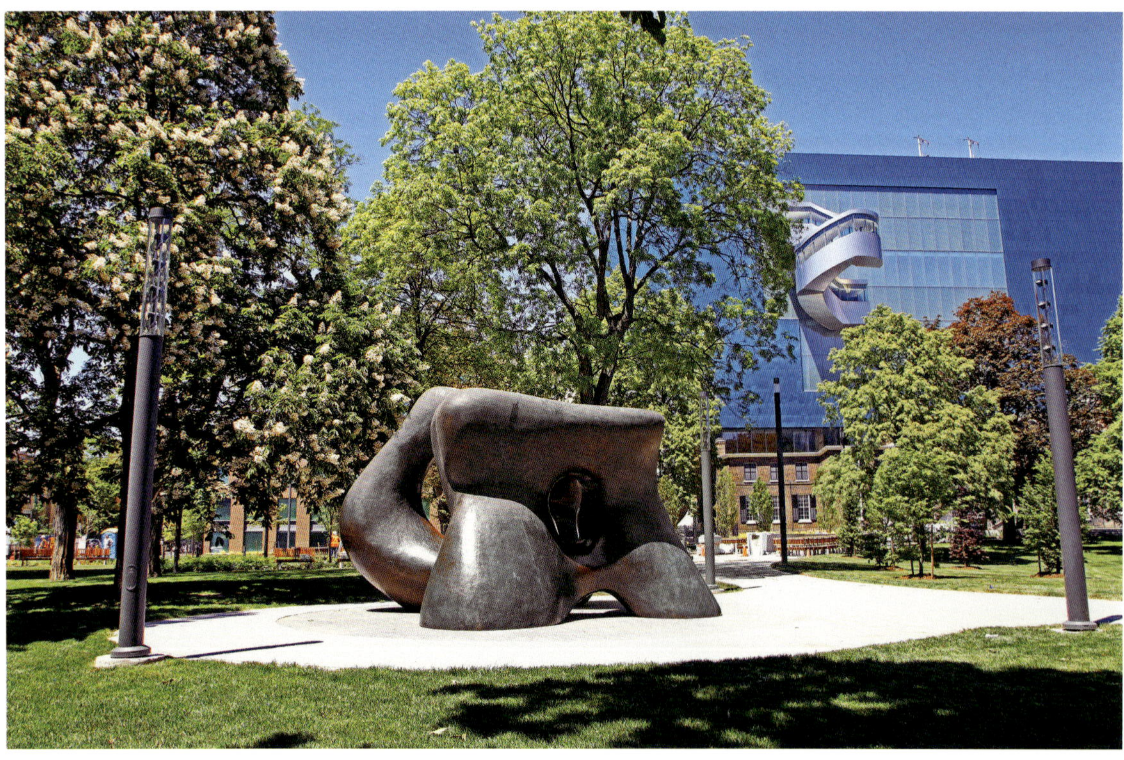

bottom: Henry Moore's *Large Two Forms* (1966–1969) in Grange Park, 2017.

BJ Yes, I have. When I was asked to work on this project, I felt very honoured, and I began to spend a lot more time in Toronto. I started taking photographs of people interacting with the Henry Moore sculpture. One thing I noted is that people used it kind of like furniture. They lounged and reclined and leaned against it, and that's something I quite liked. Another thing I noticed while visiting Toronto is that at the end of the day, people would put things that they were discarding out on the sidewalk for the garbage men to pick up. I started taking photographs of furniture that people were dumping on the sidewalk. I didn't make the connection right away, but those, I think, were the first seeds of [*Couch Monster*]. I did have other ideas about materials to use, and different forms and whatnot, but I always came back to furniture—and to bronze, in a desire to pay homage to the Henry Moore piece. I had worked with furniture before, leather couches and armchairs, so I thought that might be a good place to start. I like to use ready-made materials that are very common and that people have in their houses, because it's a really great way to enter the work and feel a connection to it.

JC But you've never made a work before in bronze, correct?

BJ No, I have not! I mean, it was kind of crazy because it's so massive…but I had so much belief that it was going to work really well because of my previous use of furniture. Also my use of Nike Air Jordans, which [are largely] made out of leather (page 116). I approached making this the same way I made the Nike masks: a disassembling and a reassembling of a found object or ready-made material.

JC I'm fascinated by the way that you've always drawn on your own community for inspiration in your work. You've used car parts and deep freezers and animal hides and leather sofas, [and] it all seems to come back to community. Is that fair to say?

BJ Oh, definitely. Henry Moore was very into his family, and he made pieces about his community, his family. Another thing I stumbled upon when I was doing research was the history of Jumbo, the circus elephant. I started thinking about exotic animals that are used for entertainment. I remember seeing an elephant when I was about five. I was very frightened of it because I'd never seen anything

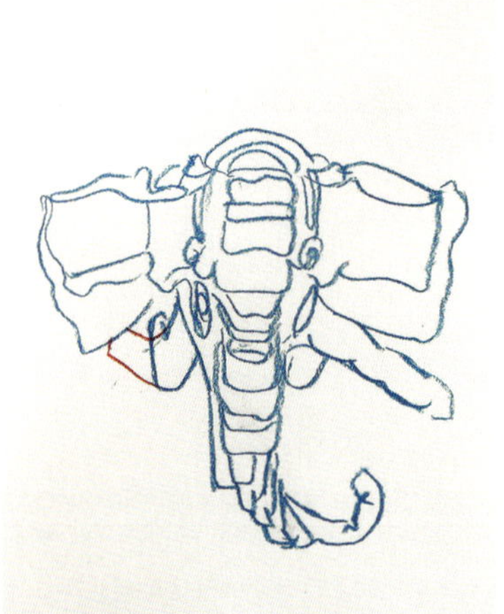

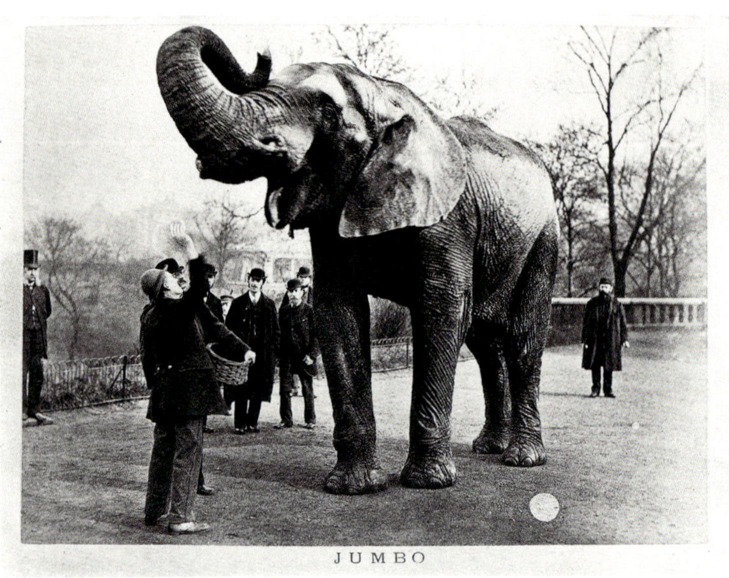

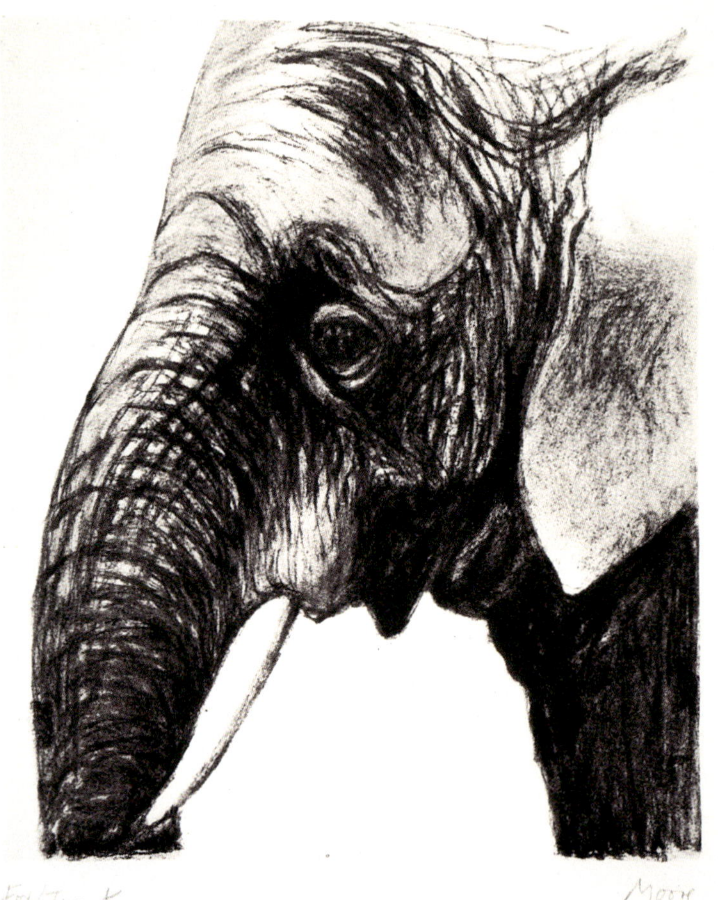

20

like that. So I asked the elders in my Indigenous community when they first saw an exotic animal, like a tiger or an elephant. A lot of them remember seeing [one] in the 1940s or 1950s, and they thought it was, like, a spirit animal, and they observed that it was in distress because it had obviously been manipulated by the trainers. So they felt great compassion toward this creature. This got me thinking about trying to portray that, and figuring out how to talk about it. Because when I look at the photographs and illustrations of Jumbo the elephant, they appeared very heroic (page 20, left) and. I don't think that's accurate. I think that poor animal was in distress and was miserable. These are all thoughts I was playing around with when I was researching the project.

JC This is not the first time that you have made an animal the subject of your work. I'm thinking of your monumental sculpture of a marine mammal, *Cetology*, and your *Cats Radiant City* installation.

BJ Exactly. I also wanted to make something that people would instantly recognize. But I didn't want to look at any images of elephants; I wanted to just use my memory of seeing them in popular culture—the Disney version or the nature program version. I wanted to base the work entirely on my memory. Because I think that's another thing an elephant is symbolic of: memory—and family and intelligence. Those are elements I wanted to work with.

JC We even refer to the memory of an elephant as a figure of speech! Speaking of representations of elephants: you're known mainly as a sculptor, but you also make beautiful drawings. Can you tell me about this drawing (page 20, top right) and how it corresponds with the creative evolution of the sculpture?

BJ Because the border was closed, I couldn't come down to finish the piece with the folks at the Foundry, so I had to rely on FaceTime and photographs and taking notes. I did a series of drawings to try out different positions of how I wanted the elephant to be standing. The drawings were very fast, in crayon on crappy paper. [laughs] I wanted to show the folks here at the Foundry what I was thinking. I use drawing as kind of a last resort. Making sculpture is like drawing in space. That's how I look at it.

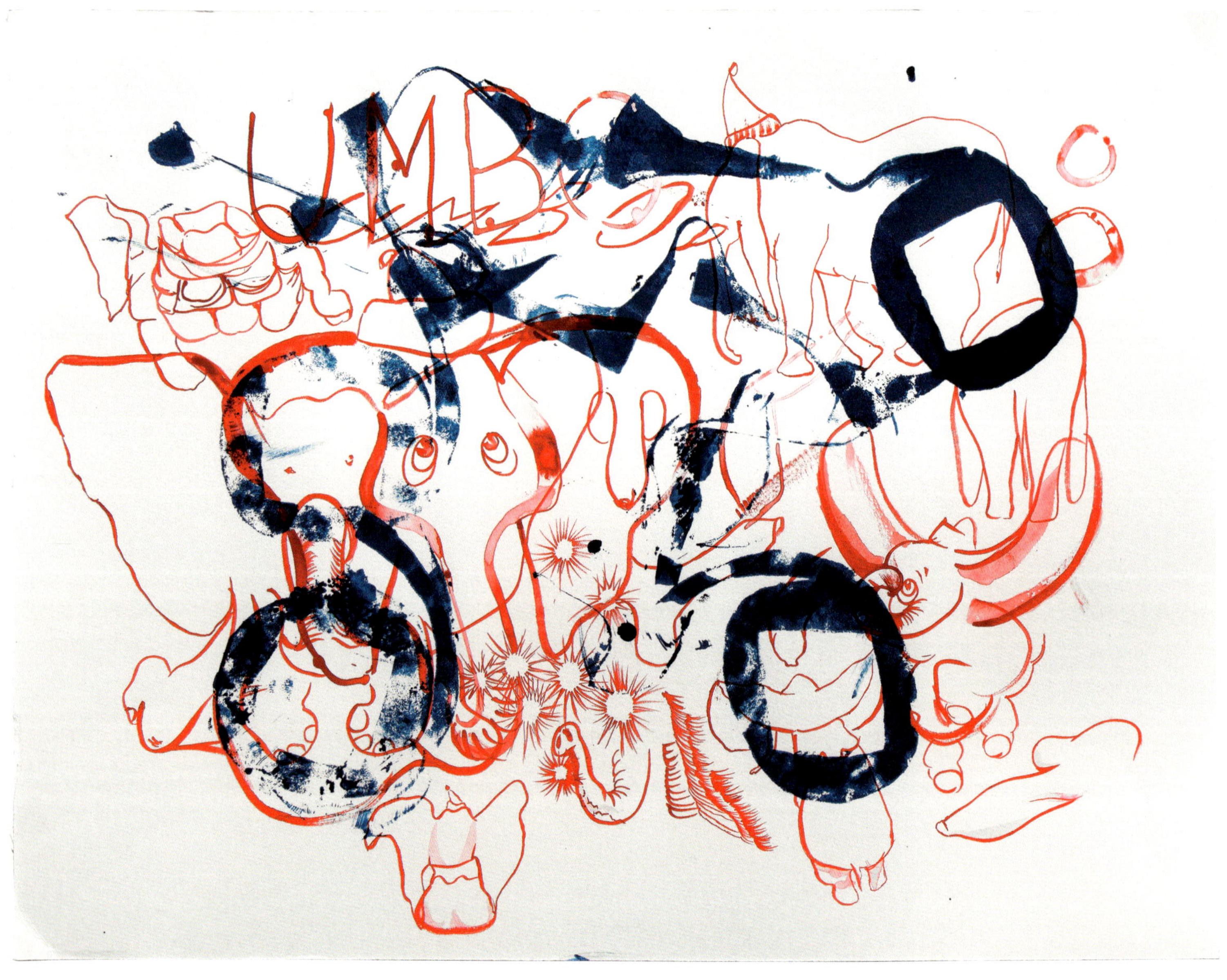

Brian Jungen, *Umbo*, 2020. Ink on paper, 45.72 × 60.96 cm. Courtesy of the artist and Casey Kaplan, New York. © Brian Jungen.

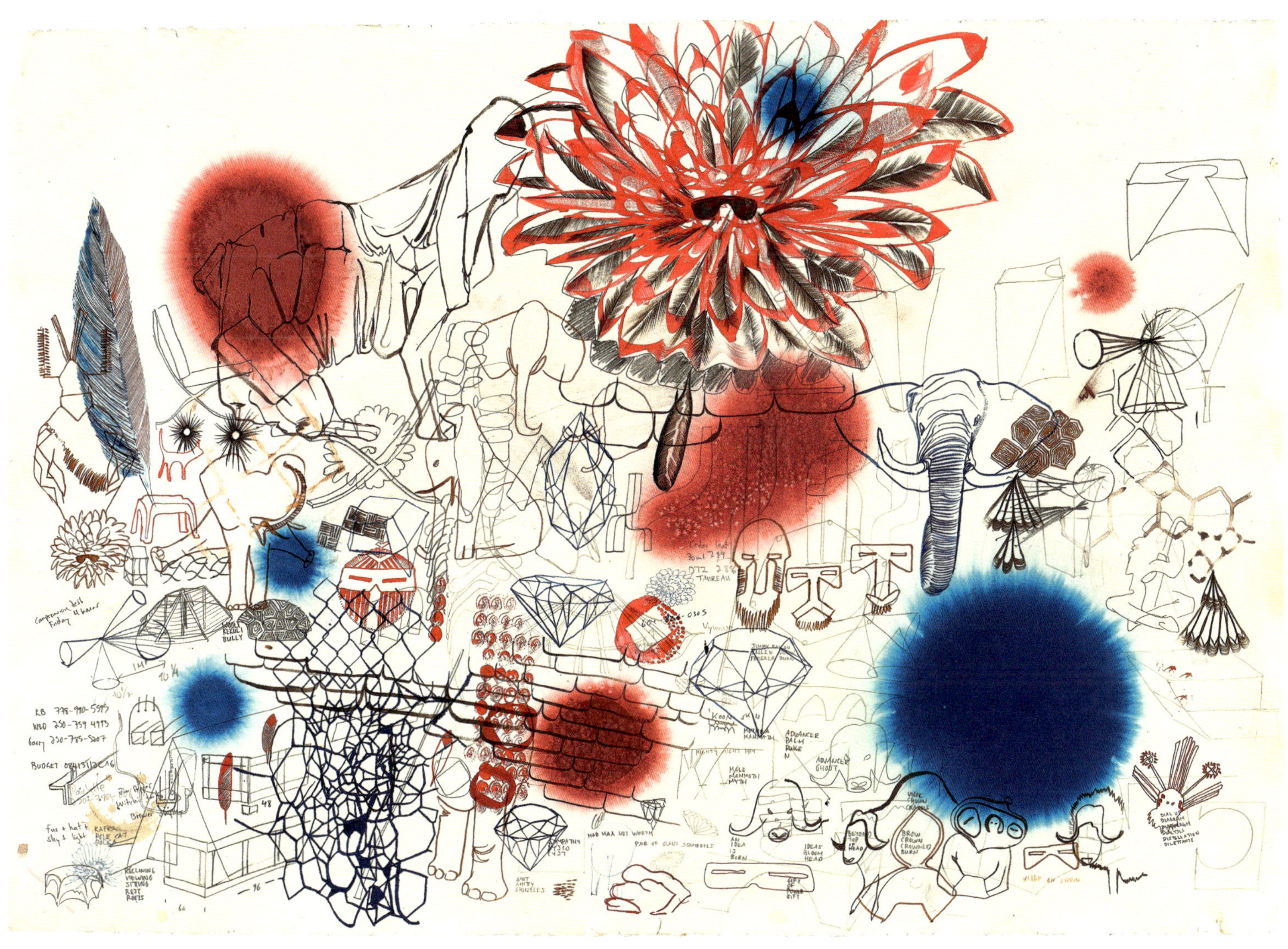

Brian Jungen, *In Perpetuity*, 2010–2020. Ink and graphite on cream paper, 77 × 111.5 cm. Purchased 2021. National Gallery of Canada, Ottawa. © Brian Jungen.

JC You are describing your drawings in a playful way as "a last resort," but I think you make beautiful drawings. You perhaps understate how great they are. And I know that in the early 1990s, when you were based in Vancouver, you did public pastings of your drawings on Hastings Street. I'm simply making the point that drawing, as one part of your creative process, has been visible in public space before. That's interesting to me—it feels like a political act. Can you tell me a little about that moment?

BJ When I lived in Vancouver in the '90s, I was young and I was poor, so drawing was something that I could afford. A lot of those drawings were very political and they were very explicit, and I wheat-pasted them on the boarded-up buildings in the Downtown Eastside. And then I noticed that people started adding to them—they weren't really vandalized, but people started peeling them off and stealing them. [Those were among] my first attempts at getting my artwork out there. And then some serious artists and curators in Vancouver saw that work and began to pay attention and became curious about me. These were the first steps in my journey of becoming a professional artist.

JC This is interesting because you began by working in the public space, in the street, and from that moment onward, you have been producing work for galleries and have been operating within those walls and within the museum structure. It must be exhilarating to create a work like this for a public space.

BJ It is, because I feel like I'm not in captivity anymore in the museum. [laughs] But seriously, working in public space is very freeing, and viewers don't respond like they would when they enter the validating space of the museum. The work exists in a completely different context. It's back in the space where I shared those early drawings. I find that very refreshing.

JC There is a lovely parallel here, I think, with these lithographs that were made in the early '80s by Henry Moore and signed by him—you can see the inscription: "For Toronto." They were part of a major gift the artist made to the AGO in 1986. There's something about Moore's focus on the eye of the elephant which is really fabulous (page 20, bottom right).

BJ Yes, when I was shown these and other images of Moore [works], I was very surprised that he drew these, and that I was working basically with the same form. It was exciting. There's also a photograph of him with an elephant skull, I believe, somewhere.

JC Moore was fascinated by the anatomy of animals, and it is well known that his studio in Perry Green, Hertfordshire, England, was positioned in the field so he could be among the sheep and observe them. It was his favourite thing to do. Animals are central to Moore's work, and their forms make their way into many of his sculptures. But let's get back to how you made the prototype for the sculpture out of leather in your studio in the Okanagan Valley, and how it relates to the final work in bronze.

BJ Yes, well, I worked with a crew of people. We scoured Craigslist and Facebook Marketplace and classifieds to find used leather furniture; I wanted to use leather because it's animal hide, but also, it has a visible history of the people who used it, with the creasing and whatnot in the leather. I thought it would transfer really beautifully to bronze. So we spent a couple months gathering furniture, and it was stockpiled and then gutted out (cut apart and disassembled) in the studio. Then I started building the form, which was based on my memories of elephants. It was a trial-and-error process of cutting apart [furniture items], reassembling them, stitching the leather back together. It was an exciting time. It's the last major piece I made in that studio.

JC How did you figure out how to engineer the sculpture?

BJ Oh, well, we used gantry cranes and engine hoists, because the furniture got very heavy the more compacted it became. We used two-by-fours to build the structure, and then we realized that the more two-by-fours we were using, the more it was taking up space over the lower body. So we had to disassemble it, and then we welded a steel frame for it, which existed right until it was cast in silicone. It was a complex process of making something in the studio and knowing that in the end it would be turned into metal. All of that was new for me because I'm used to making the end-product itself. There was a great deal of back-and-forth with the Foundry. I wasn't sure what was possible. And they just kept greenlighting everything. They were so optimistic that it was almost unnerving. I was asking myself, "Wait, what? Are you sure?"

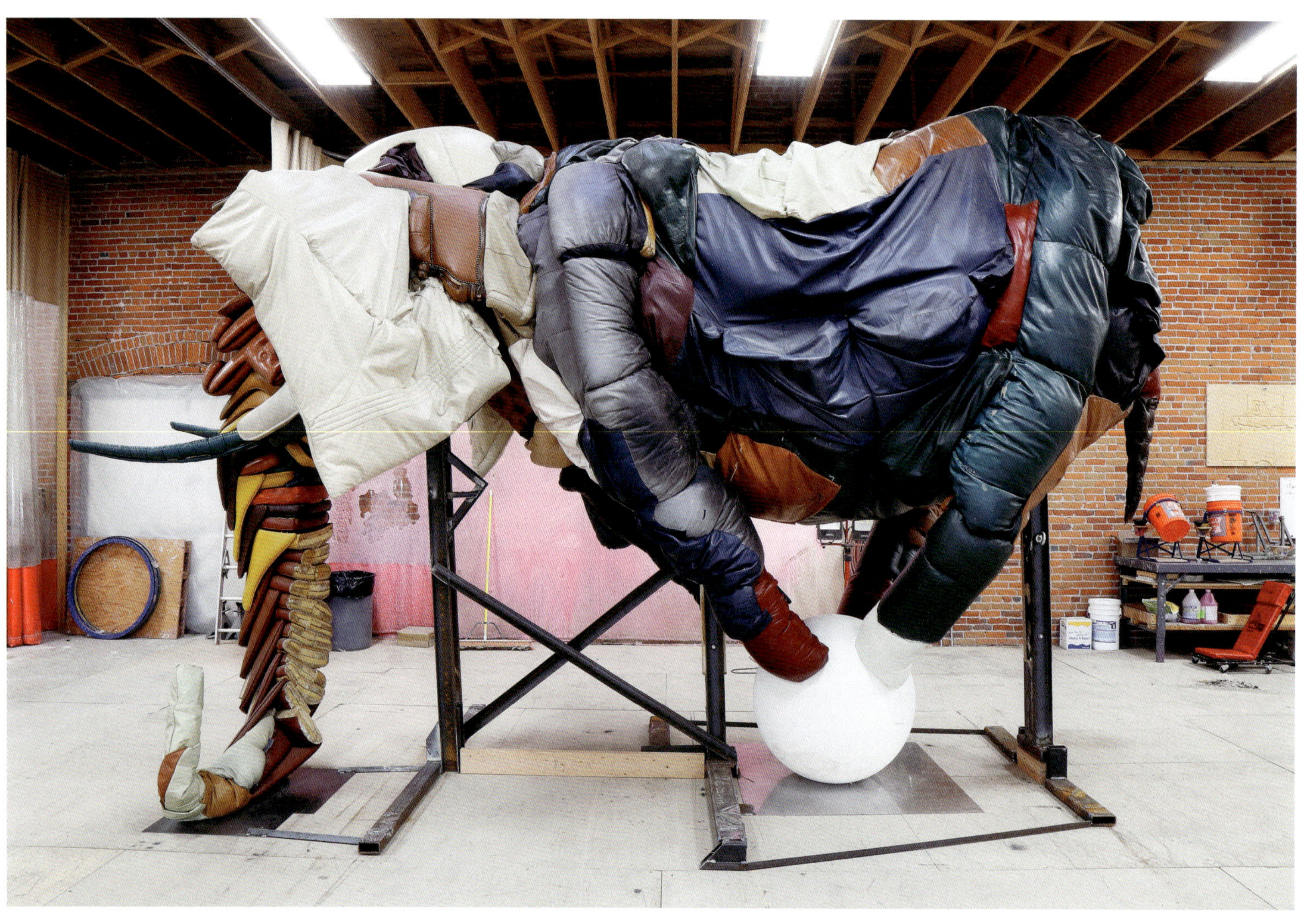

JC That was a huge leap of faith on your part, trusting the team at the Foundry to translate your leather prototype into bronze.

BJ Yes, and I really wanted all of the textures, the creases, the buttons, the stitching, and the seams to translate in the bronze. The best way to do that was to make a one-to-one scale prototyope that could be replicated at the exact same size. There's all sorts of different technologies now where you can have large-scale sculptures 3D-printed, but you lose the surface texture when you do that. That's why we decided to go with the one-to-one system.

JC At a certain point in the process, you changed the pose of the elephant. Rather than standing on its four feet it now balances on a sphere. What led to this decision, and why did you make that shift?

BJ Basically the head, the trunk, and the body are stacked, and I designed it so the legs were flexible, because I wasn't sure about the final placement. I wanted to go down to the Foundry and work with them on that, so that was the original plan. But COVID hit and the border was closed. In fact, the piece itself made it down there just under the wire. It arrived in Walla Walla the same week in March 2020 that the border closed. At that moment we realized that there was going to be a significant delay, and that gave me time to really think about how I wanted the legs to be. I also decided to take some of the stuffing out of the couches, and have the piece sag more, to give it a more palpable sense of weight. We used many different types of furniture to make the work that you see now, and the leather was in a variety of colours. But of course I had to think of it all as one unified colour.

JC Sourcing the leather was akin to hunting and gathering; as I understand it, you were acquiring these sofas from wherever you could find them and then improvising how they could relate to each other in the form of the work.

BJ I had a really great sewing machine that's used for making saddles, so once we skinned the sofas we were able to sew every one of them together. I worked with a gifted colleague who specializes in theatre design, and she helped me figure out how to make patterns with the individual components. As I mentioned earlier, it was somewhat similar to making the Nike stuff but on a much larger scale. I could not do it all by myself. At one point it required six or seven people to pull the couch skins overtop of the frame. Everything was more complex and took longer.

JC It's a big pivot to go from of a position of self-reliance to working with a team of people that are bringing very particular skills to help you realize what it is that you need.

BJ Yes.

JC So the sculpture got across the border in the nick of time. Can you talk me through the developments that took place after it arrived at the Foundry?

BJ The Foundry closed for several months in the spring of 2020. When things started to open up again that summer, I worked with Matt Ryle and his team to finalize the pose of the elephant so they could start the process of casting. There was a great deal of back and forth; that's where a lot of the drawing happened. I said I wanted the form to be balancing, [the way] a circus elephant would balance for entertainment. We tried all sorts of different positions. At one point it was balancing on one foot, almost like a ballet move, which I really liked, but the internal engineering structure would have been very, very difficult. So I decided to have it balancing on a ball, which made the engineering much more manageable. This also made the casting process a little less of a challenge.

JC What sort of evolution did the legs have to go through to be in the form that they are now?

BJ Well, I sent a variety of extra leather pieces with the shipment that I was hoping to use myself when I came down here. When I wasn't able to do that, I had the Foundry take photographs of all the pieces and I indicated which ones I wanted to use. We shortened some of the legs and improvised changes to other pieces. This was challenging because, being at a distance, I essentially had to leave some of the decision-making in the hands of the Foundry. Once I had decided that the elephant was going to balance on the ball, they had to move and tuck in a lot of the leather to make it anatomically correct. They worked quickly and efficiently on this because we had a tight production schedule to adhere to, and they had to start casting it in silicone.

JC With the final form, the public will be able to literally walk right underneath the work, correct?

BJ Yes, I'm underneath it right now. And I'm sure lots of kids will be crawling under here and having fun.

JC You said that with a smile on your face. It sounds like you're excited about how people will interact with the work.

BJ Yes, I want people to touch and feel it. One of the things I love about bronze is that over time it becomes burnished by the elements and human touch. The more this happens, the more it will look like old leather.

JC You are reminding me again of the Henry Moore in Grange Park. People often lounge in the sculpture's central open orb, and the bronze becomes burnished and worn over time, like a medieval church pew, and that ever-changing surface carries the history of the work.

BJ Yes, you become more conscious of the passage of time and very aware of how the public develops a certain affection for the work. I like that very much.

JC Bronze is a metal and, of course, is classified by most as a hard material, but there can be a softness to it. I glean this from the way that you have talked about *Couch Monster* and your quest to translate leather into bronze.

BJ Well, yes, the puffiness of the leather couches lends an inherent softness, but the waxing does as well. The wax brings out the softness of the form, with its creases, crinkles, and folds, and warms up the work overall. It's wonderful!

JC This work has a very distinct title: *Couch Monster: Sadzě? yaaghęhch'ill*. This is a Dane-zaa phrase which you've said translates to "my heart is ripping." Why and how did you settle on this title?

BJ I worked on multiple versions of the title. Everyone who worked on this in my studio and at the Foundry started calling it the "Couch Monster" because in its various stages, it really looked monstrous. It looked like an alien, almost. That name stuck, and I liked the playfulness of it. But there was also a seriousness and a sadness, going back to the story that some of my elders told me about seeing animals in captivity—specifically elephants in captivity—and how they felt about it. They seemed to feel very connected to the subjugation of this creature. So I worked with members of my community, some of my cousins, to come up with a Dane-zaa phrase to describe that feeling. There wasn't a direct translation because there is no real term for breaking someone's spirit. Yet that's what happened when people trained animals, especially an animal like an elephant that could easily kill you. It was difficult to land on a good translation. I was given a variety of options by a linguist in the community, and we finally arrived at the one that's most accurate. The title is kind of twofold: the English version is playful, connoting enjoyment and entertainment, and the Dane-zaa term carries the sad and tragic side.

JC That seems in keeping with so much of the work that you've made over the years. There is often an undercurrent or hidden tension operating under the surface that is in opposition to what appears at first glance. I think this is a defining characteristic of your art, regardless of what materials you are using. *Couch Monster* was created under very challenging circumstances during the pandemic, but I think the end result is extraordinary. You have elevated your practice to a new level. Surely that has to be very satisfying?

BJ Yes, very much so. Life was very challenging when I was operating my ranch in the Okanagan and pursuing my my art practice simultaneously. And the destruction of the ranch by fire last summer was very, very difficult to go through. But seeing this result has opened up a whole new direction for me. It may be a bit of a dangerous one because I just want to make giant bronzes now. [laughs]

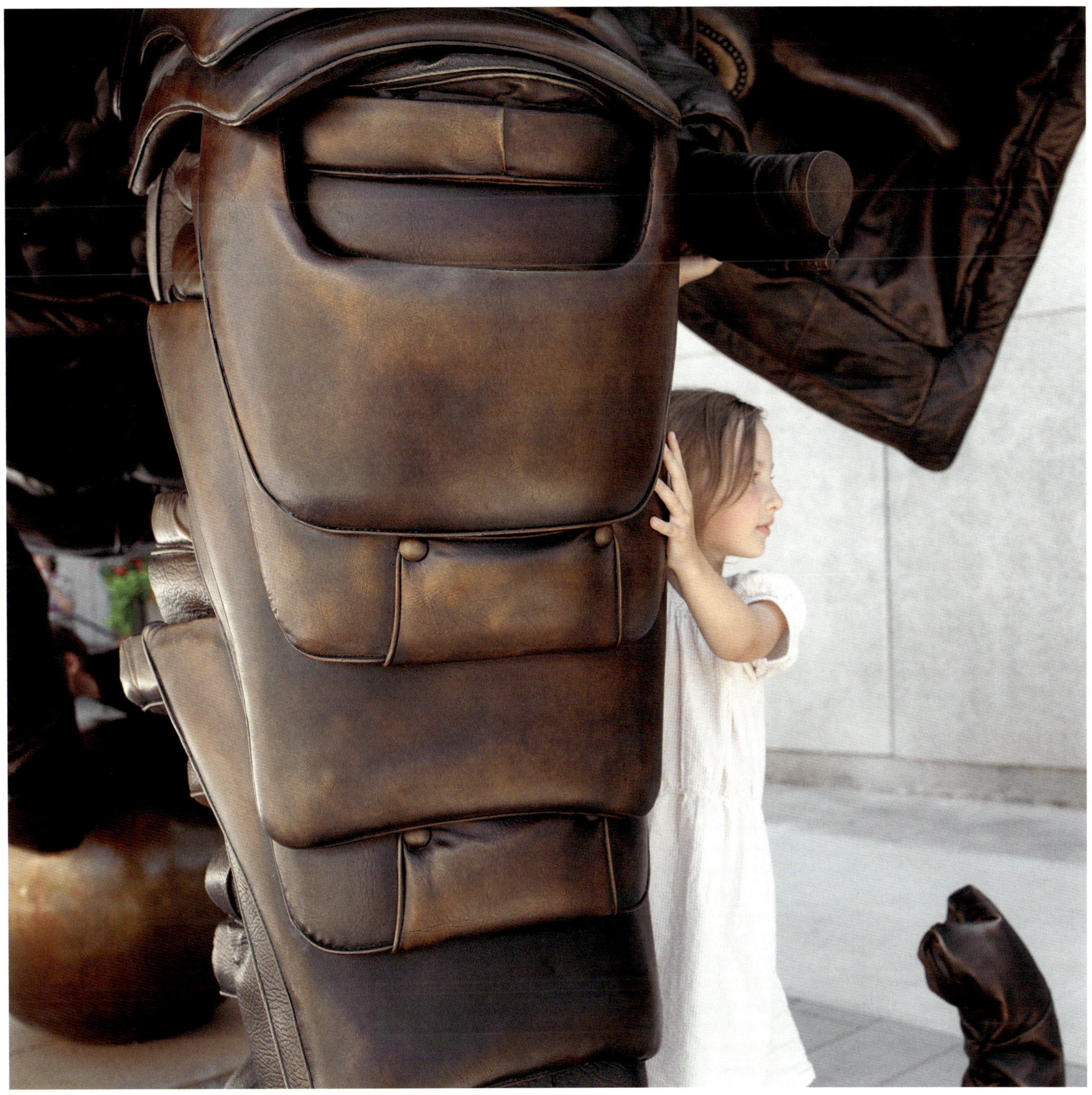

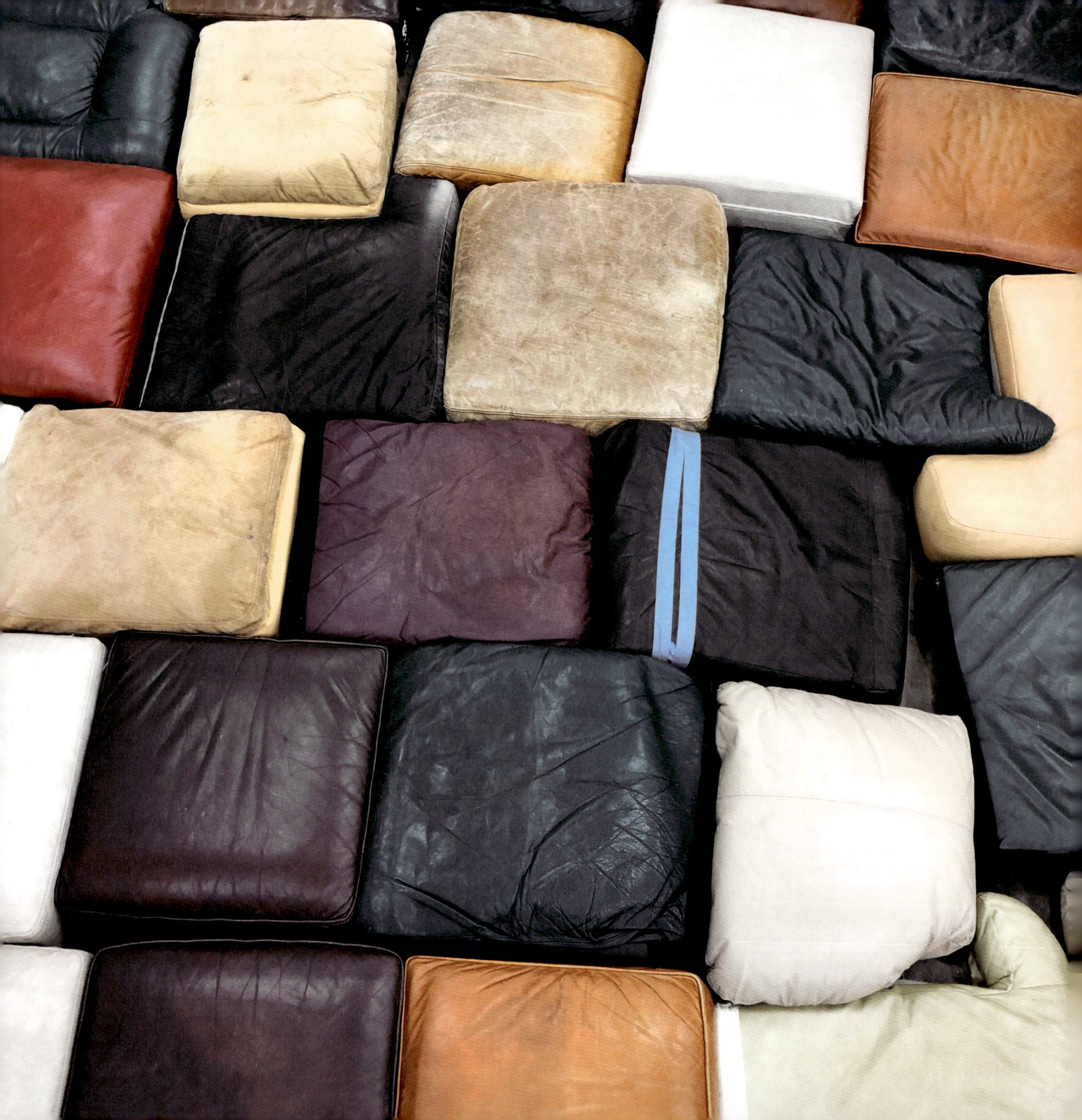

STUDIO

Brian Jungen is known for transforming everyday consumer objects into spellbinding forms through his sculptural work. *Couch Monster* is one of his most ambitious projects to date. Construction of the sofa-leather prototype took place between the summer of 2019 and the spring of 2020; during this time, his studio was enveloped by the musty thrift-shop aroma of used goods. Jungen took apart countless discarded couches and chairs to produce puzzle-like pieces, which he reassembled to make the spectacular elephant figure visitors will recognize today.

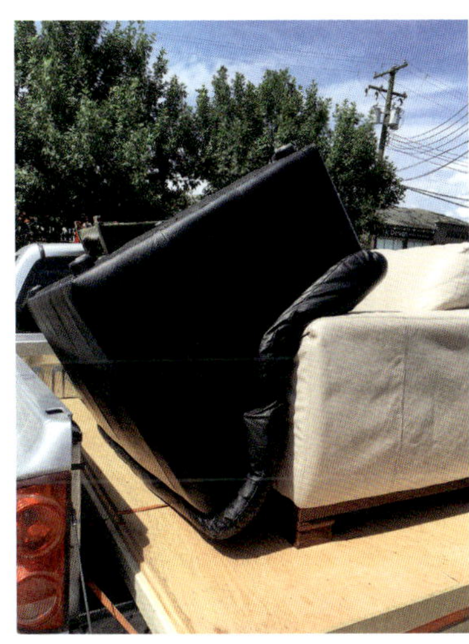
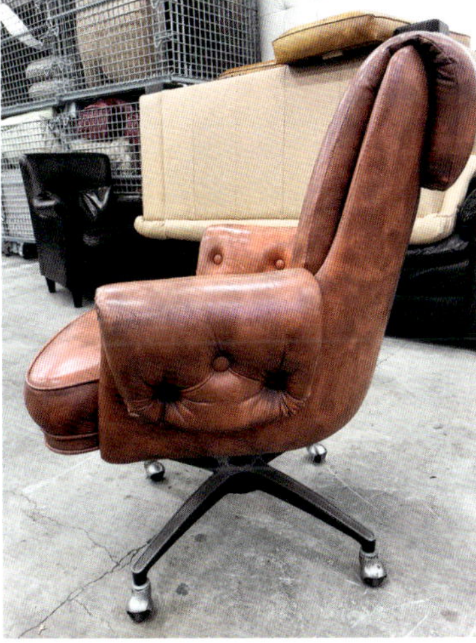
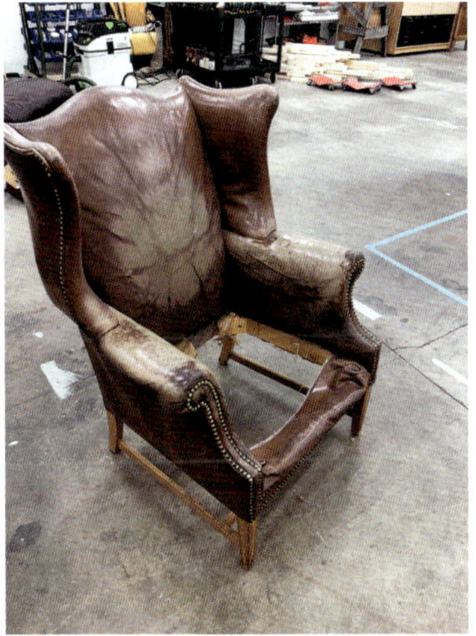
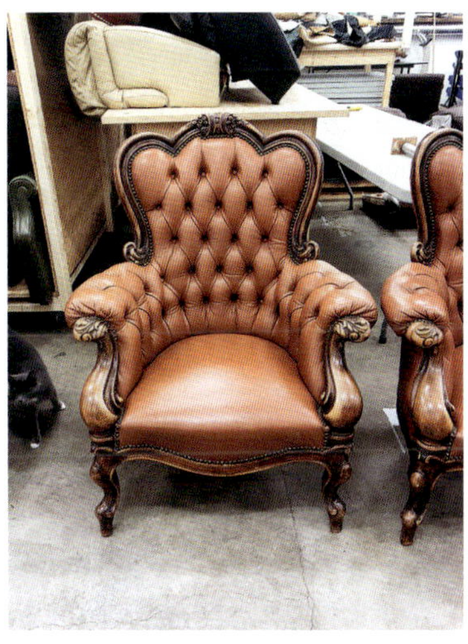
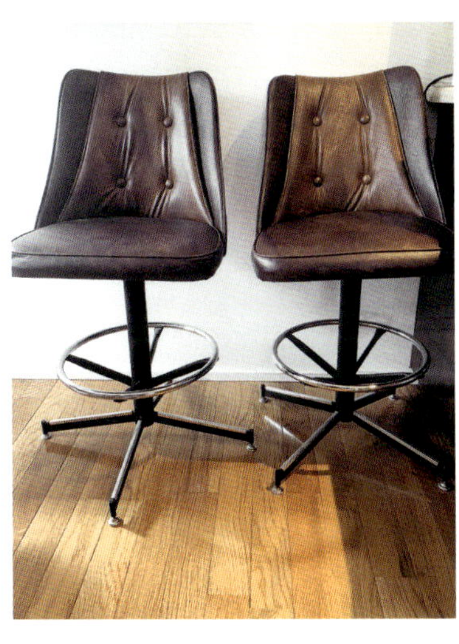
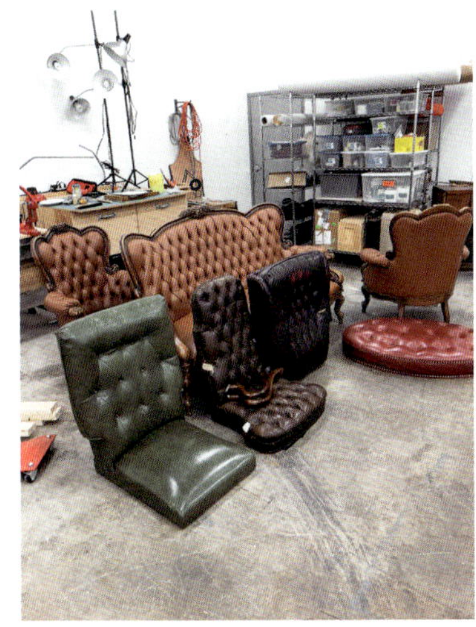
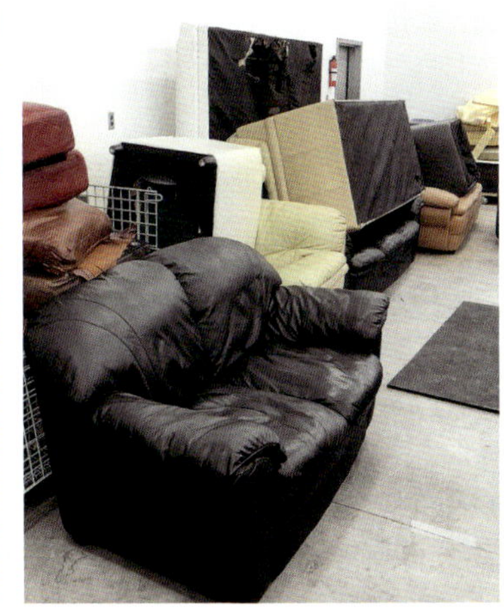
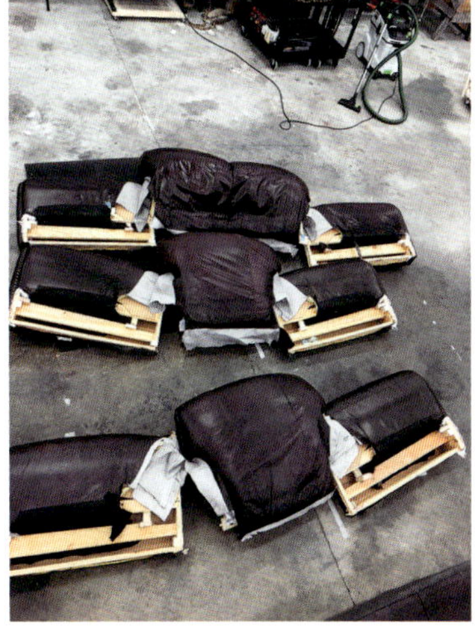
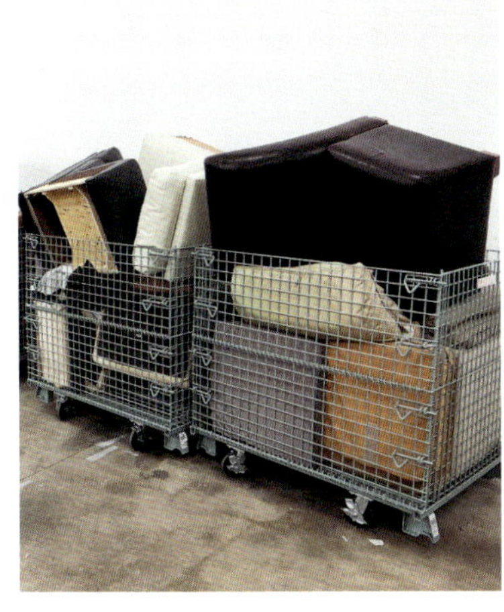
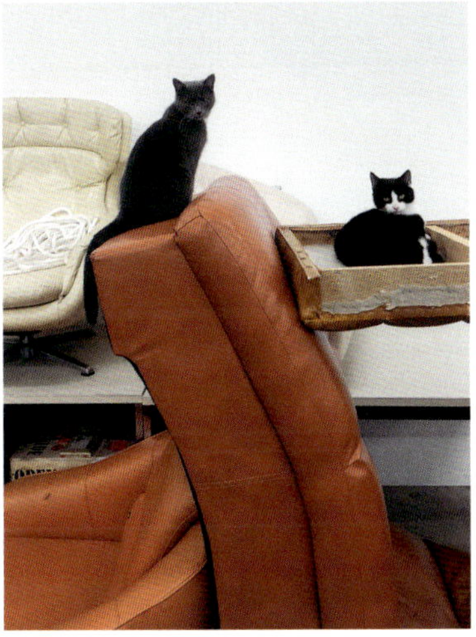
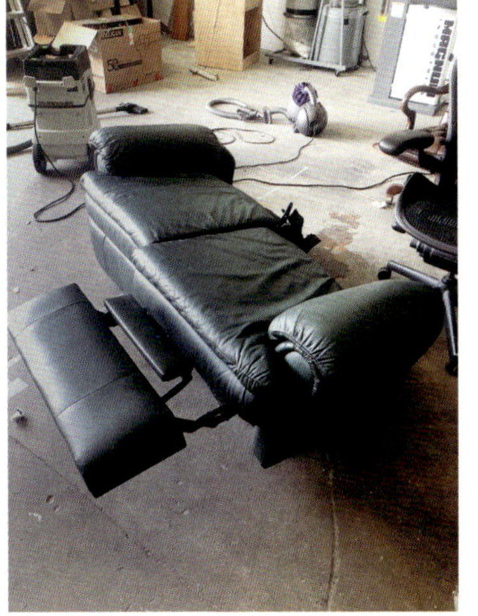
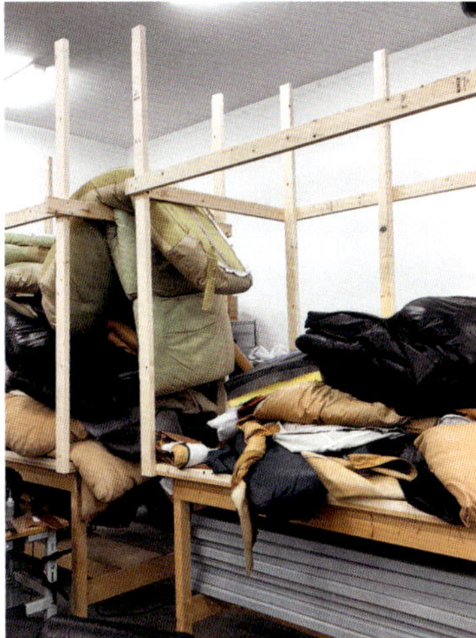

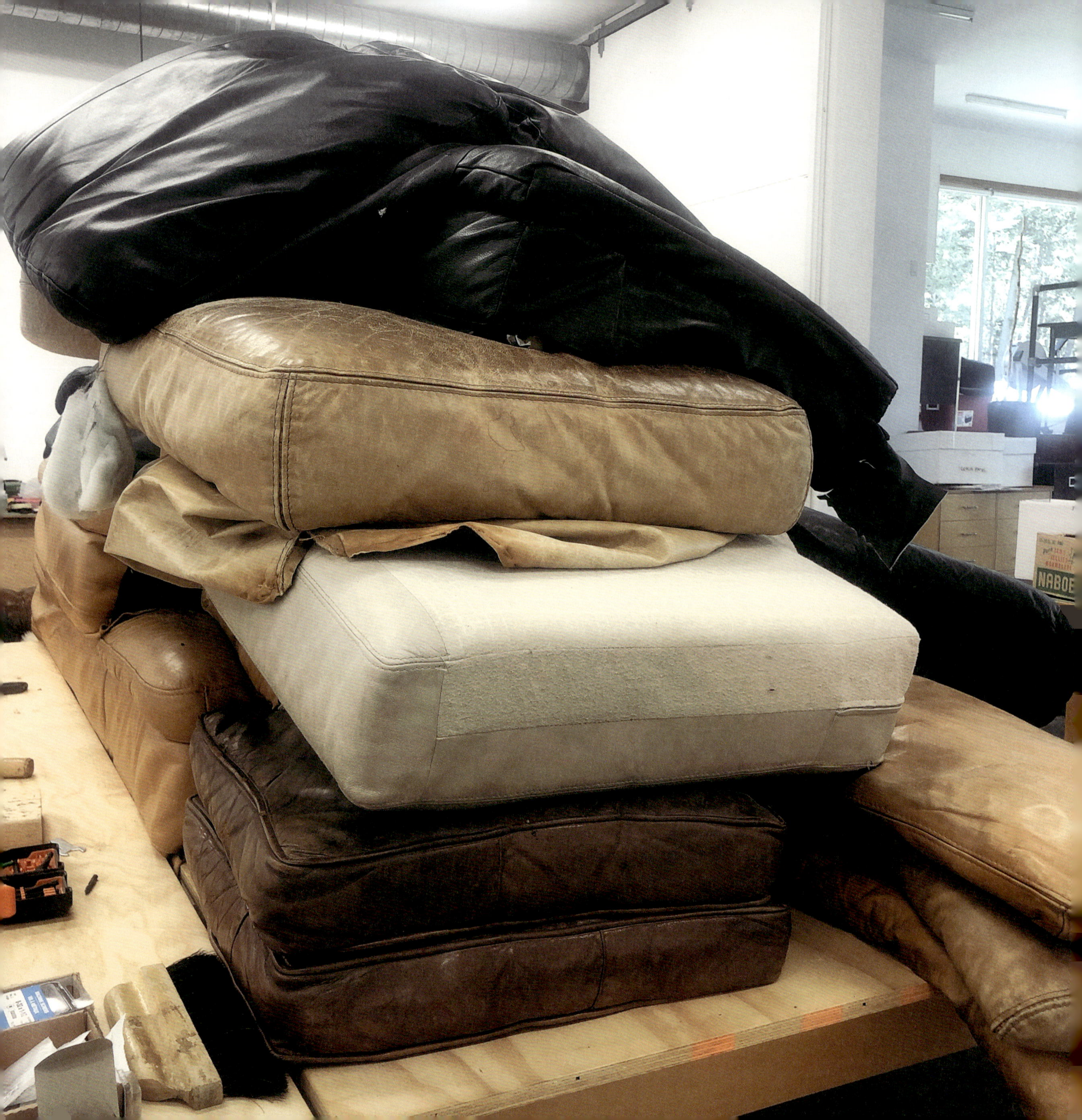

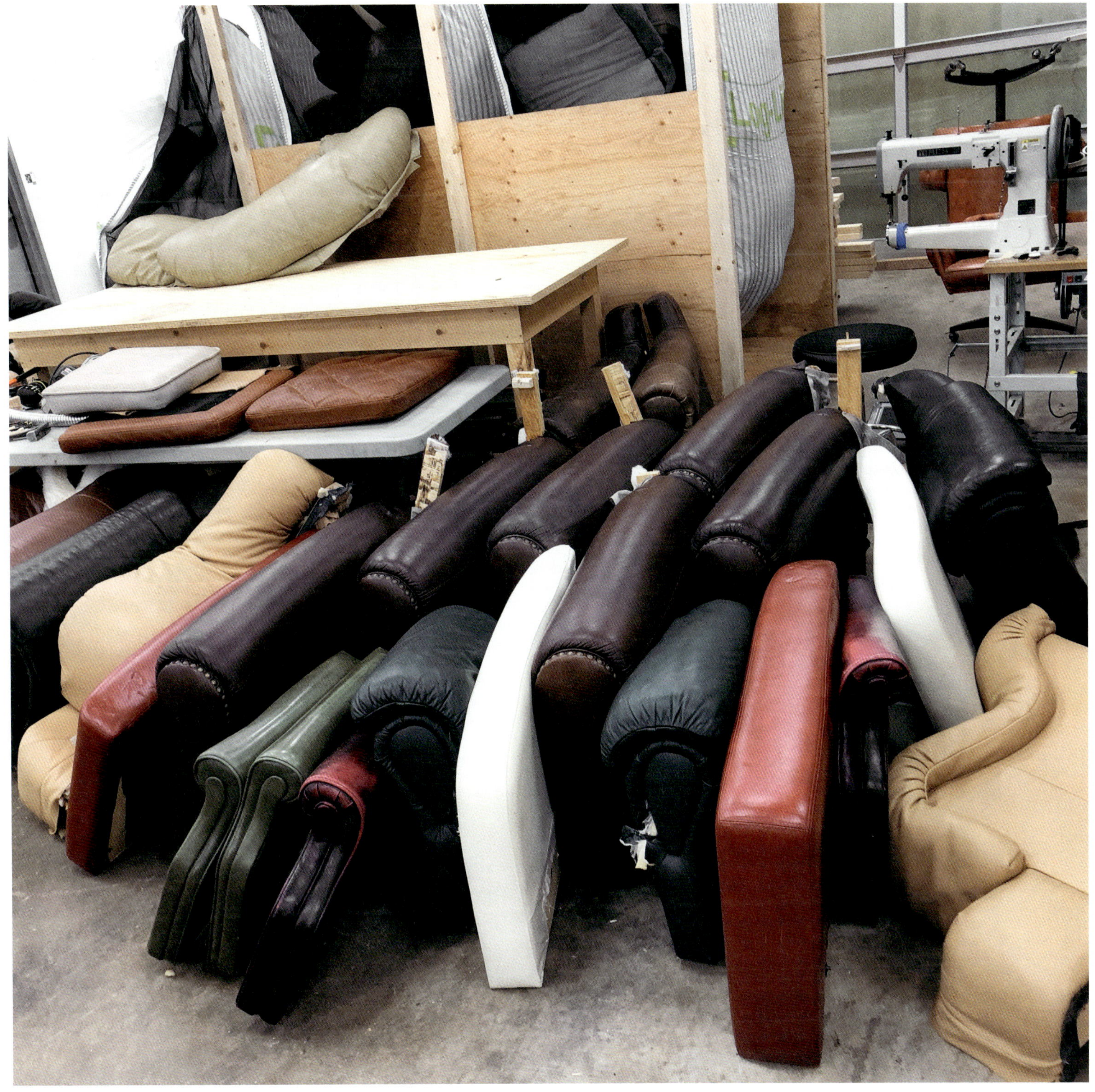

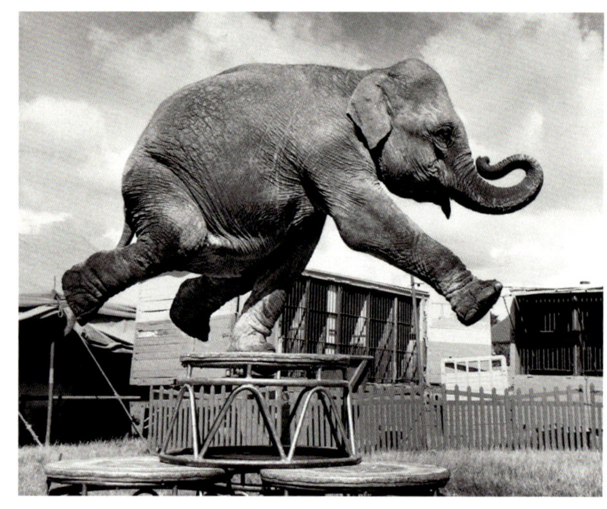

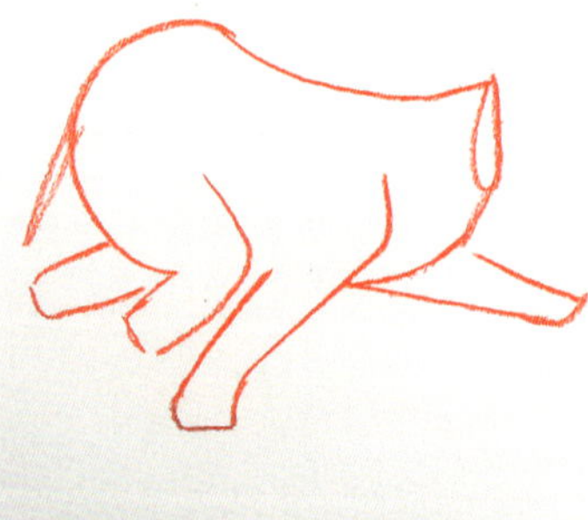

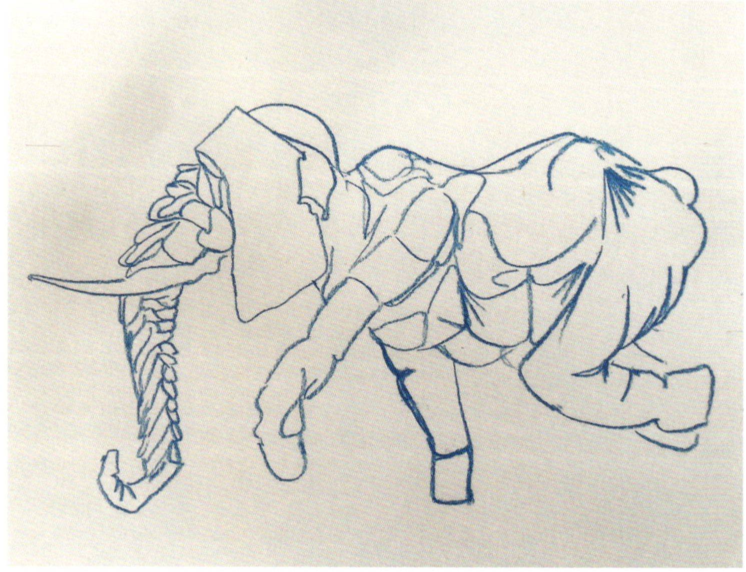

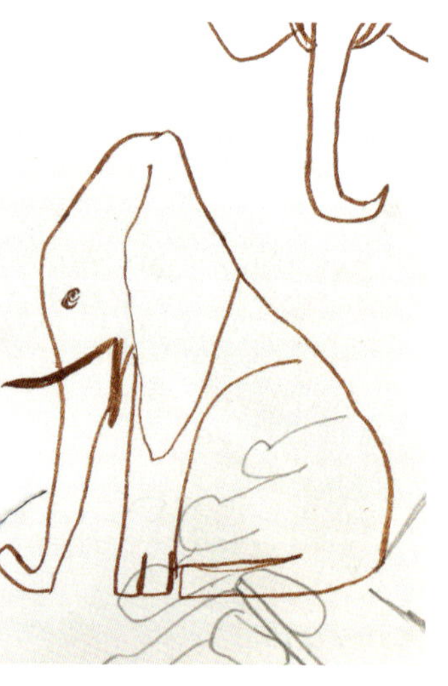

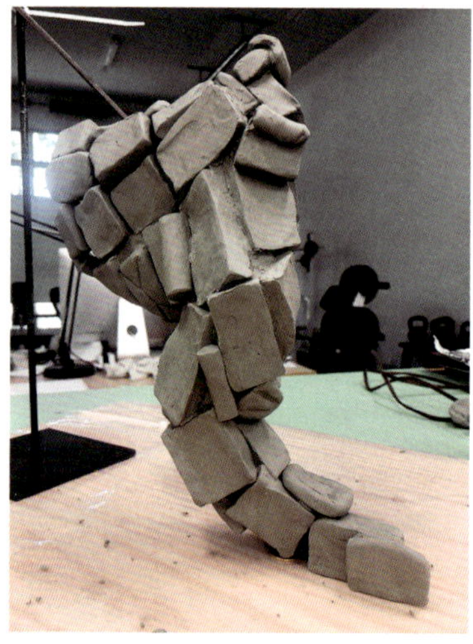

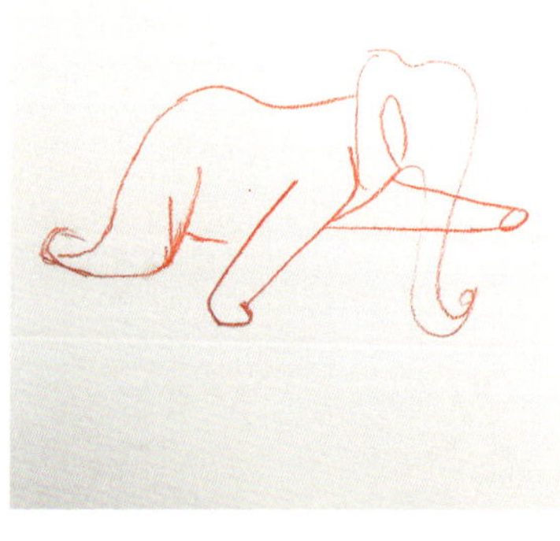

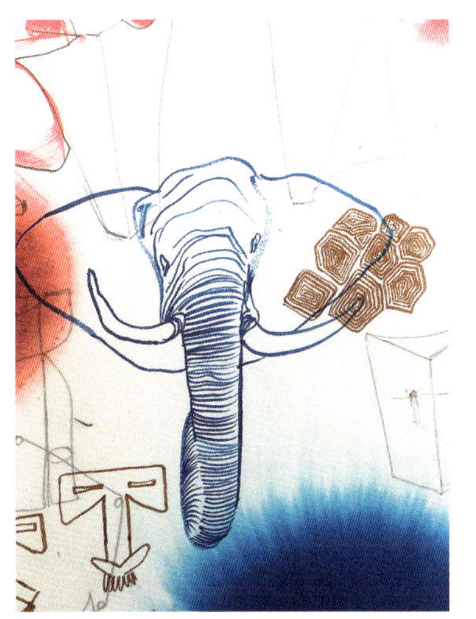

chain

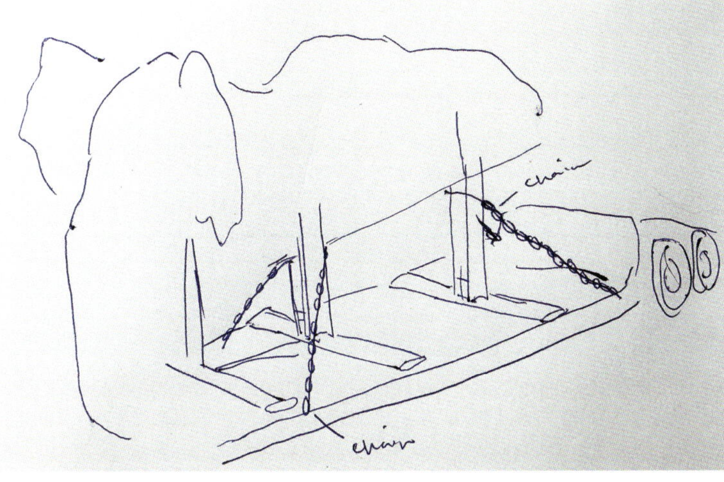

chain
chain

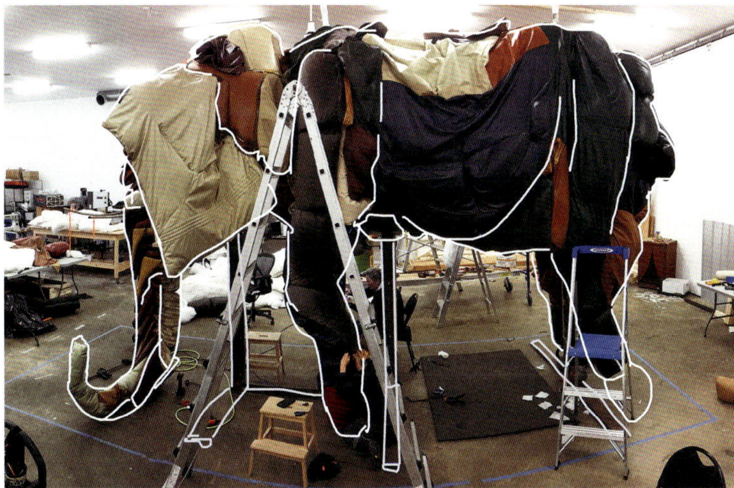

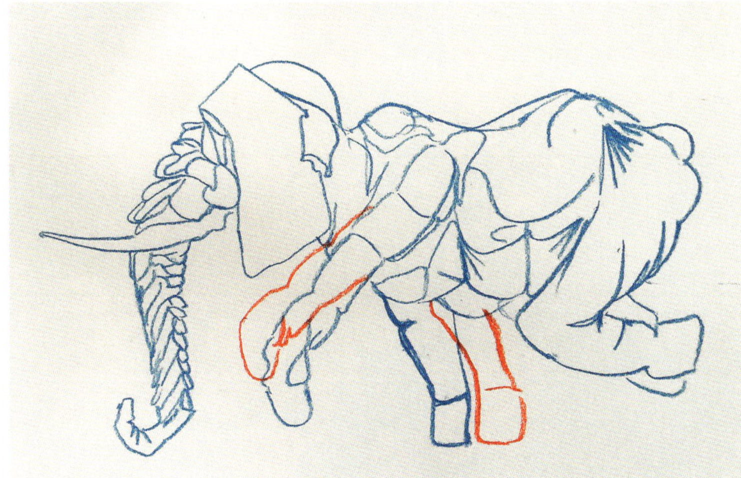

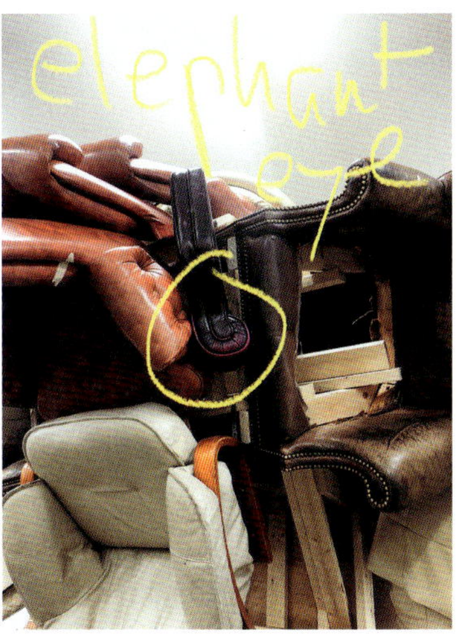

elephant
eye

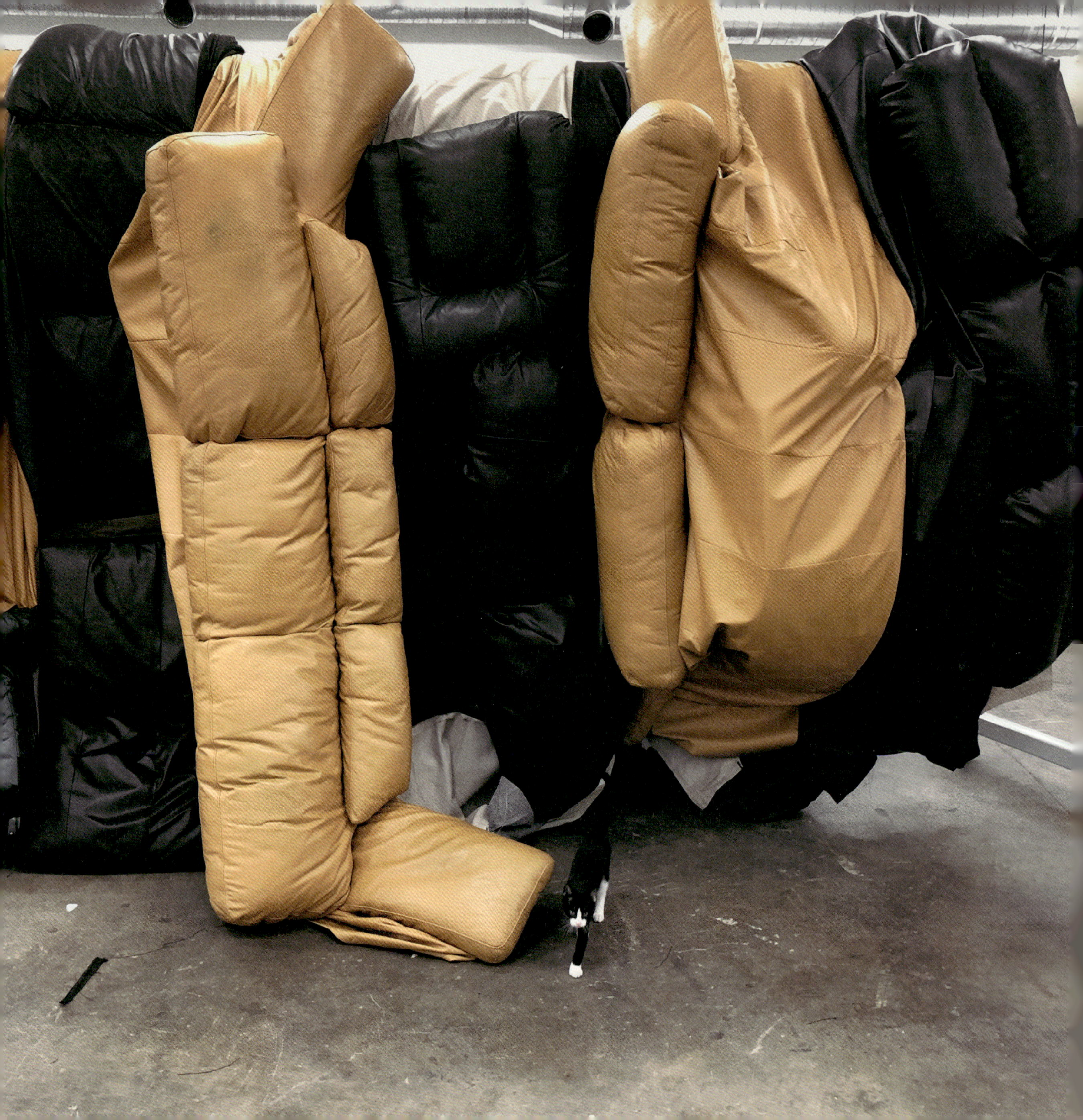

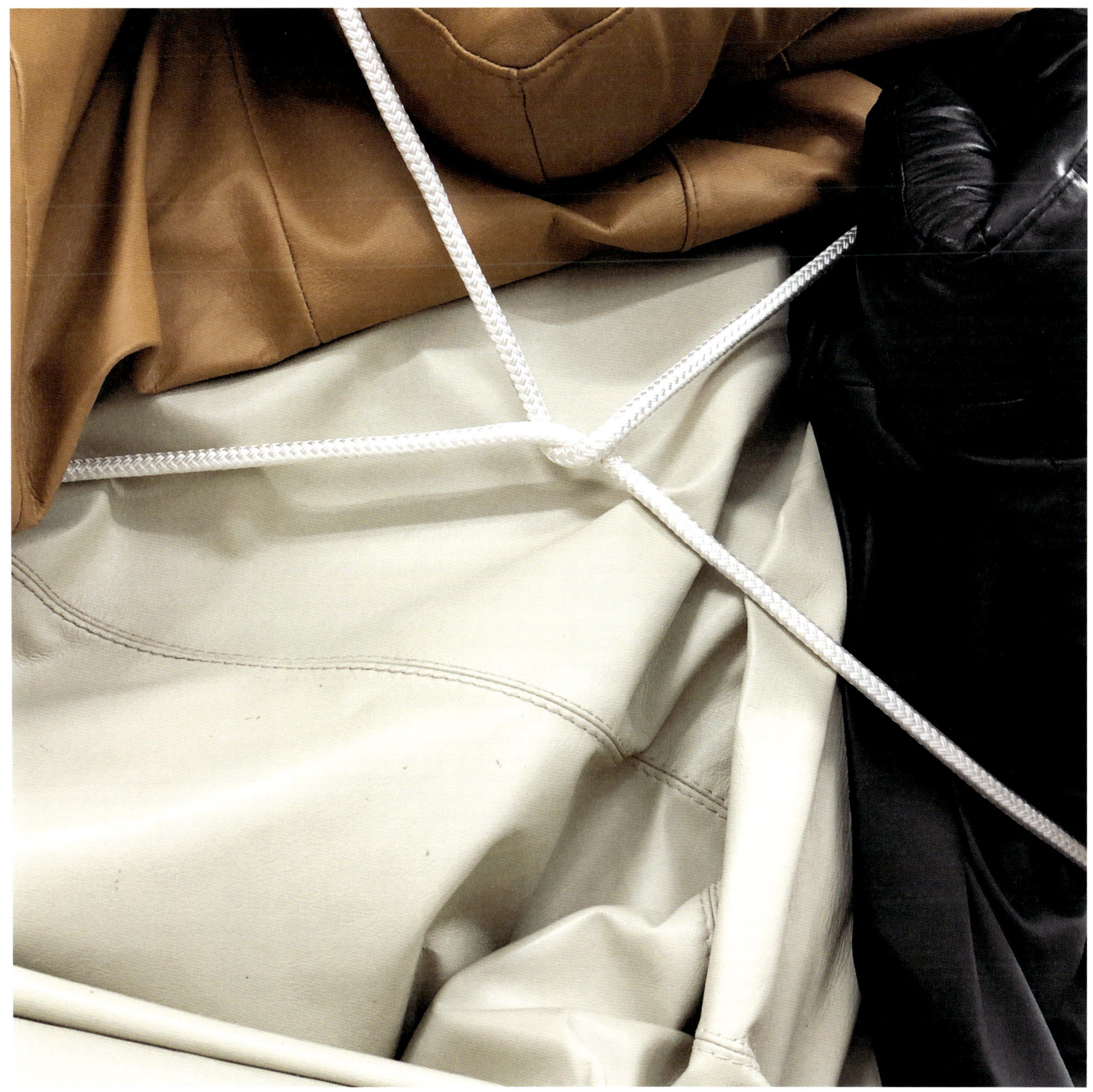

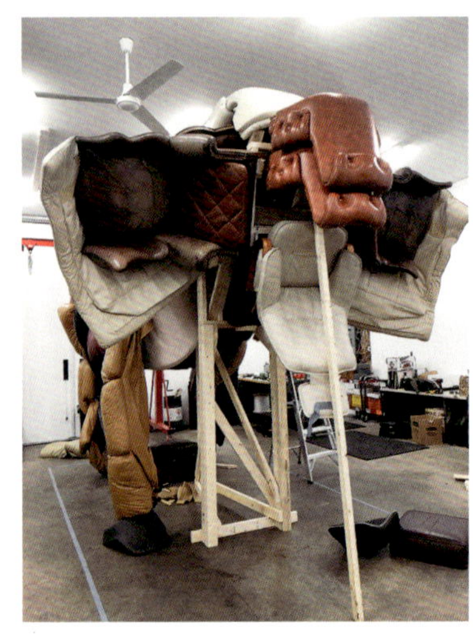 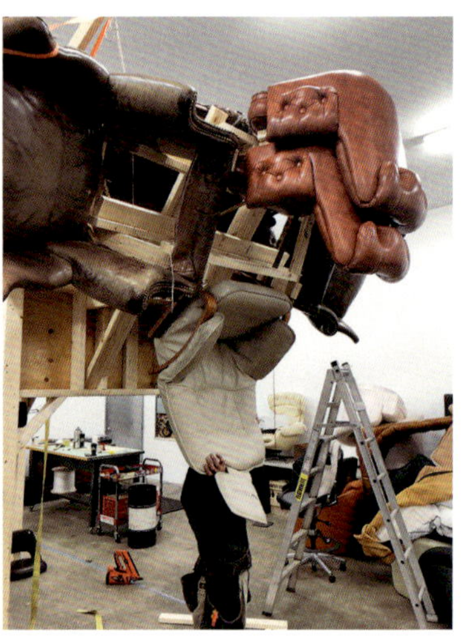 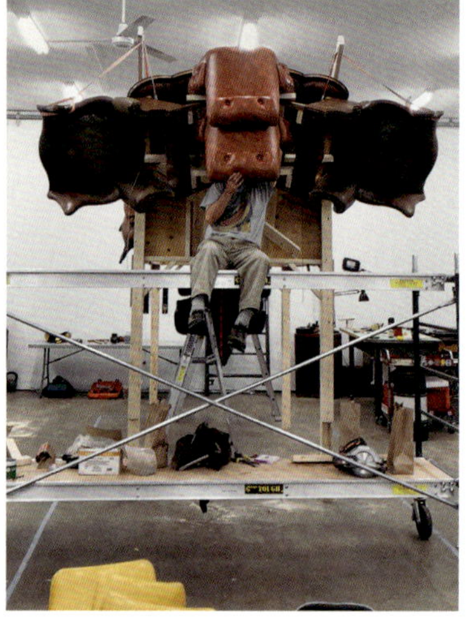 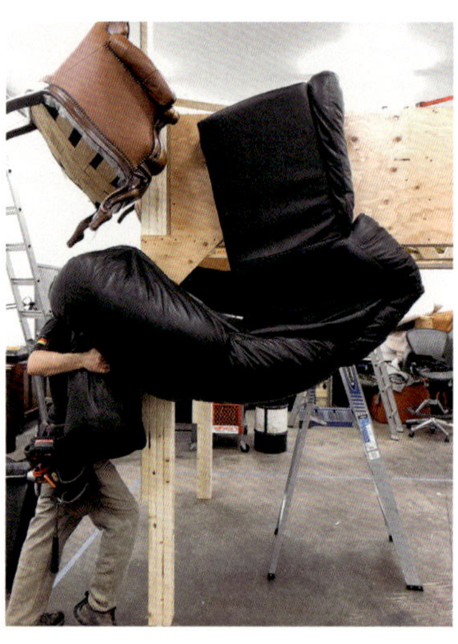

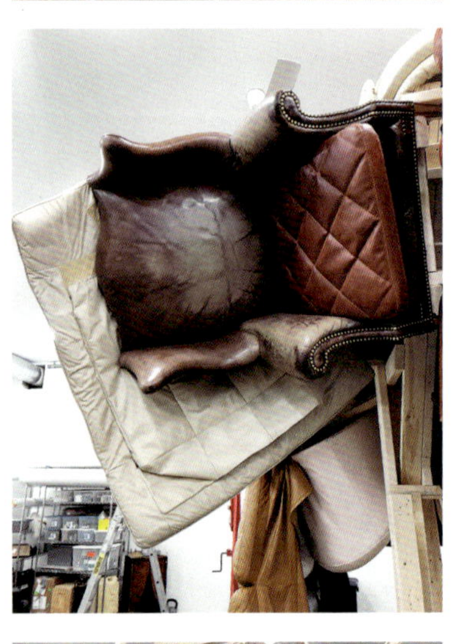 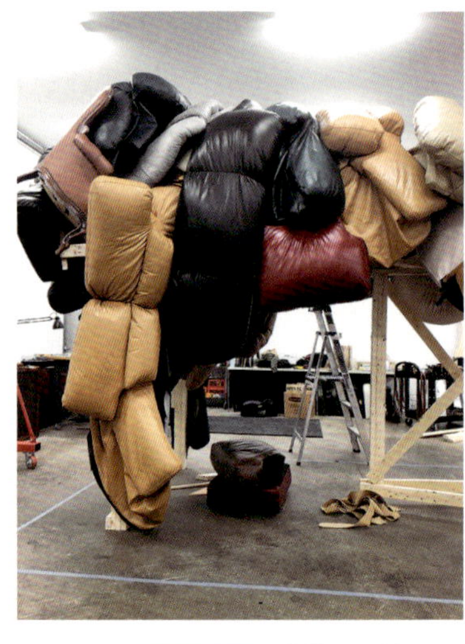 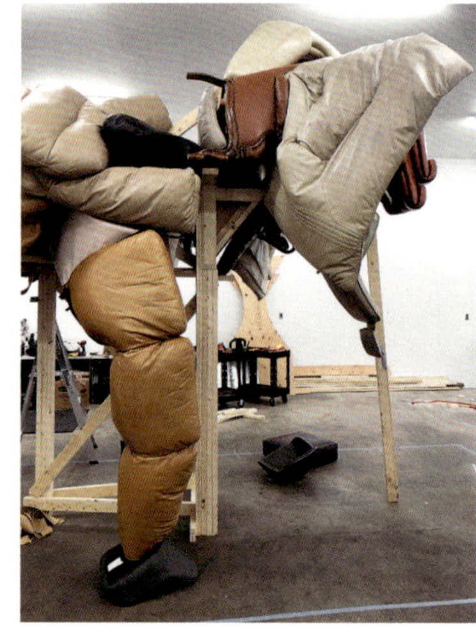 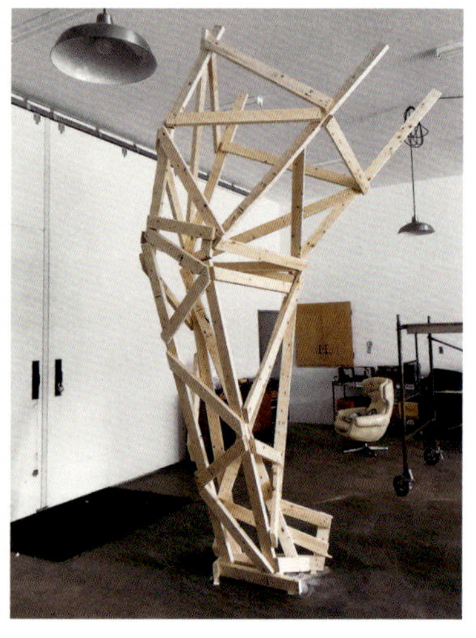

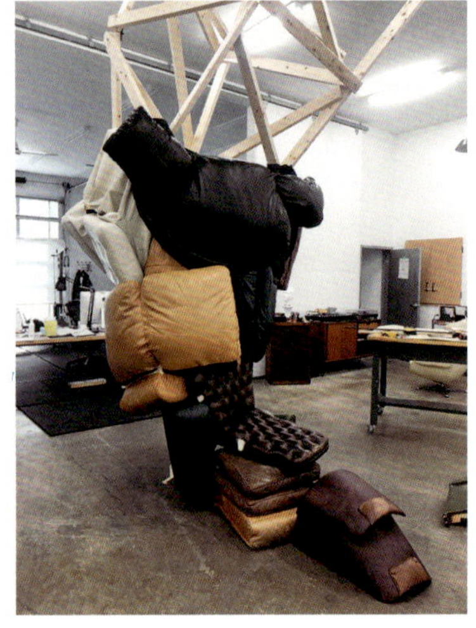 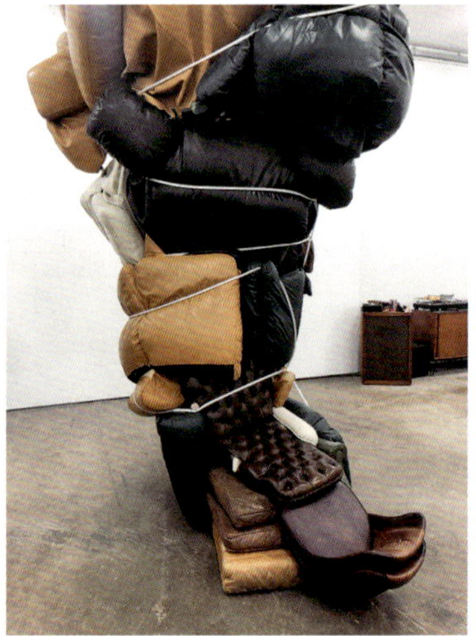 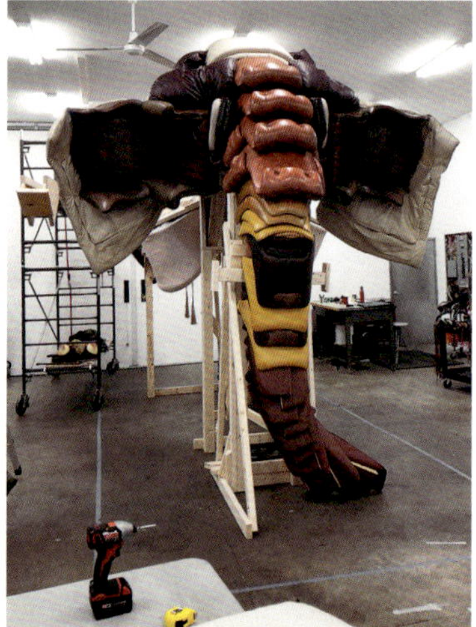 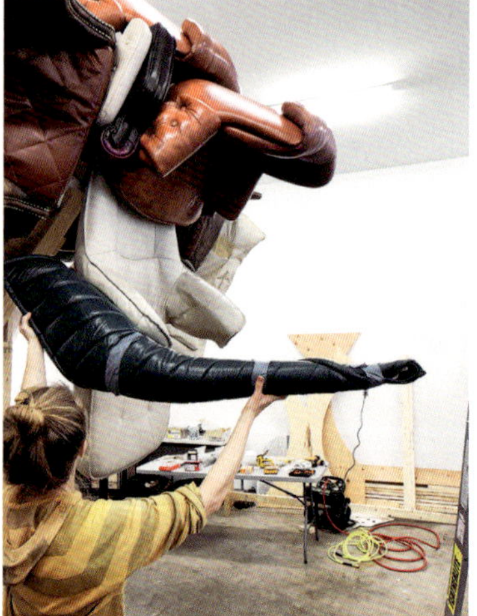

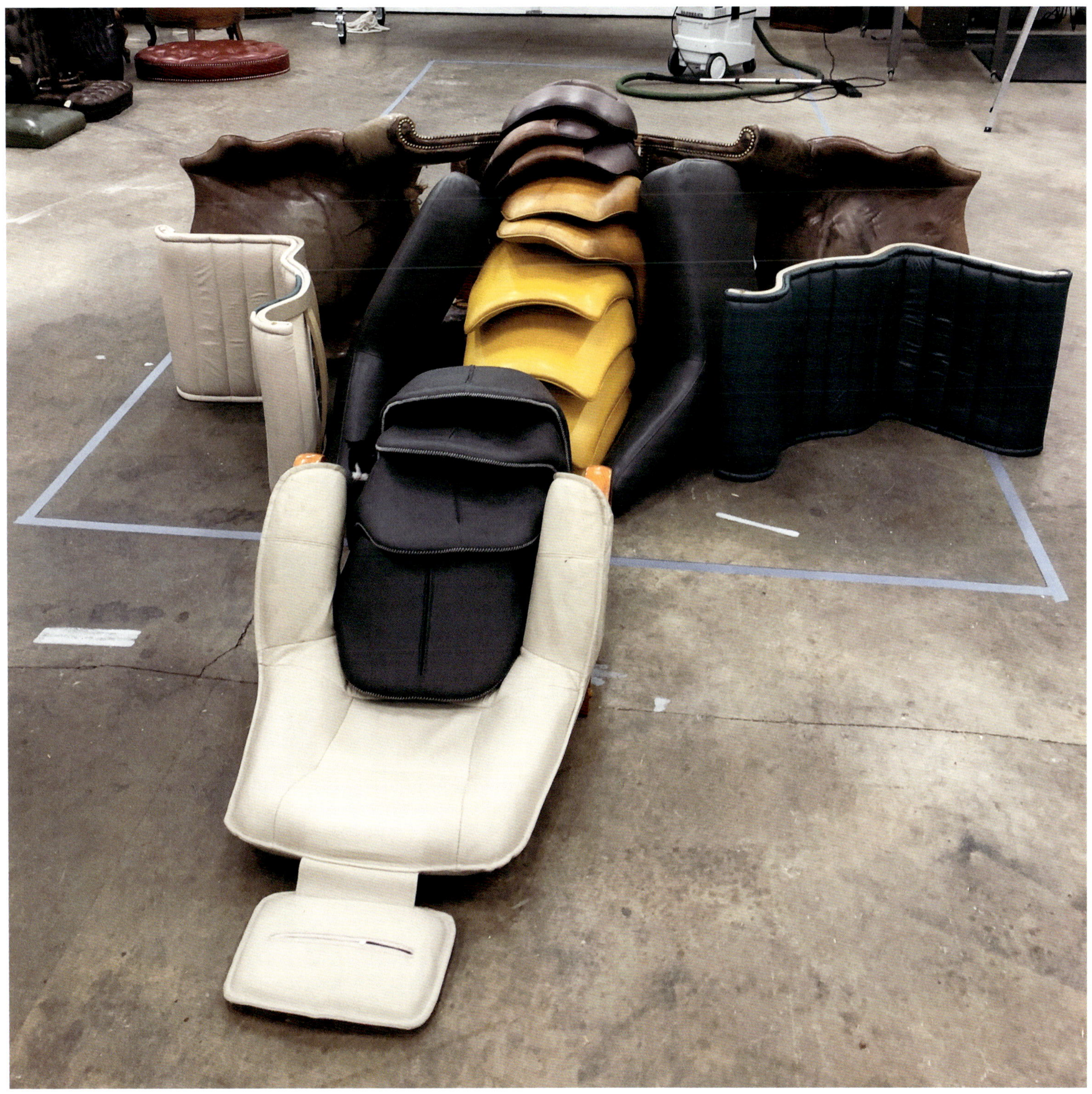

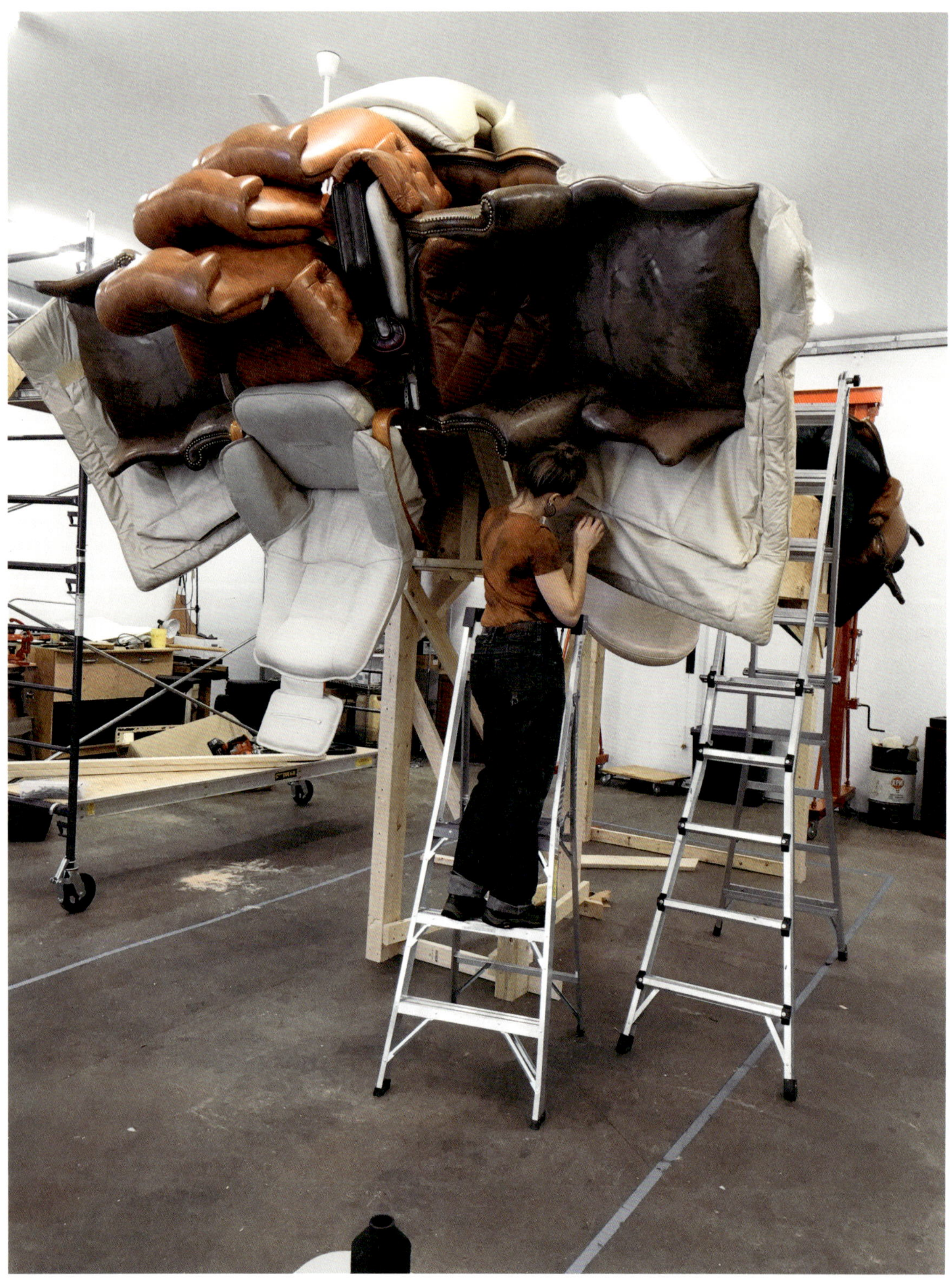

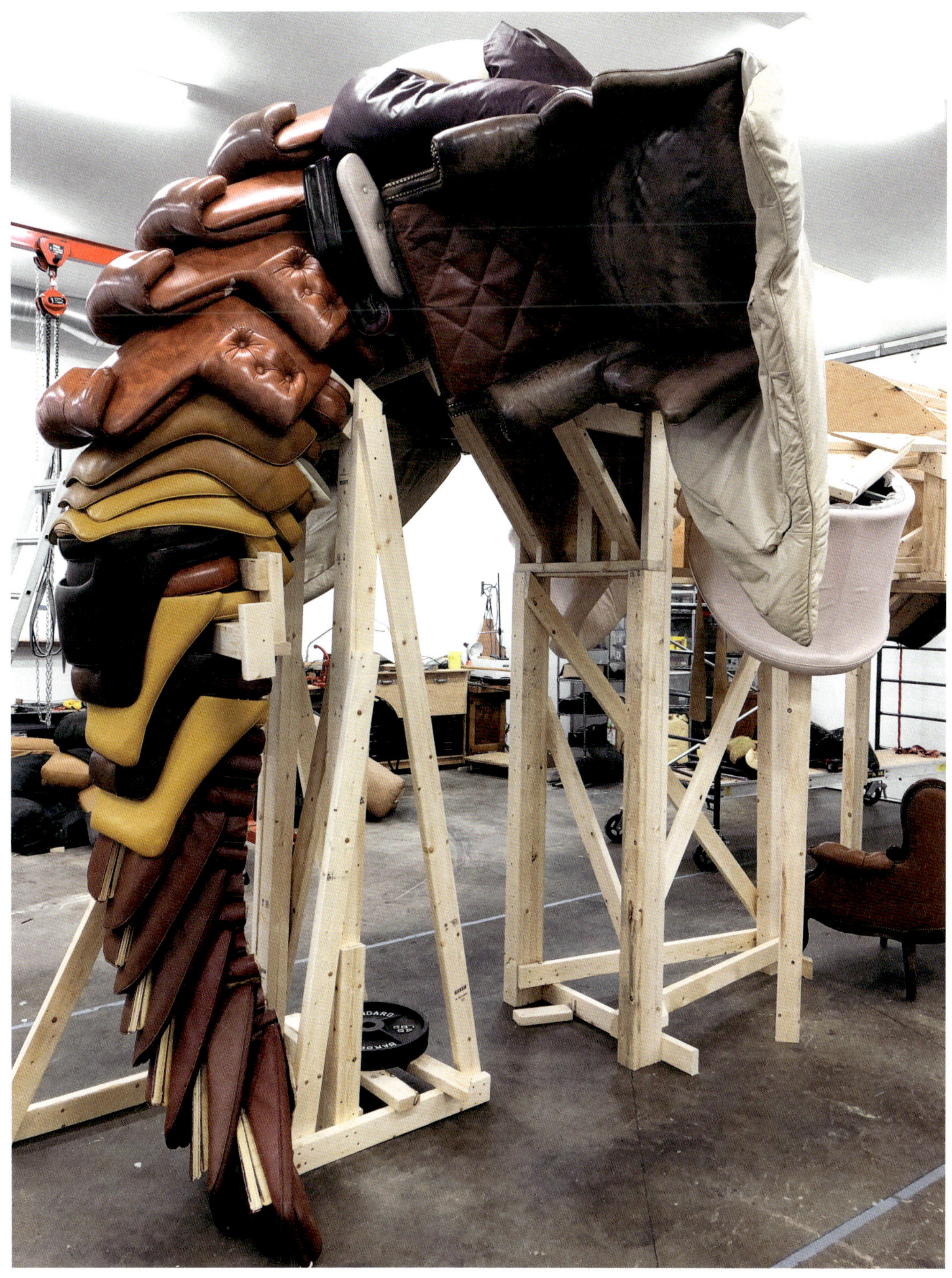

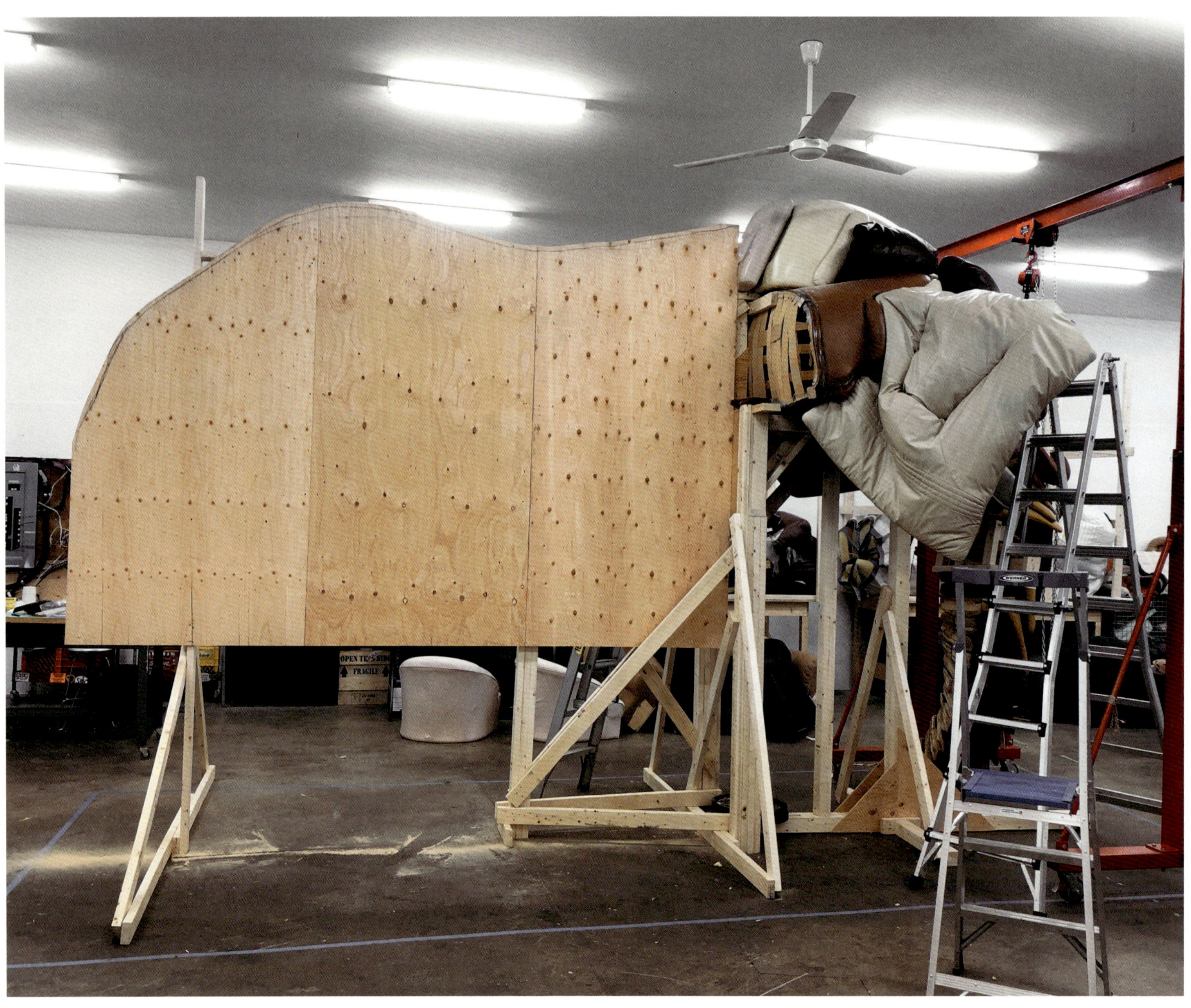

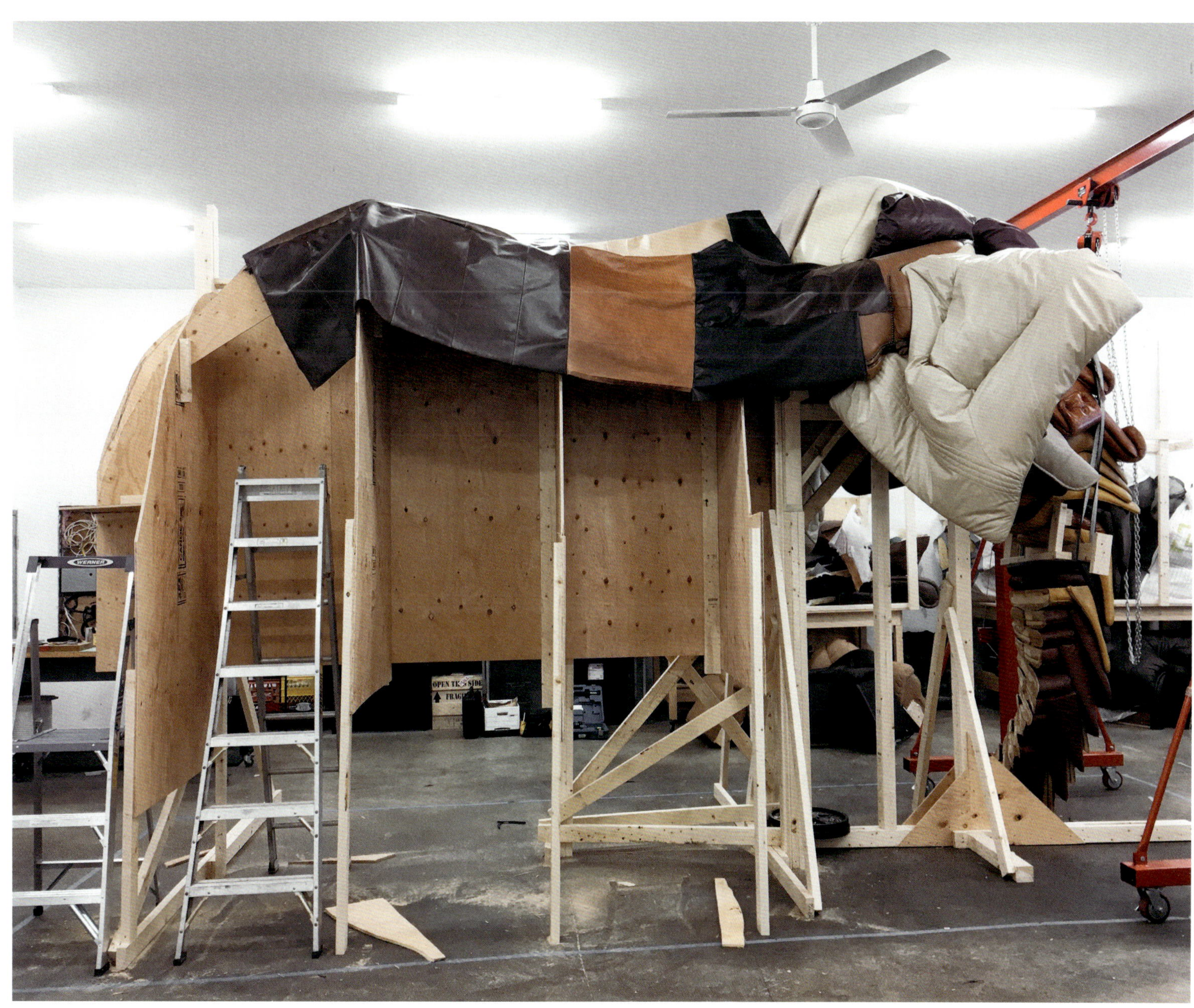

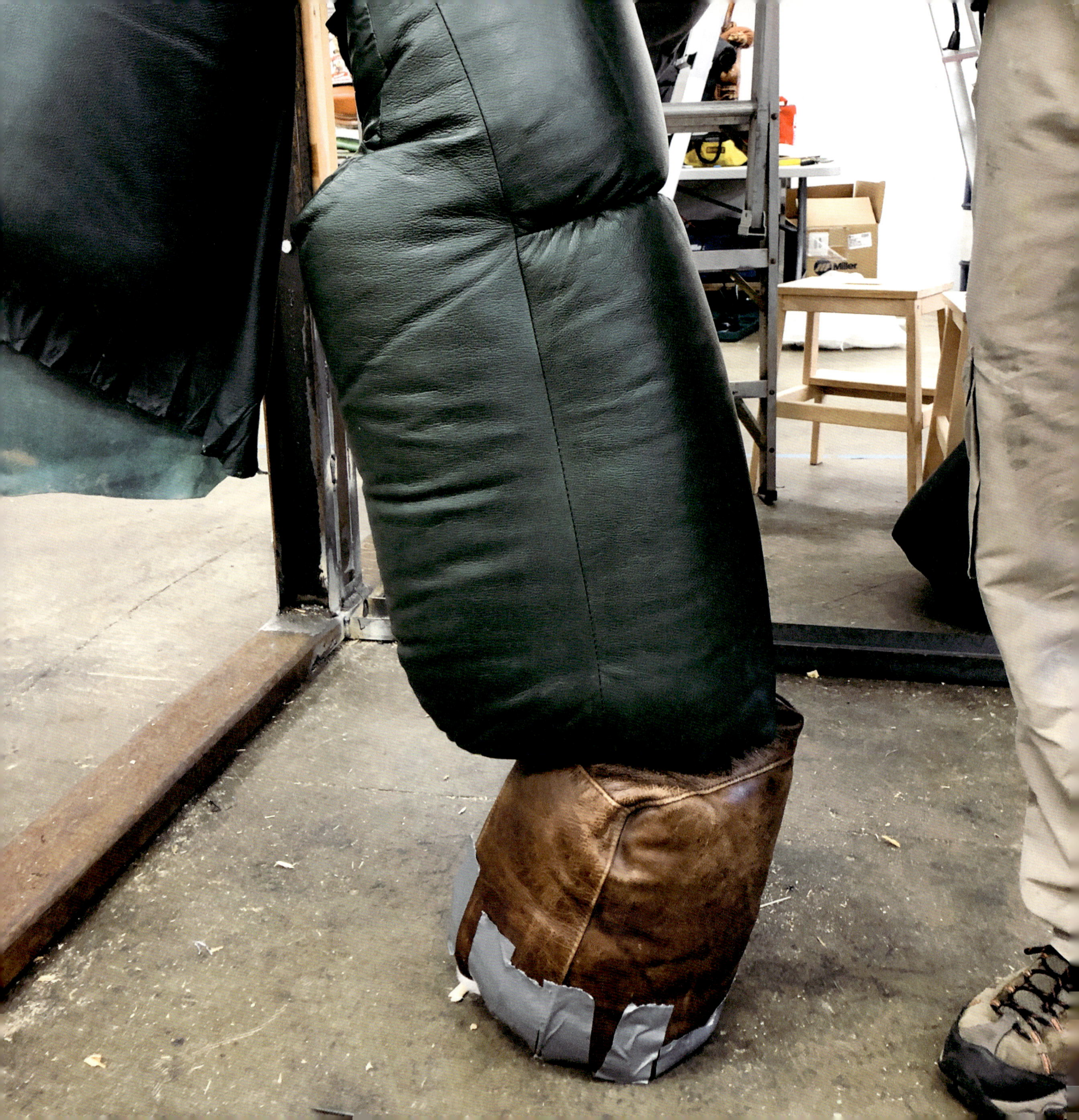

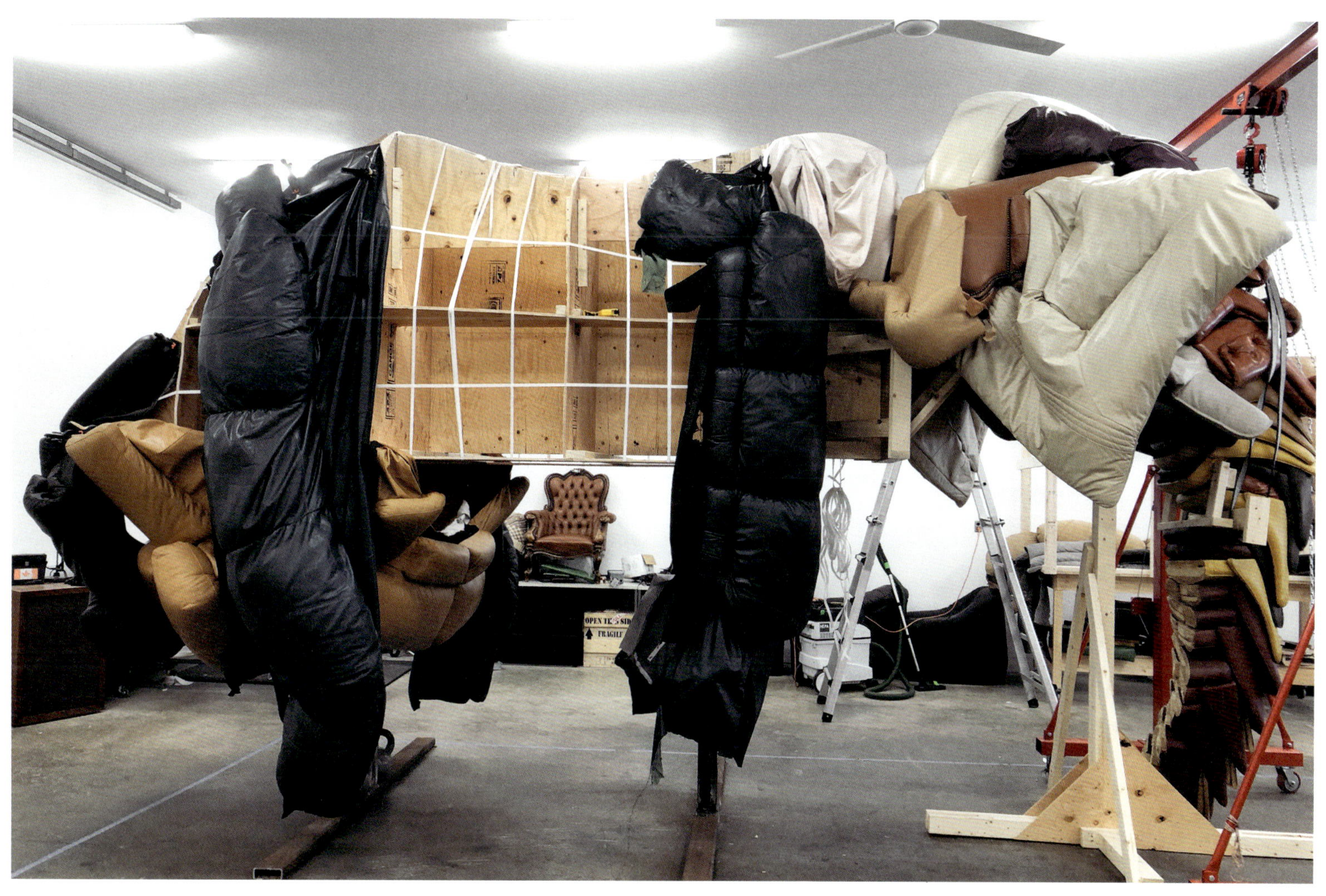

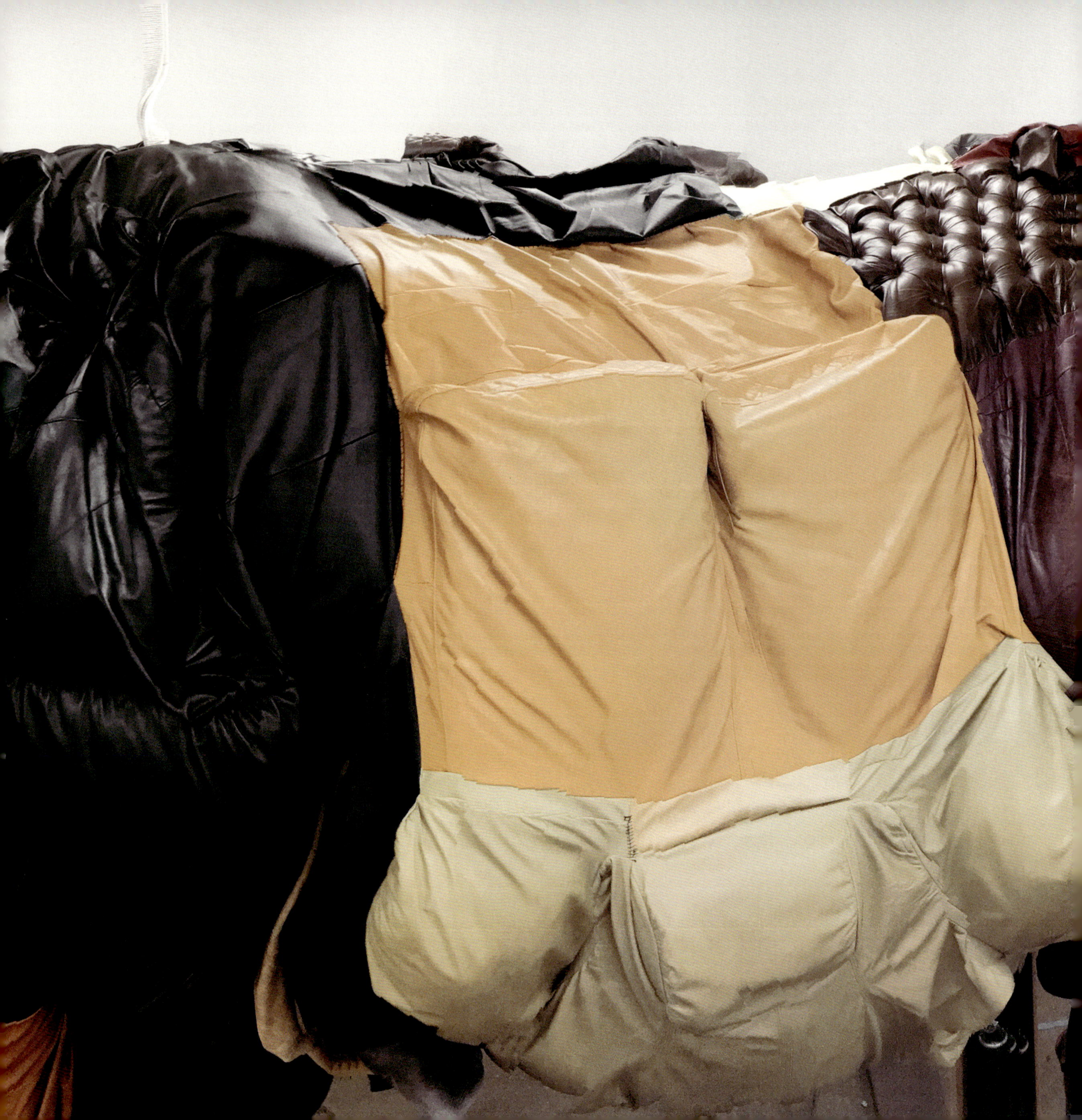

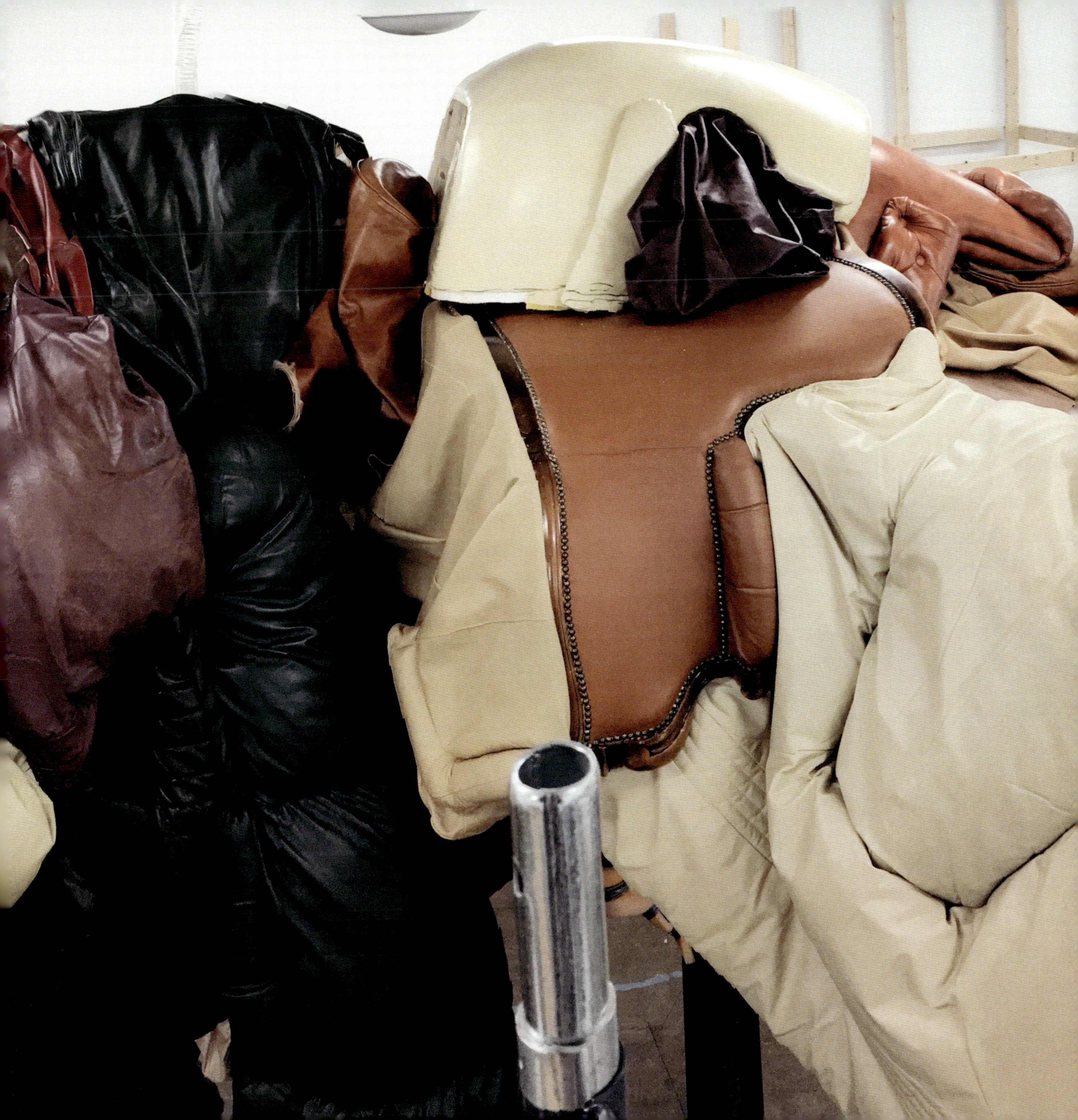

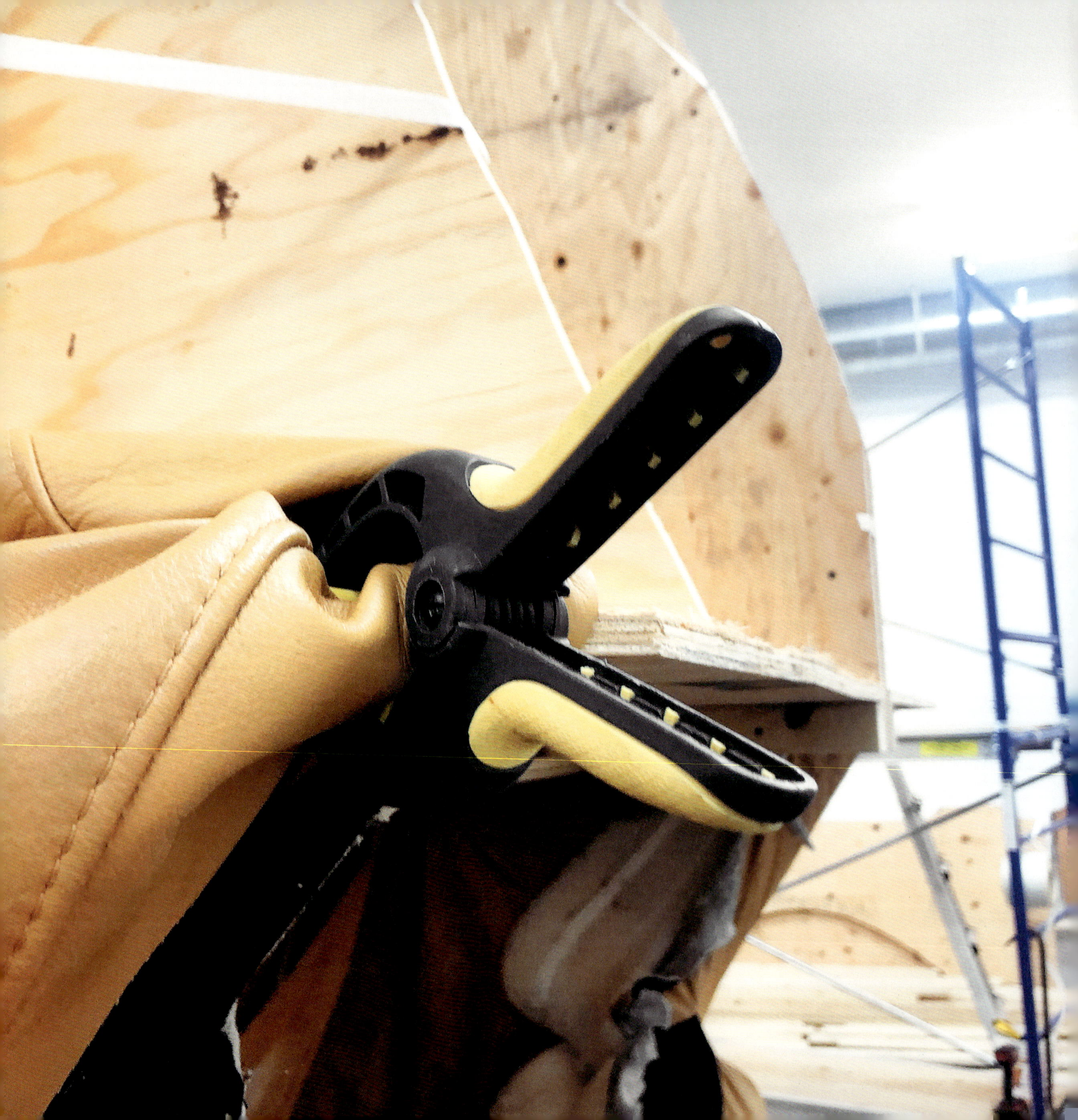

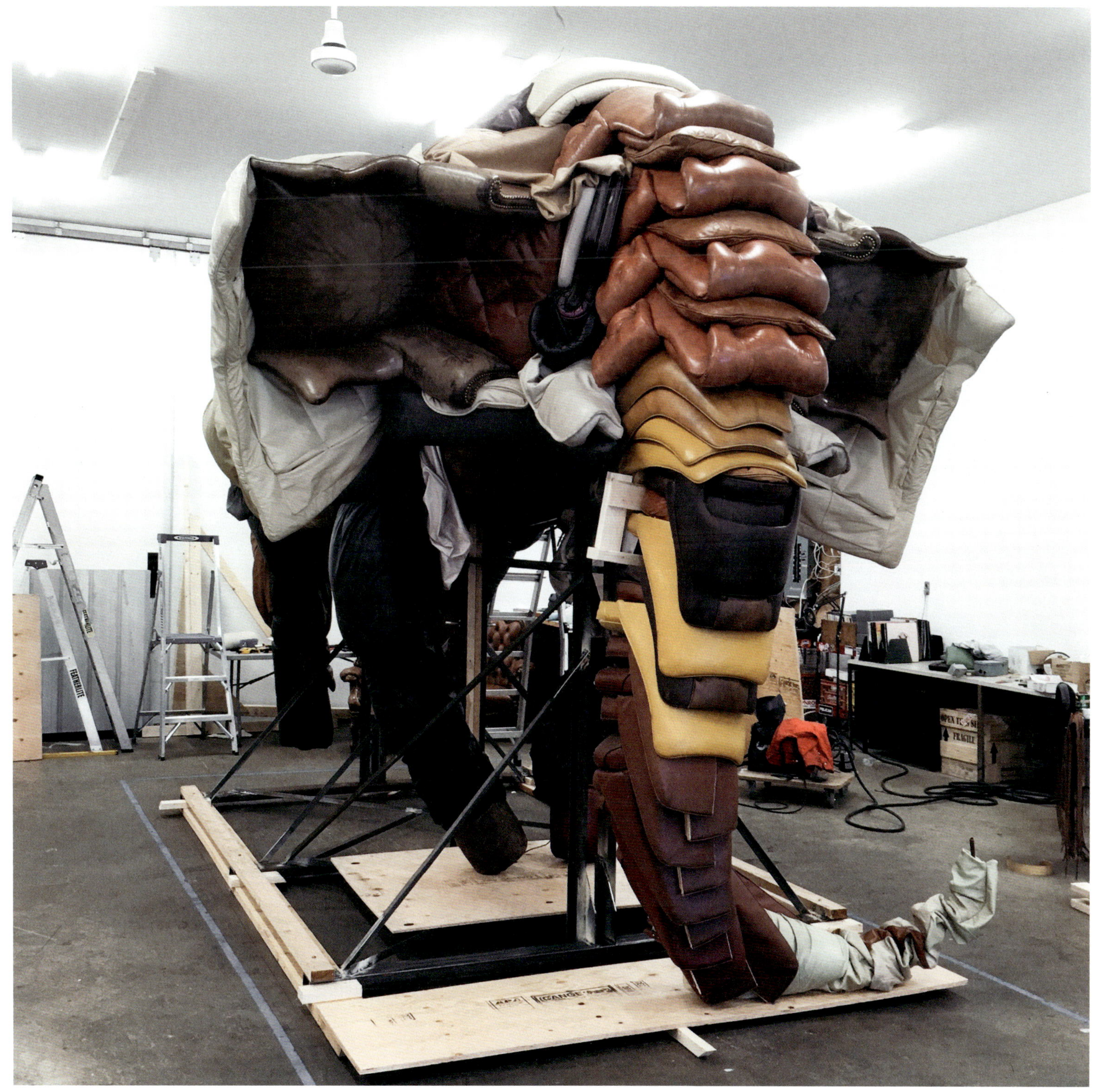

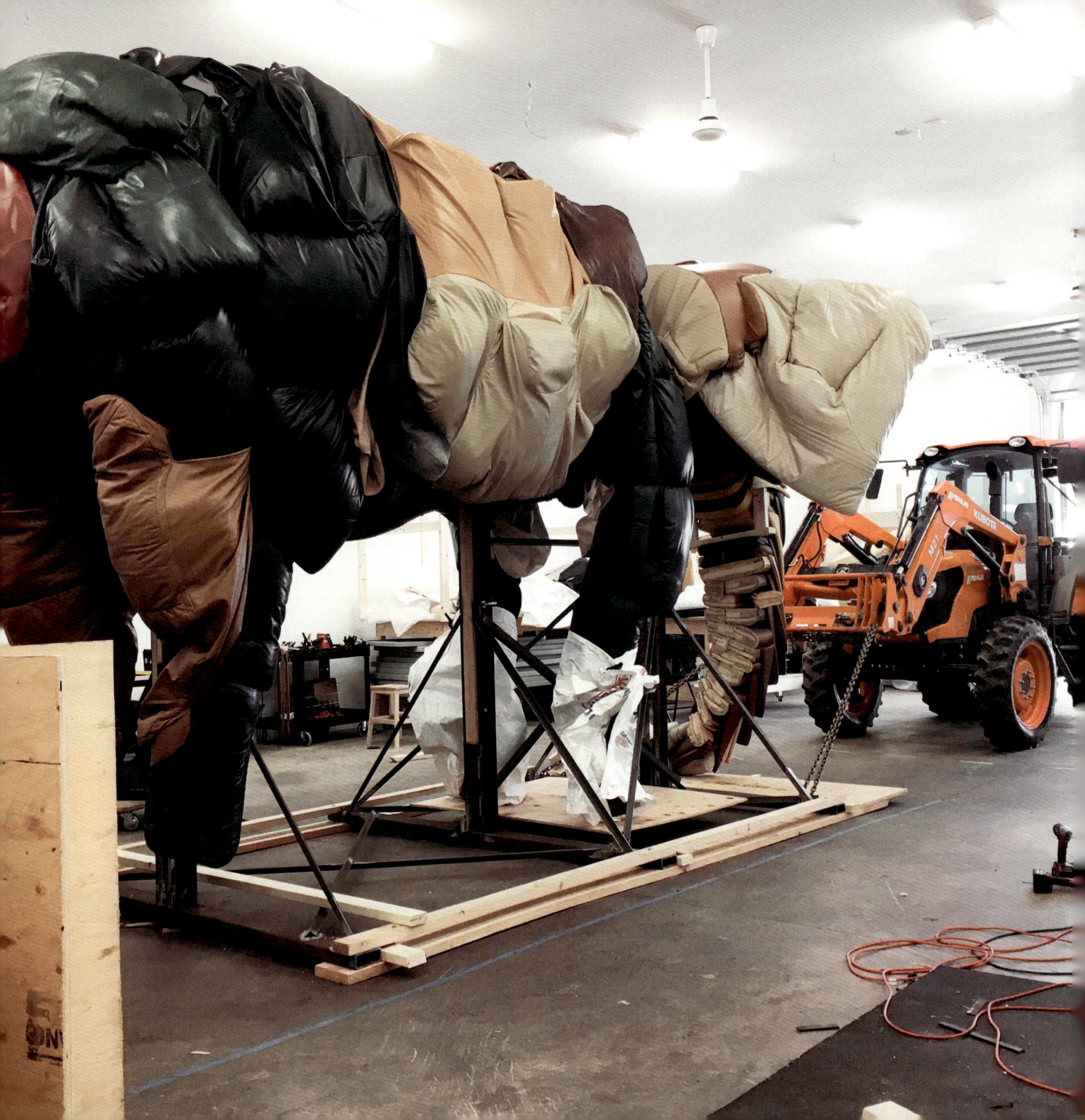

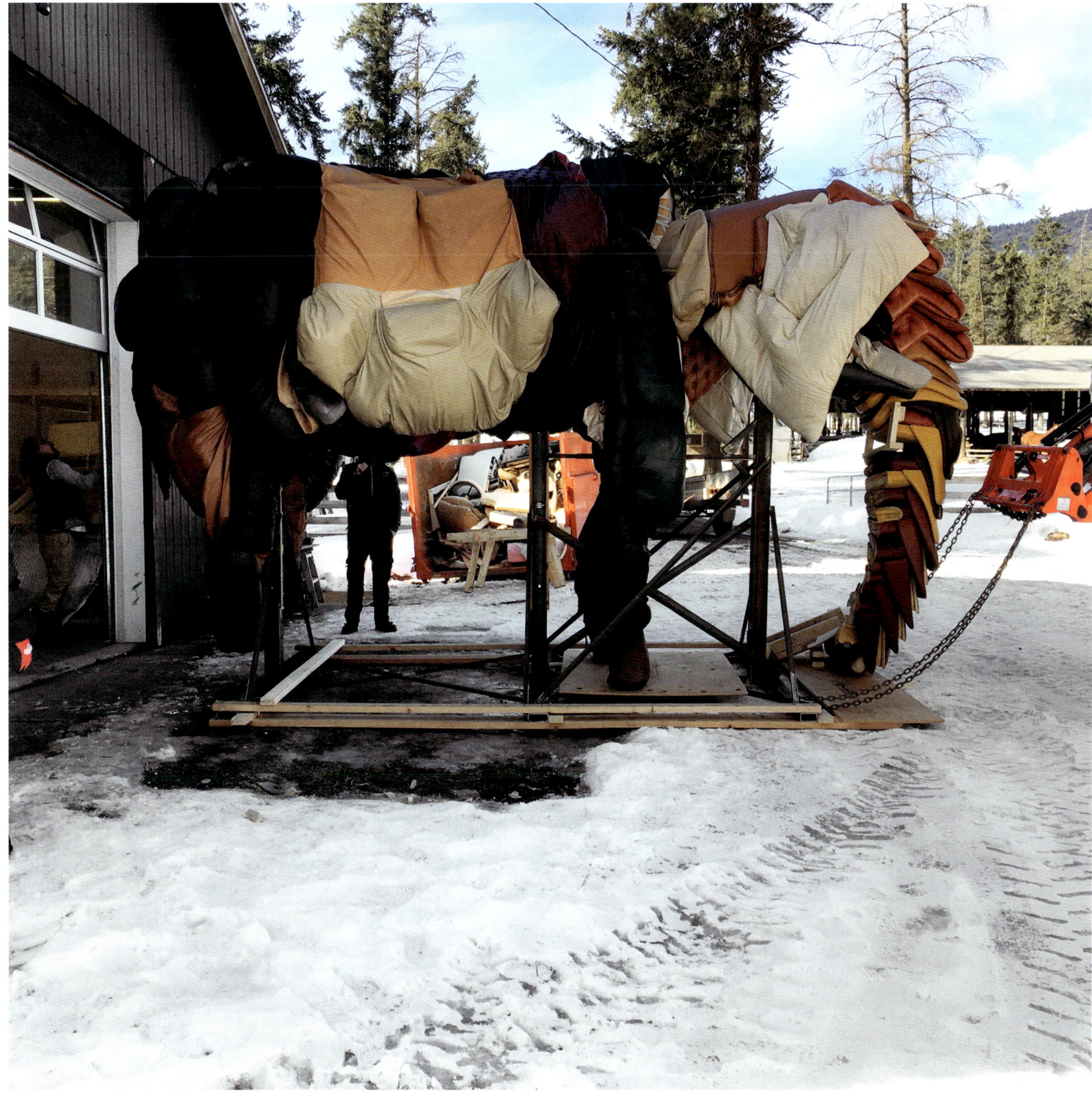

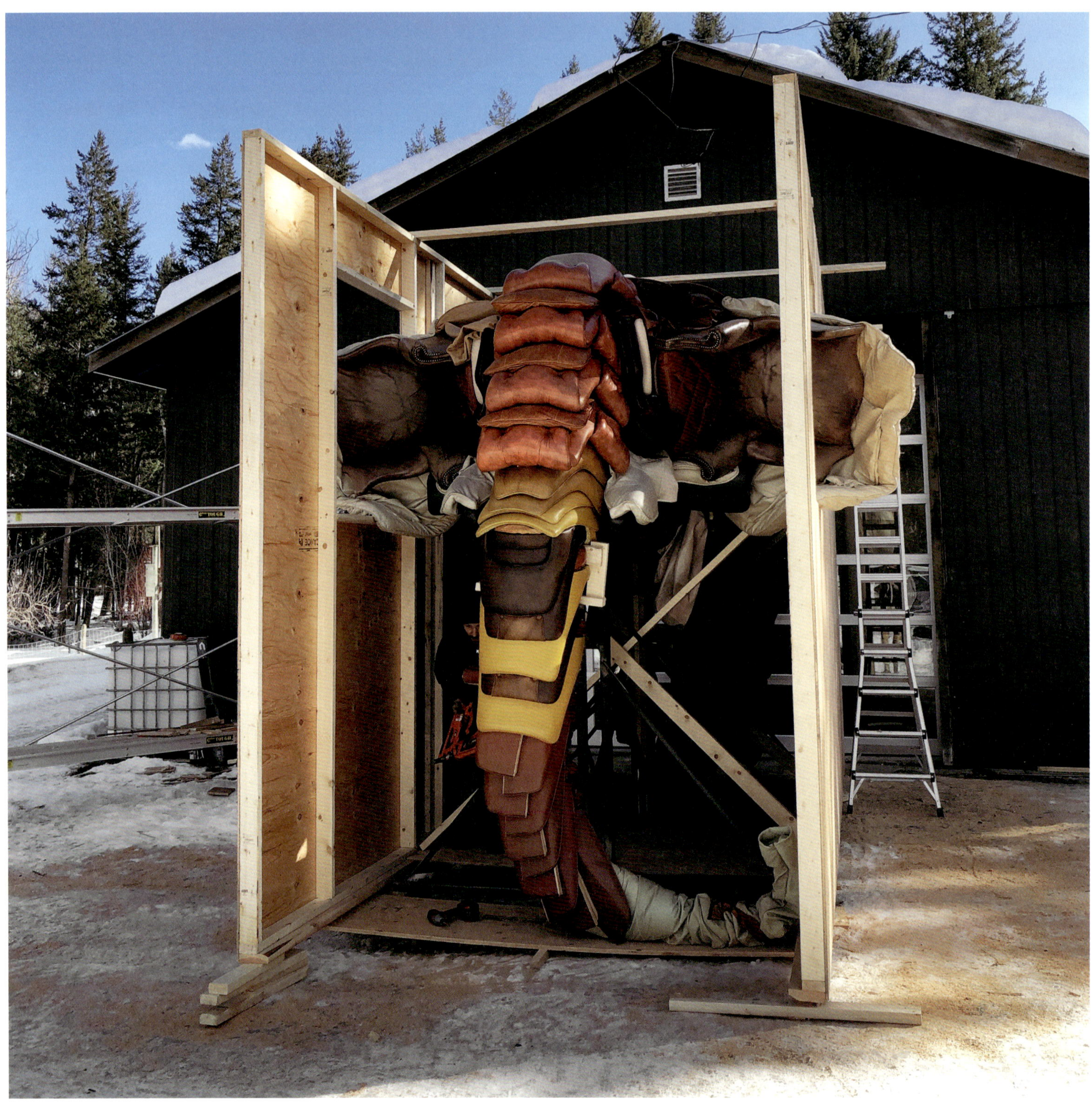

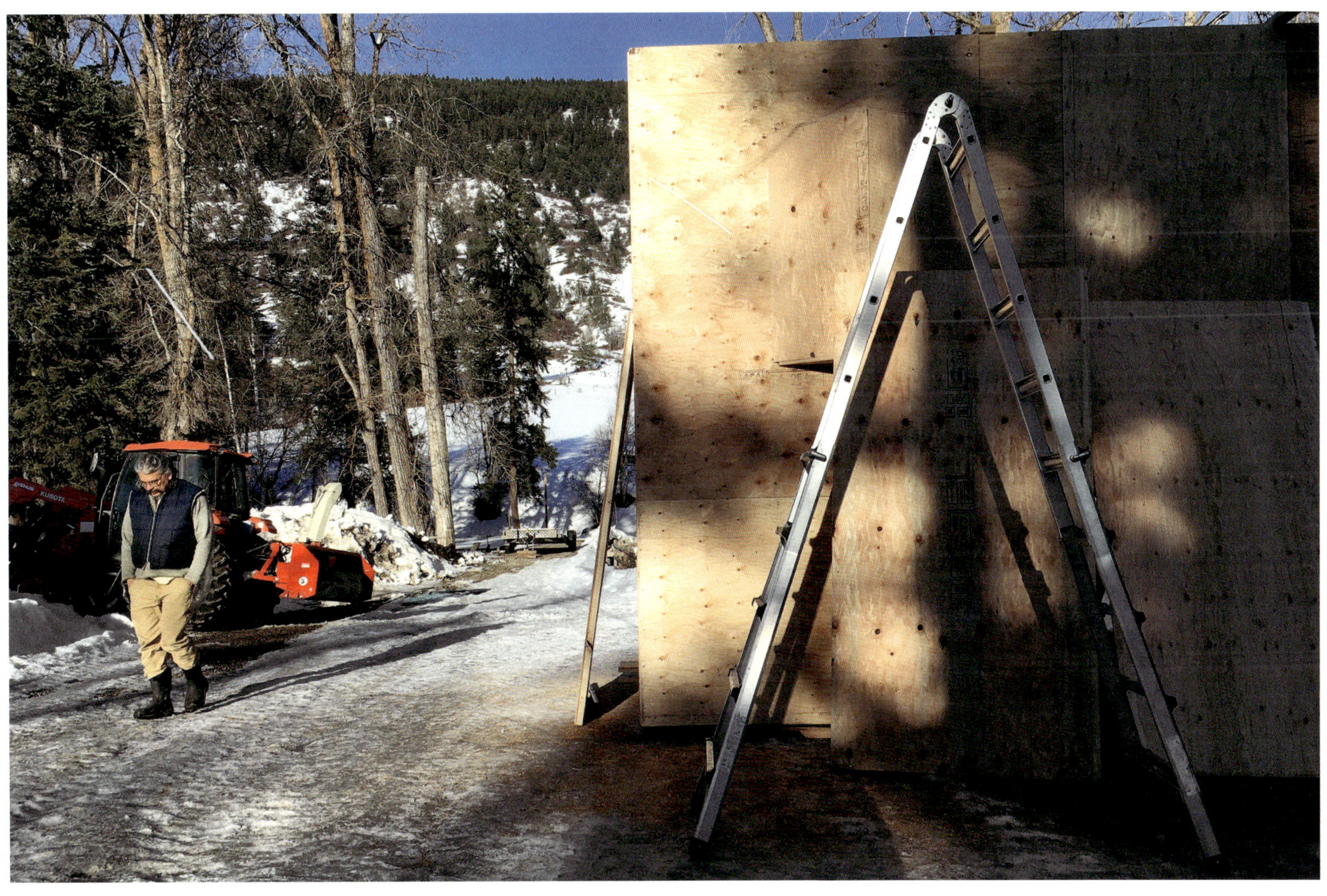

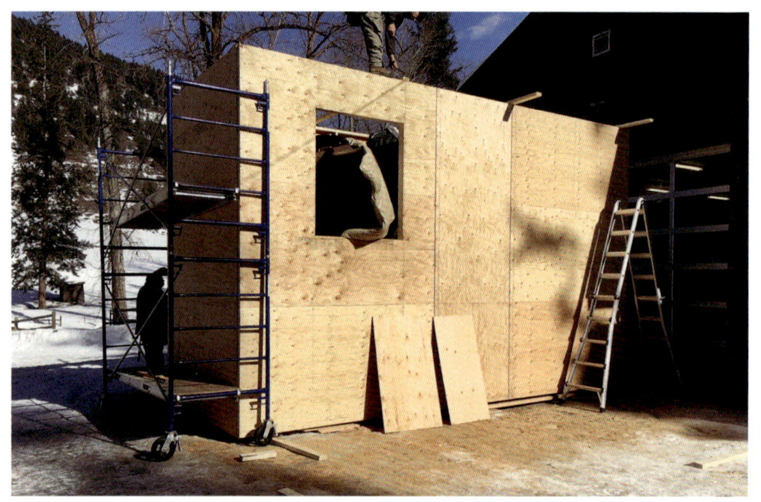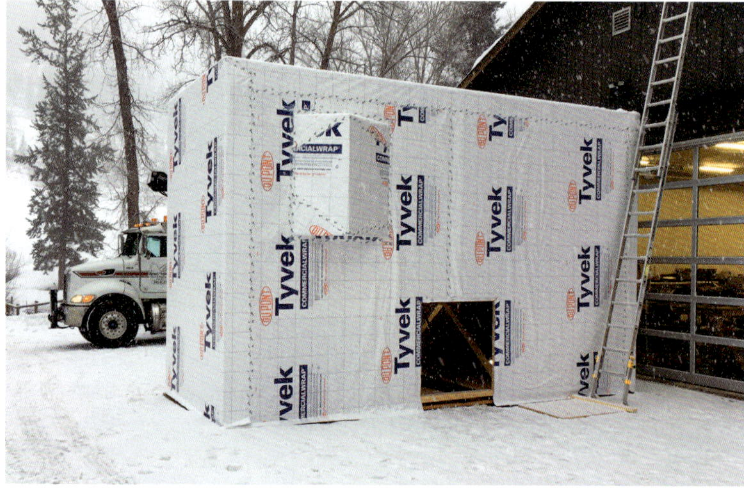

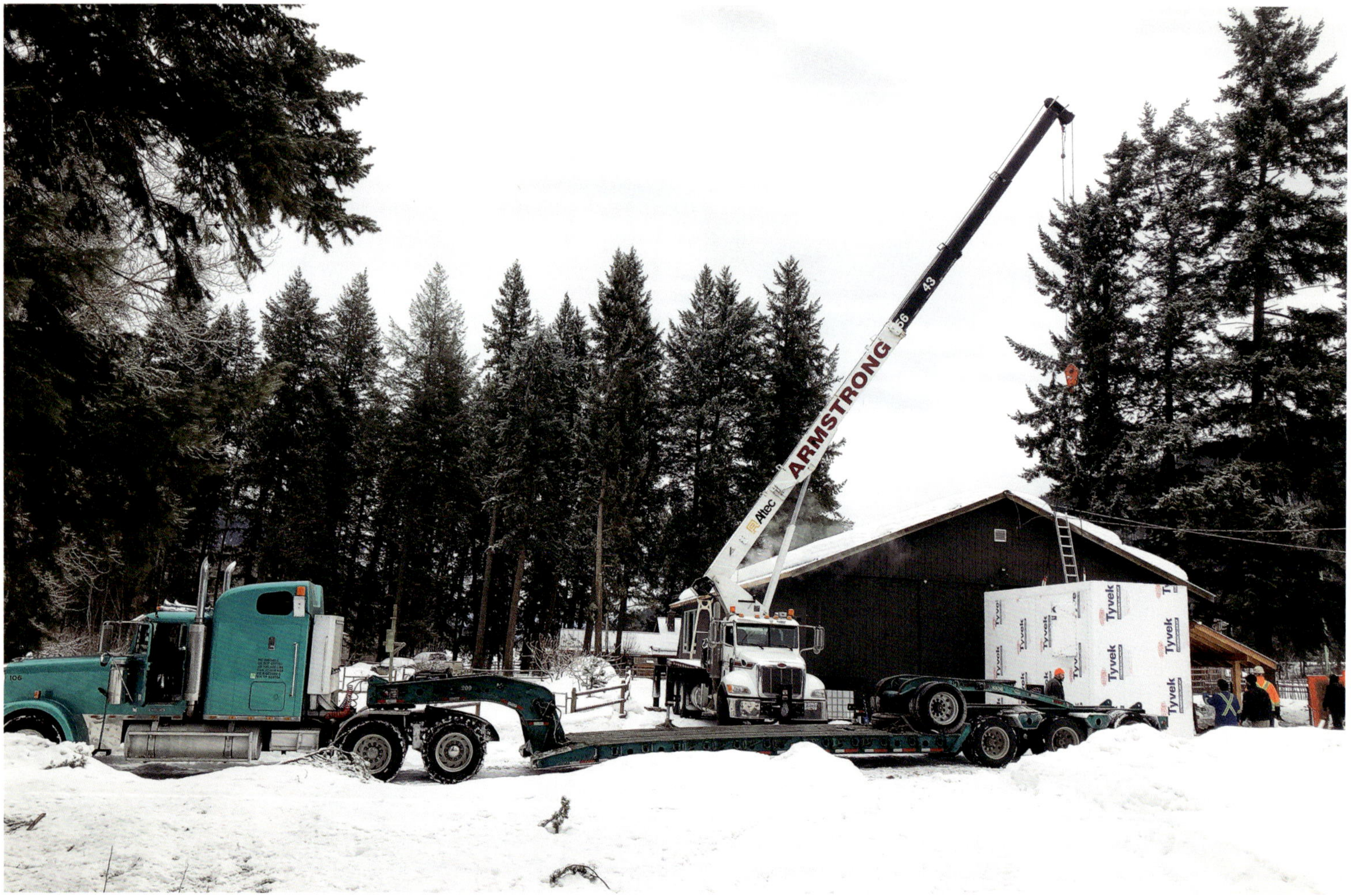

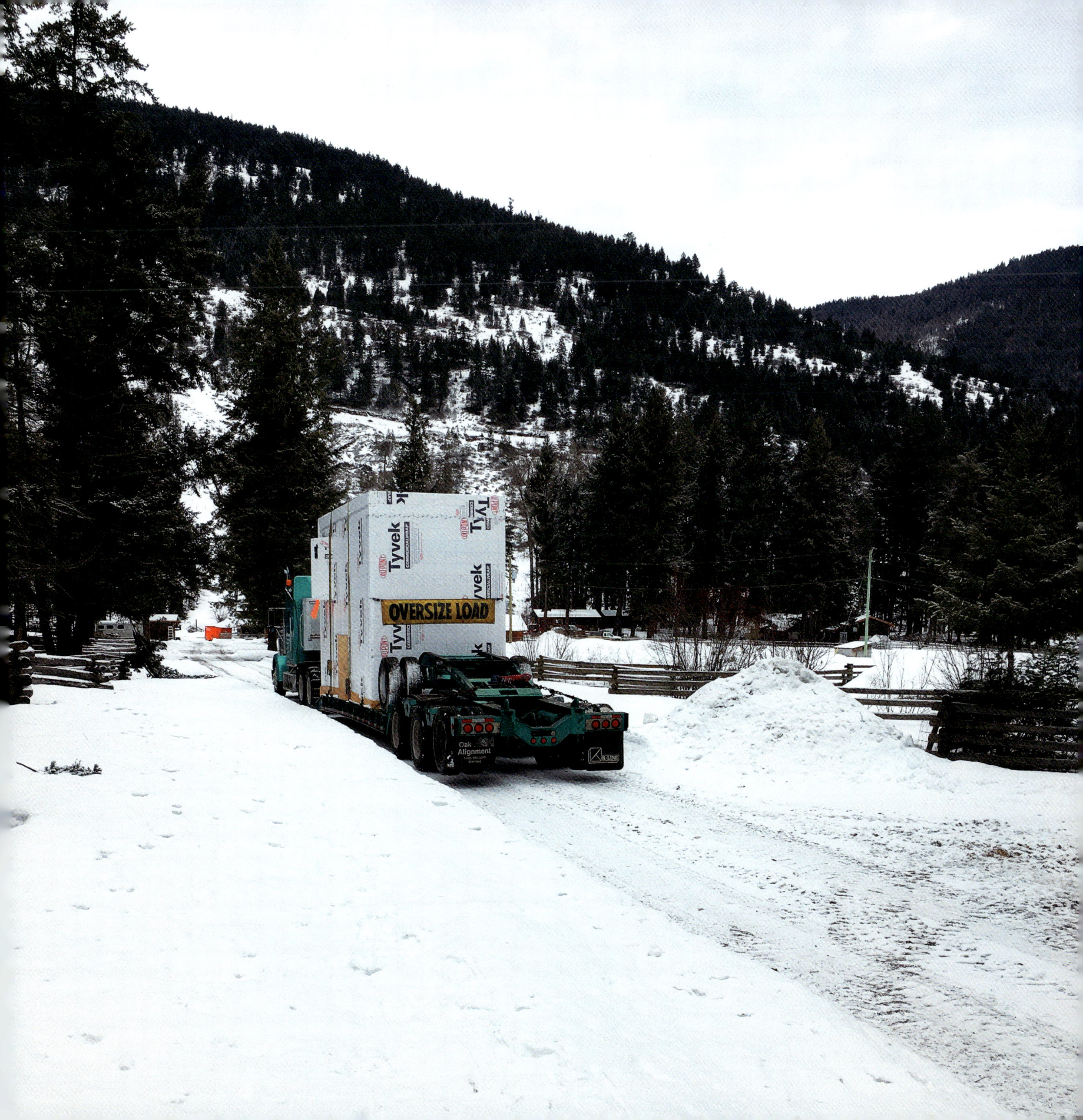
Tyvek
Tyvek
OVERSIZE LOAD
Oak
Alignment
K-LINE

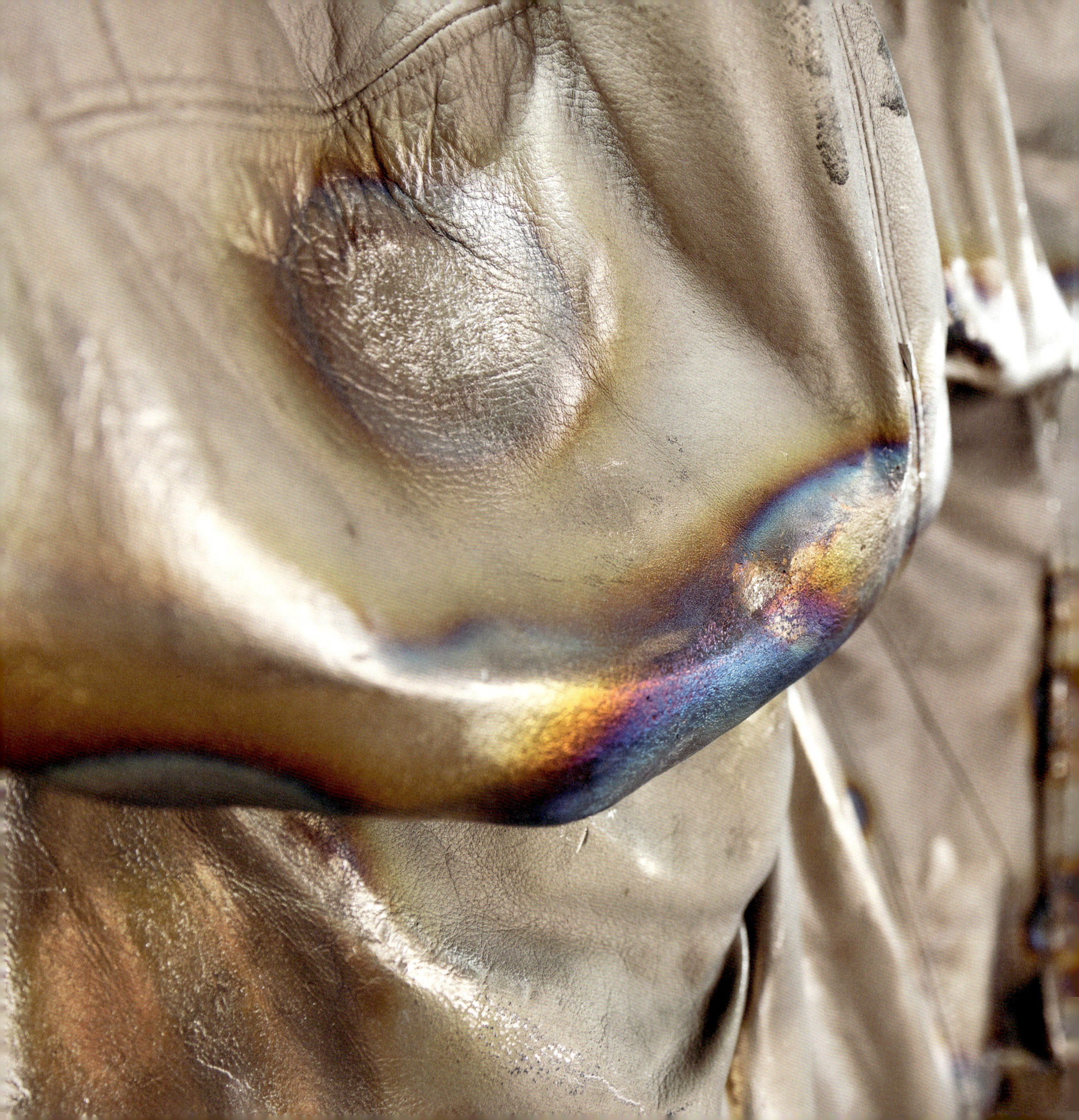

FOUNDRY

In March 2020, the *Couch Monster* prototype was transported from Jungen's studio in British Columba's Okanagan Valley to the Walla Walla Foundry in Washington, where the sculpture was cast in bronze. To capture the original leather texture of the artwork, the technicians at the Foundry created negative moulds of the entire prototype with silicone rubber and poured wax into them. Once cooled and hardened, the wax was removed, resulting in positive reproductions of the artwork's surfaces. Next, these pieces were dipped into a ceramic material, which hardened into a white shell. The shells were heated to melt out the wax, leaving behind hollow ceramic moulds, into which molten bronze was poured. 175 individual bronze pieces were then cast and seamlessly welded together around a stainless steel armature. In the final stage of production, a patina was applied to the bronze and the surface was sealed with wax.

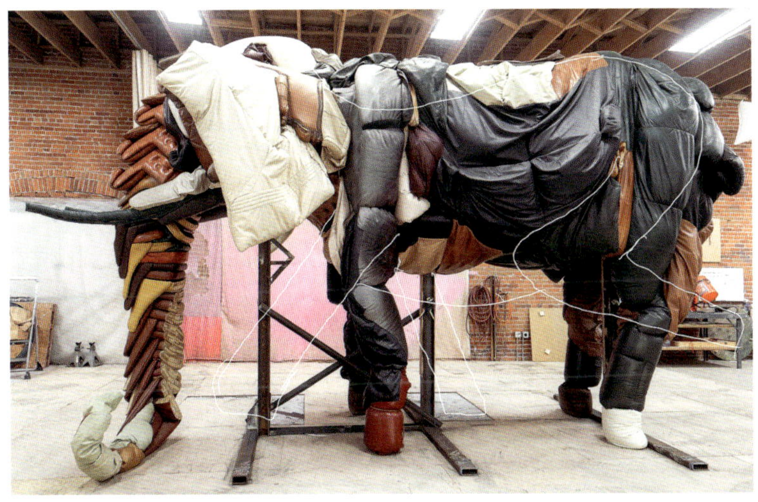

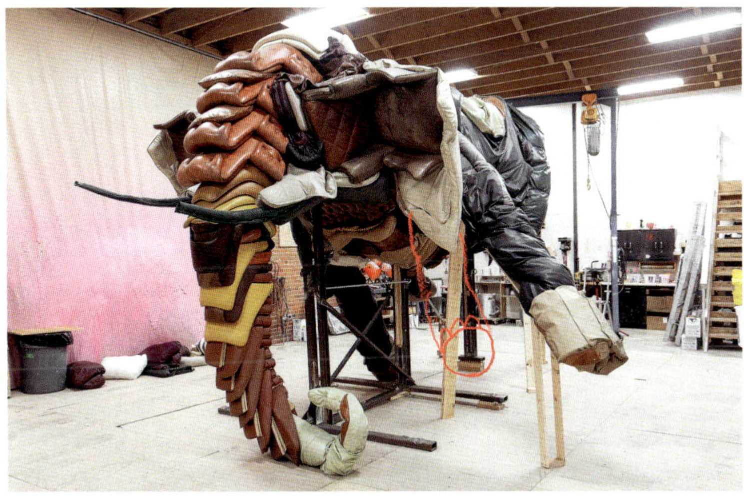

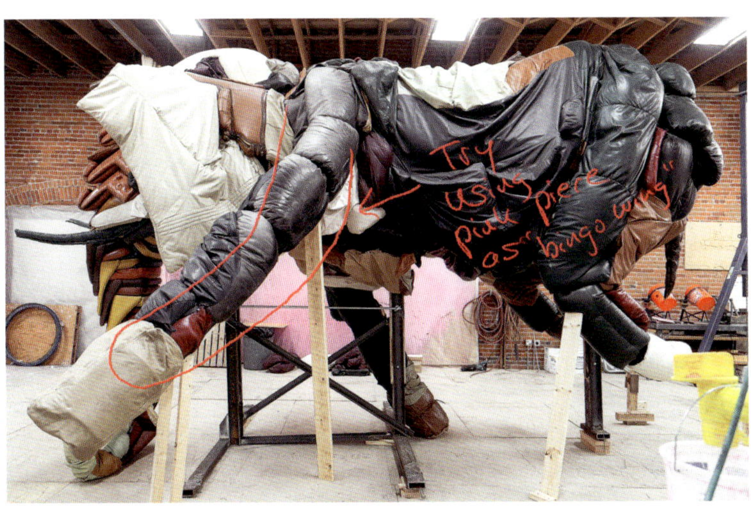
Try
using
pink piece
as a "bungalow"

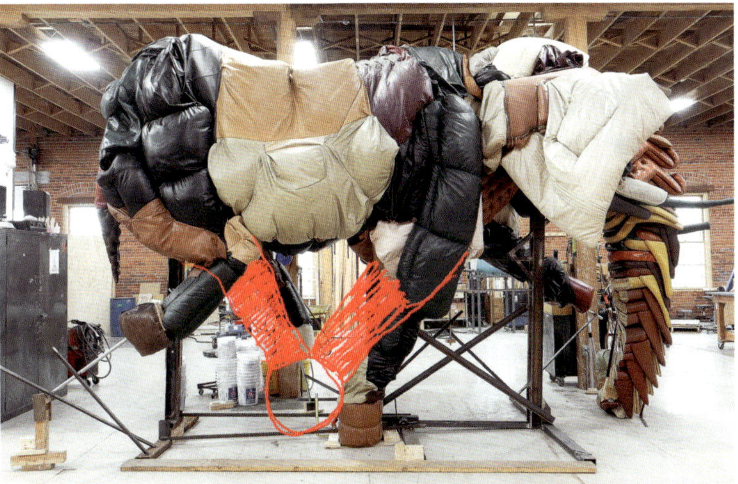

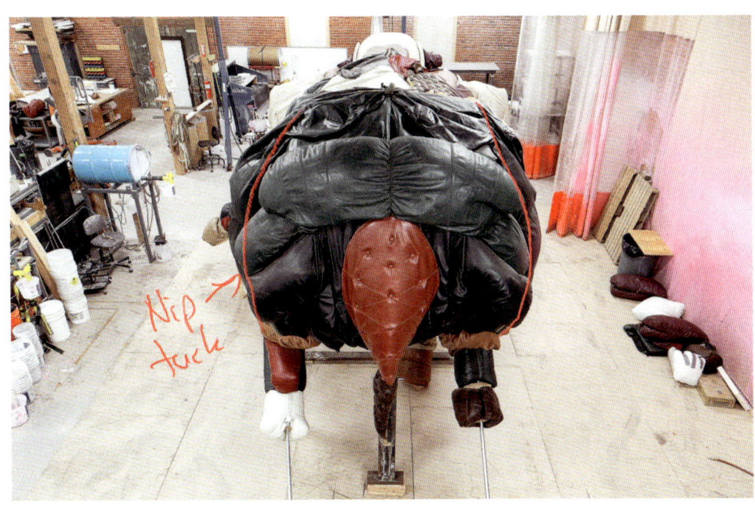
Nip
tuck

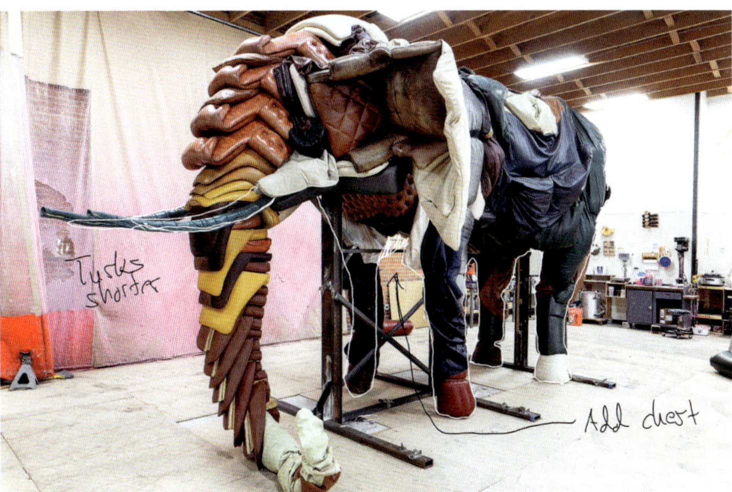
Tusks
shorter
Add chest

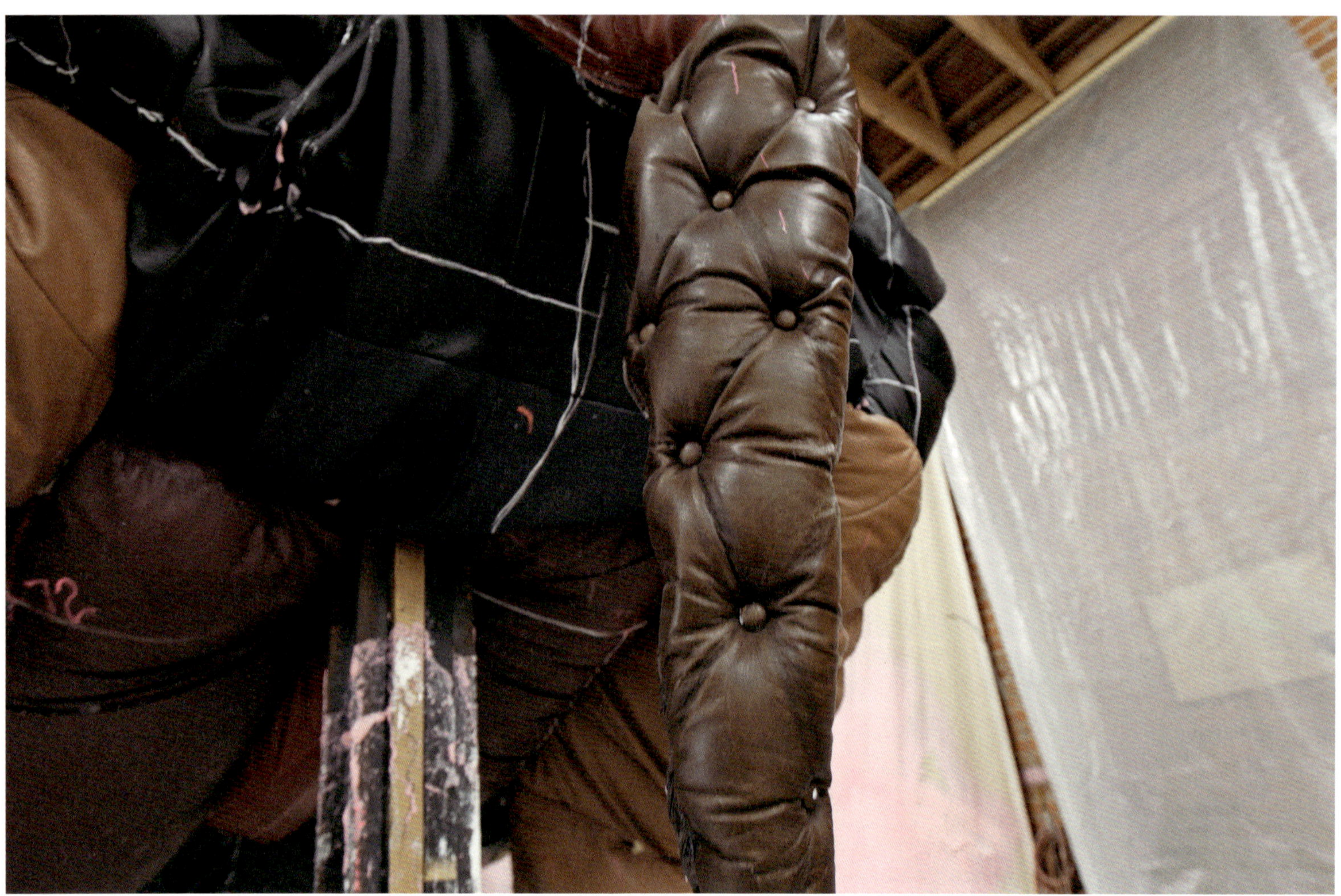

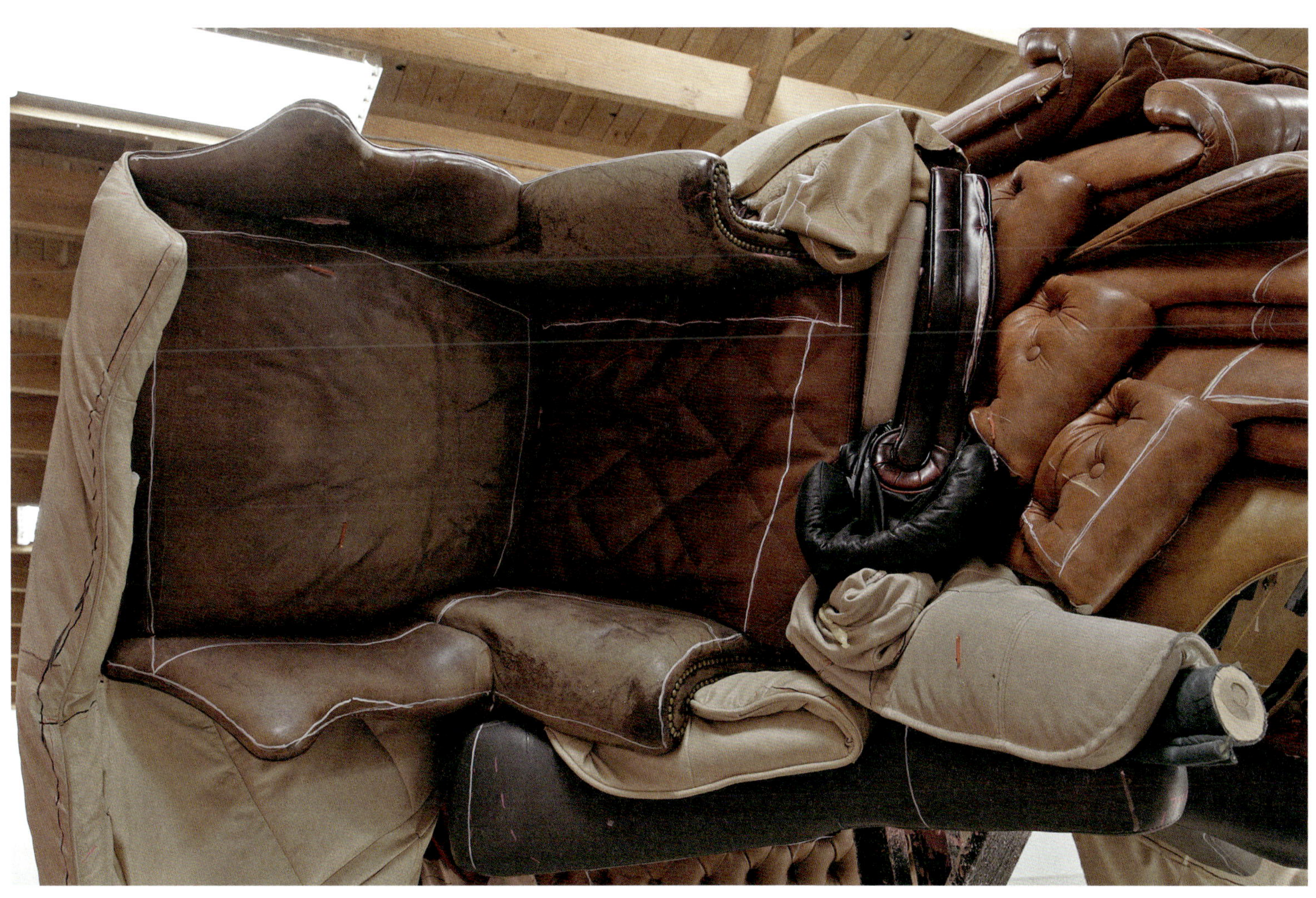

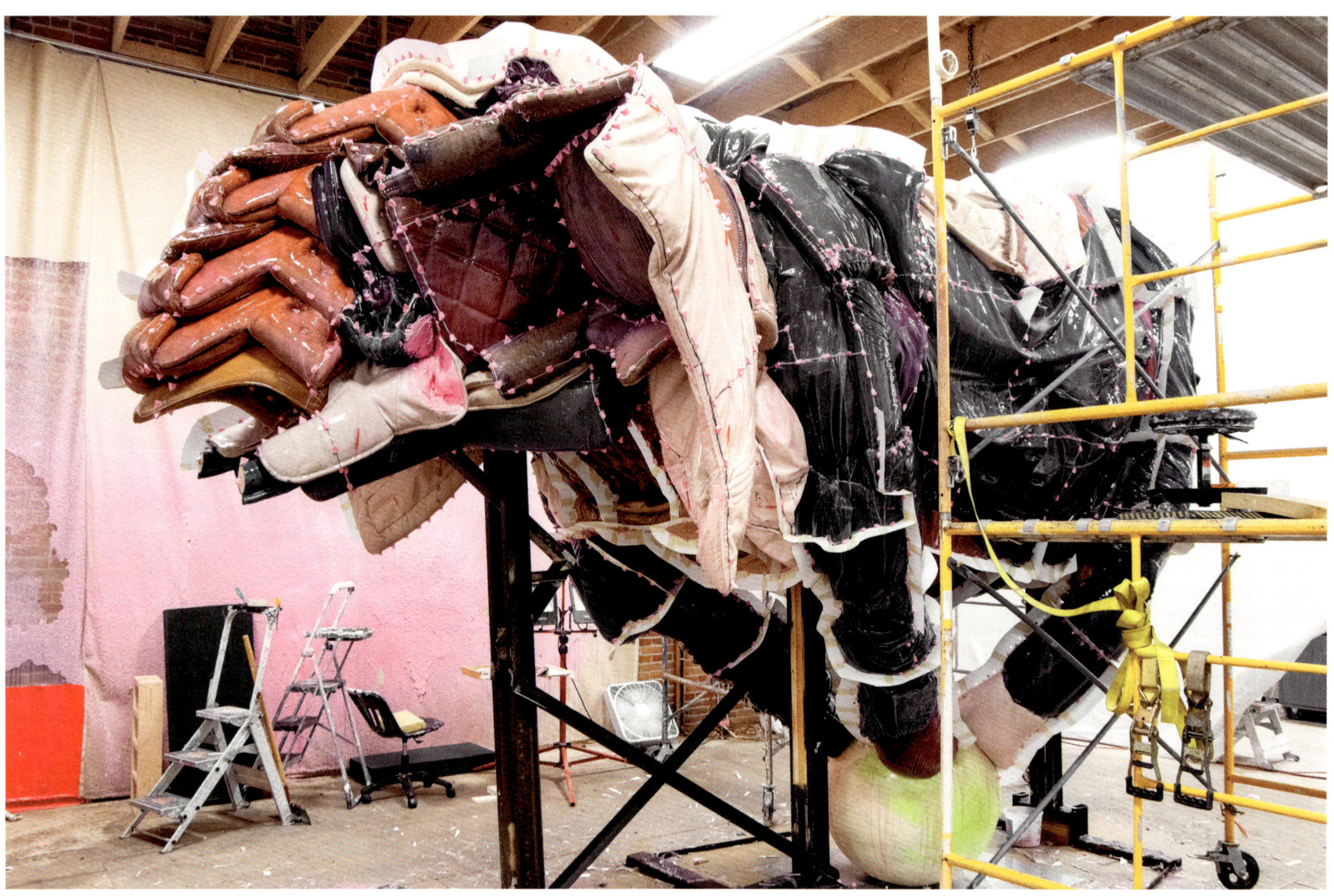

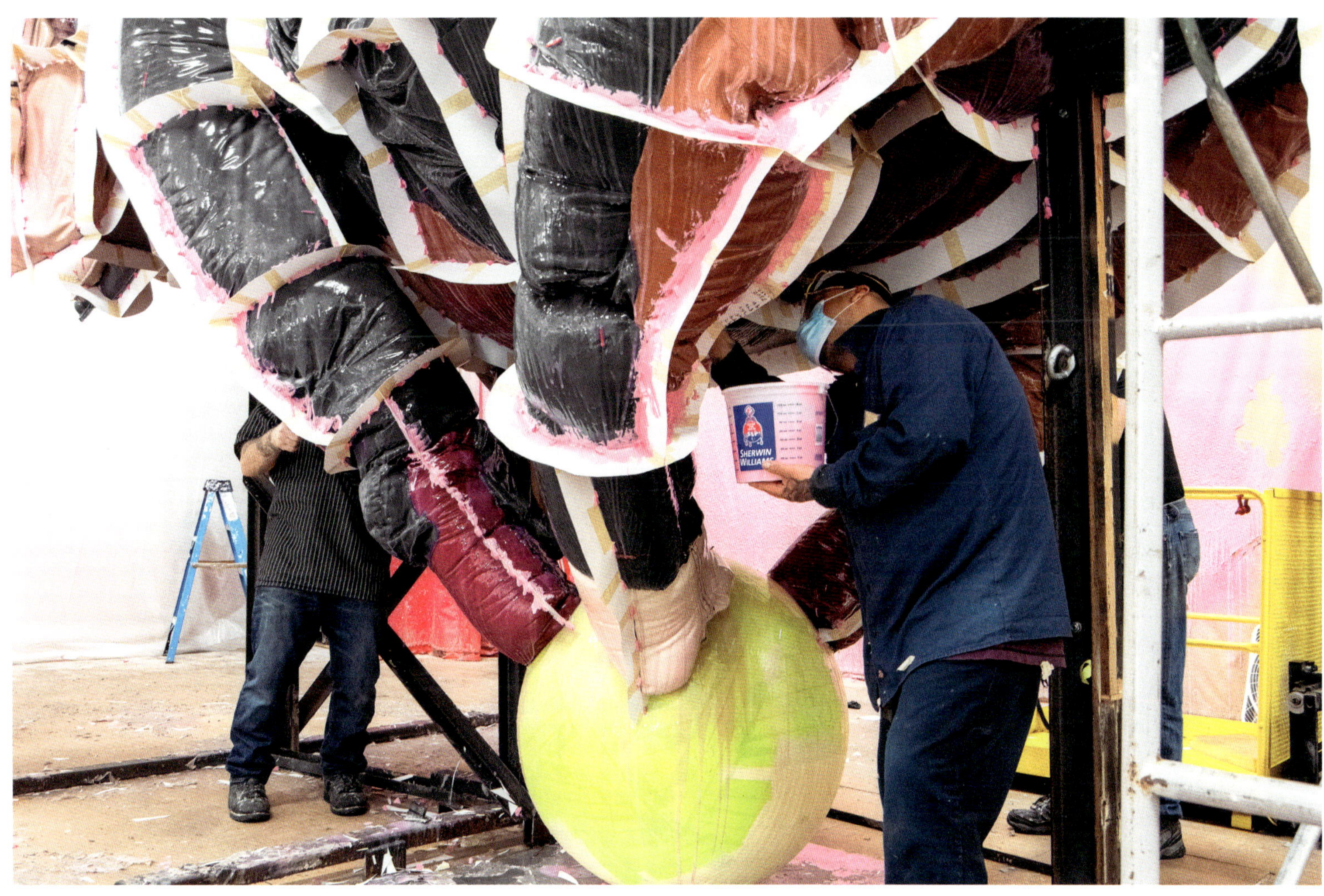

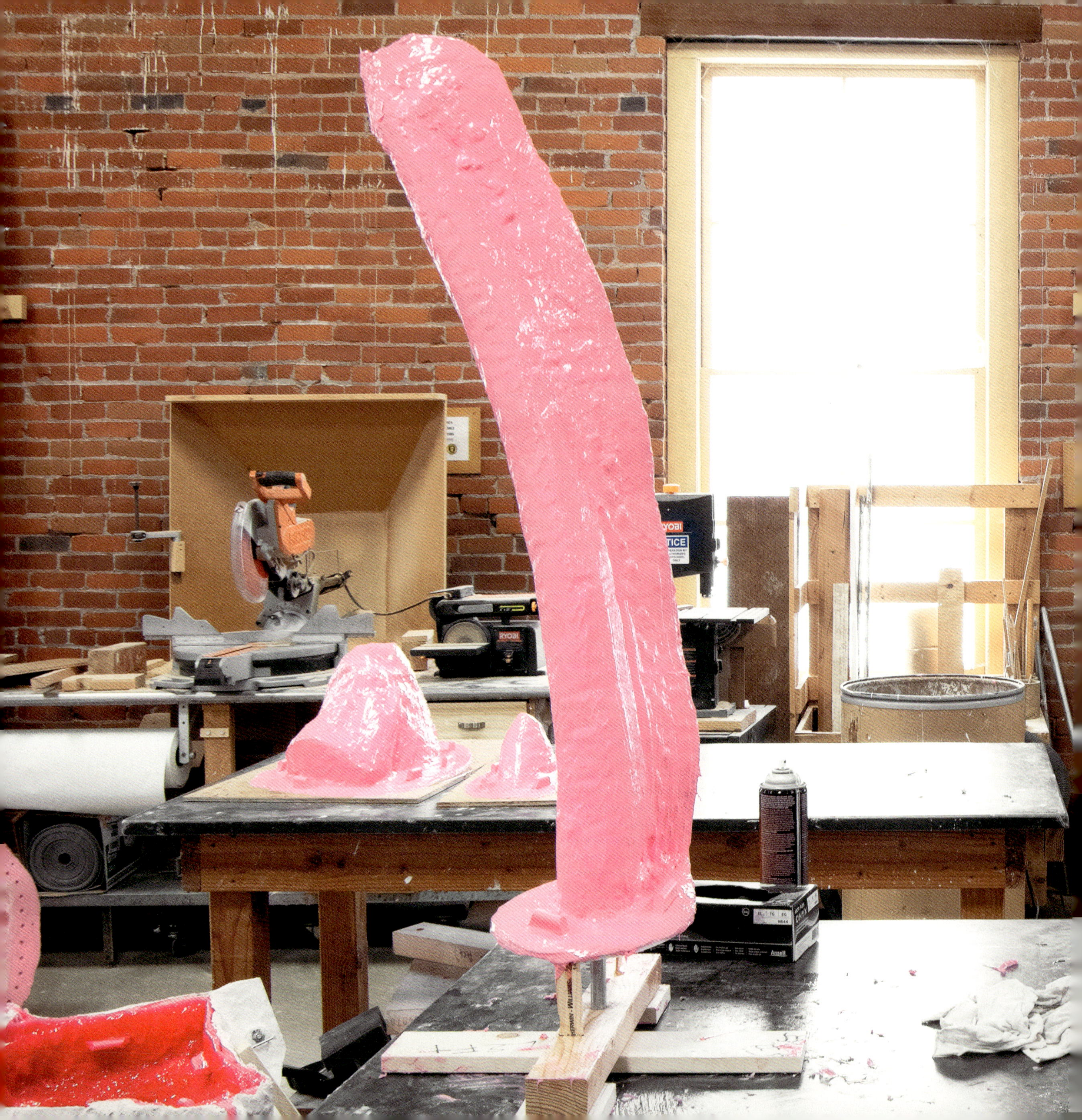

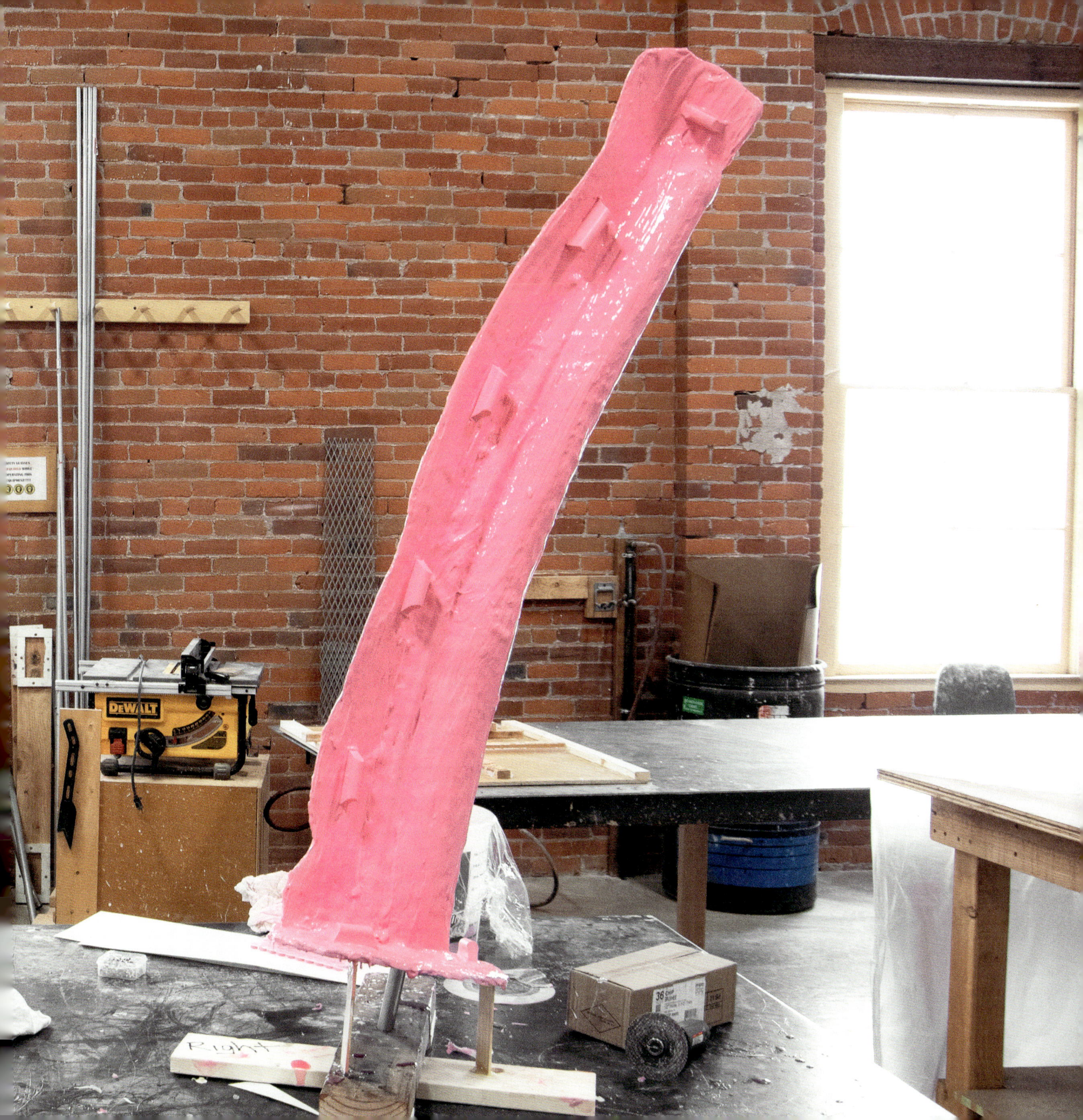
DeWALT
Right

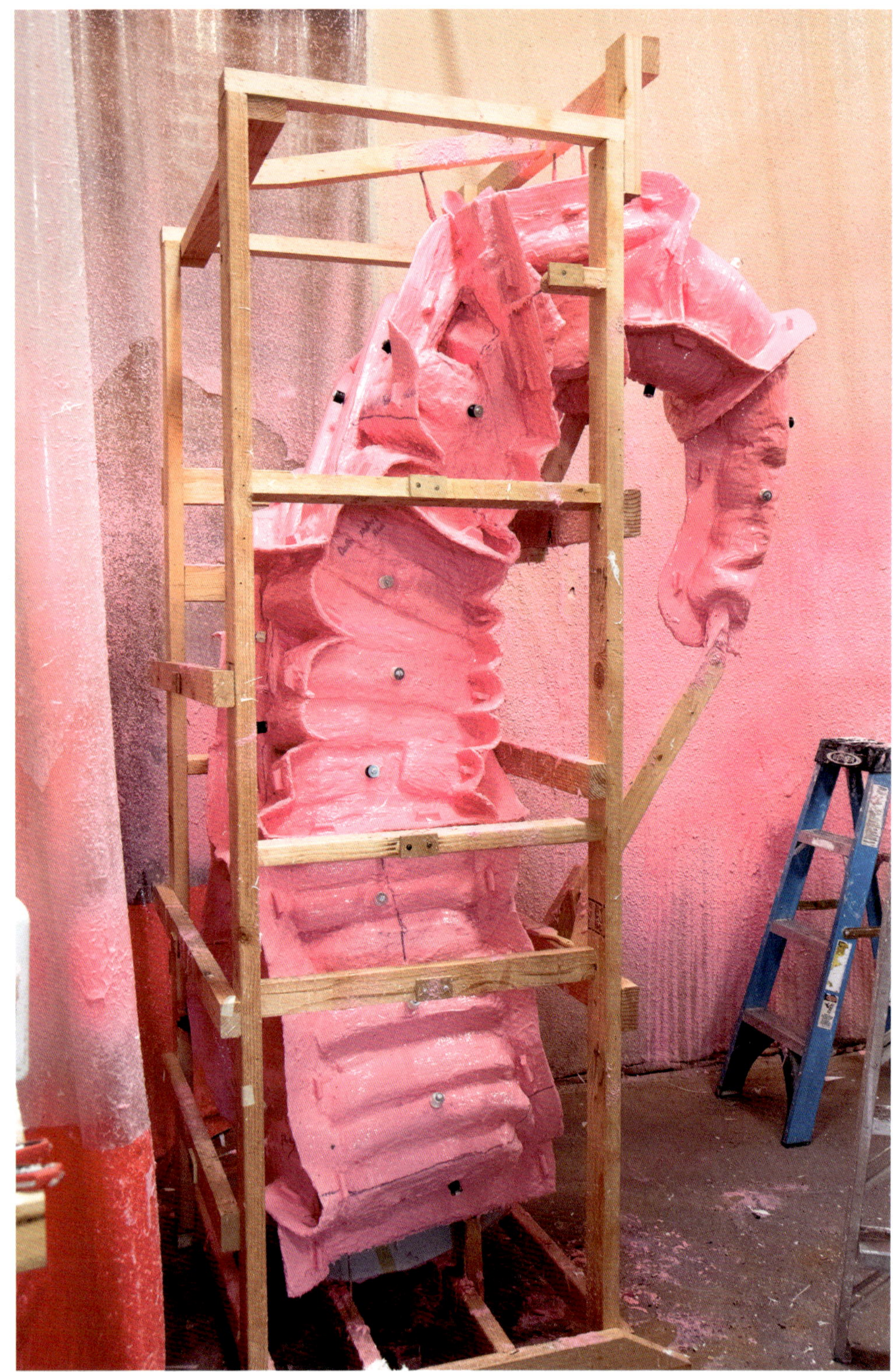

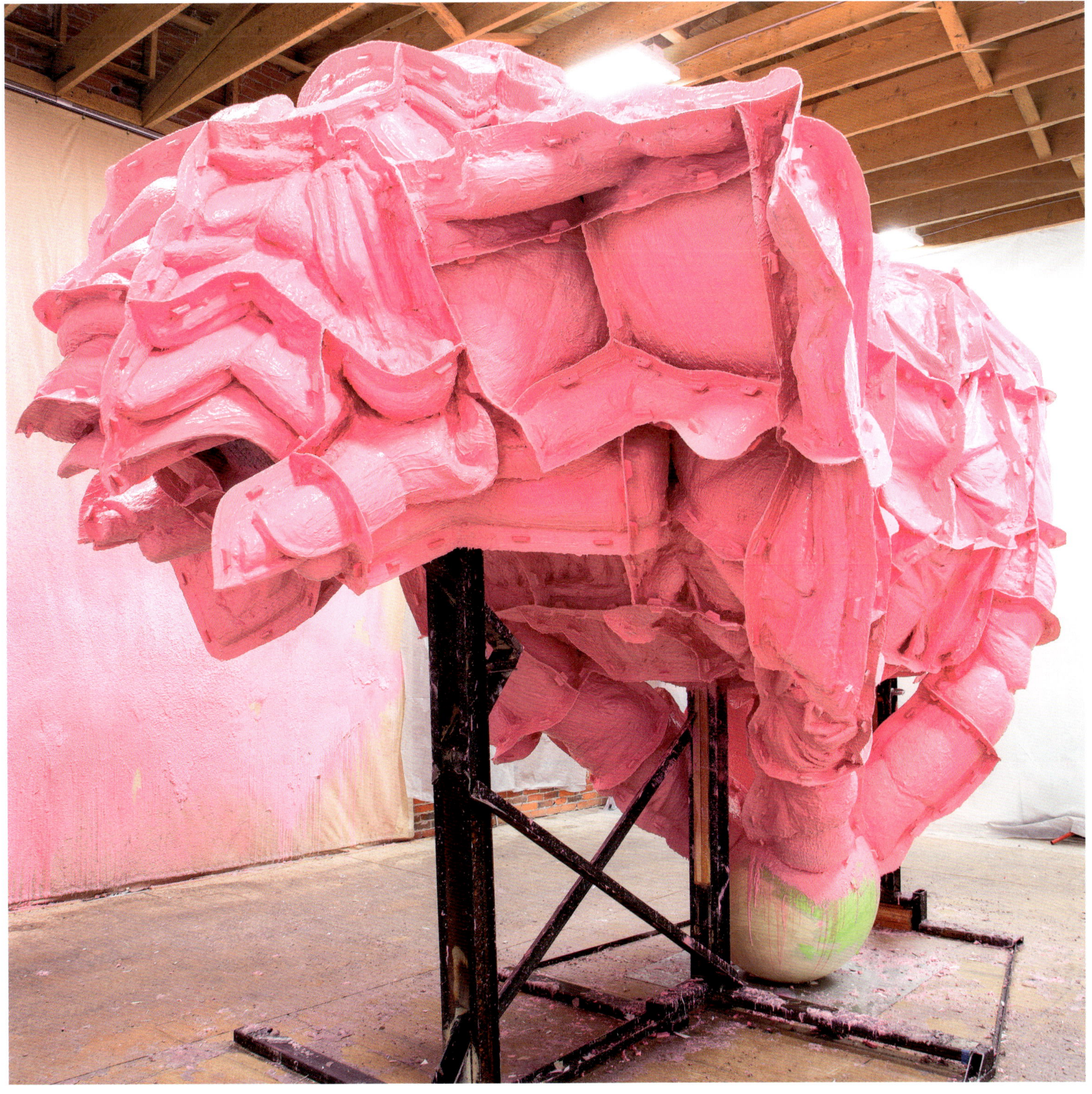

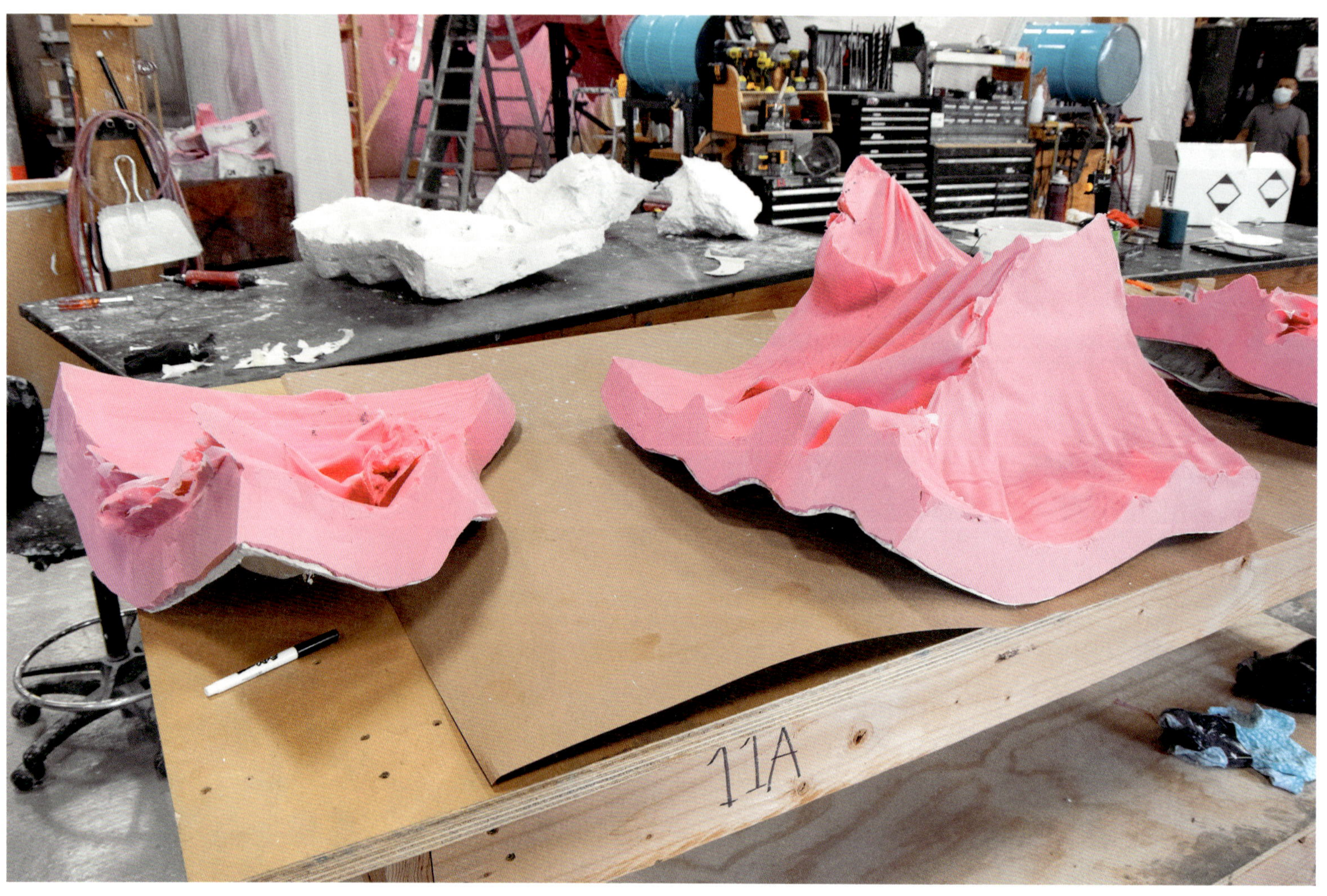
11A

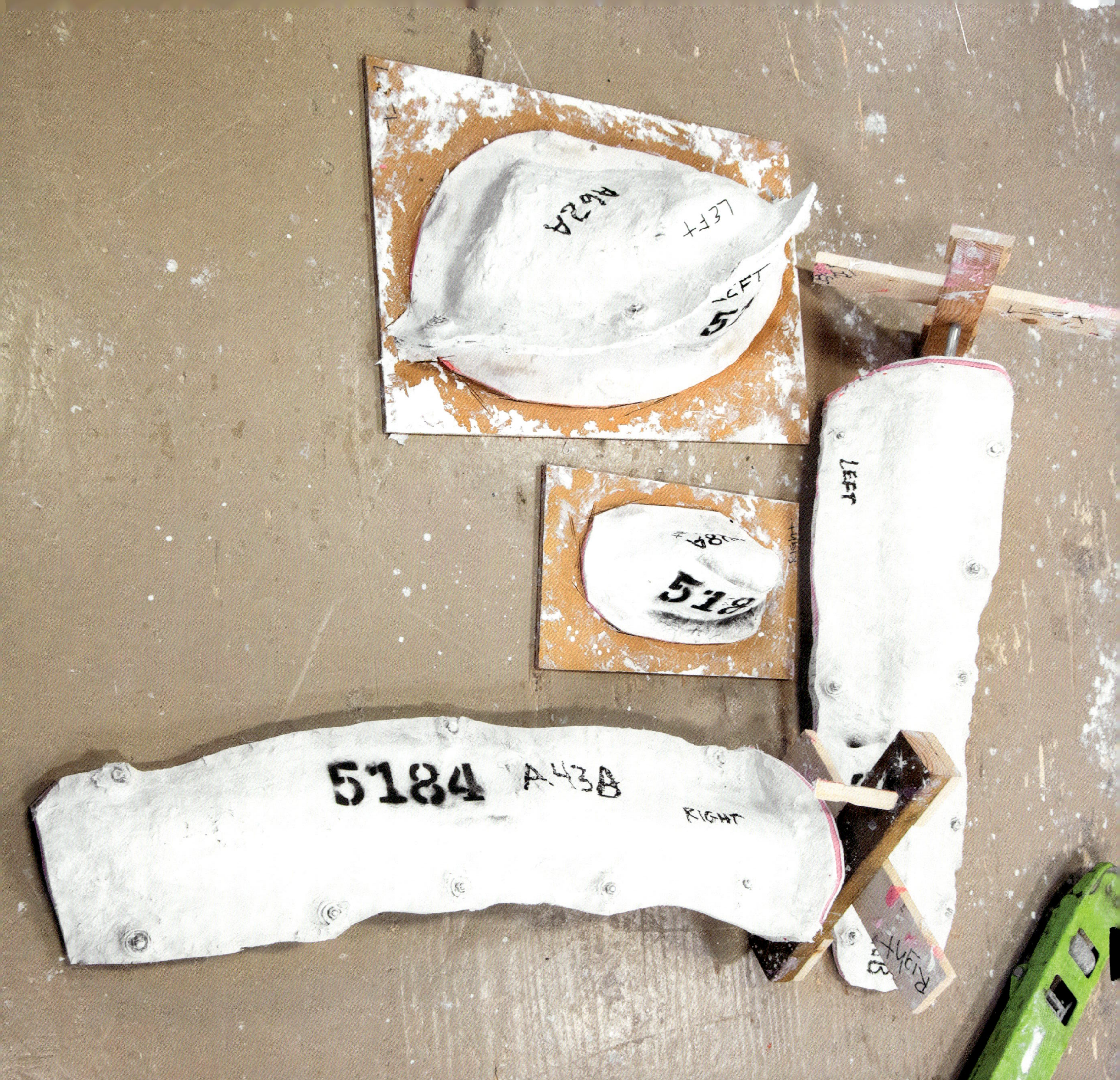

A62A
LEFT
LEFT
519
A484
LEFT
5184 A43B
RIGHT
RIGHT

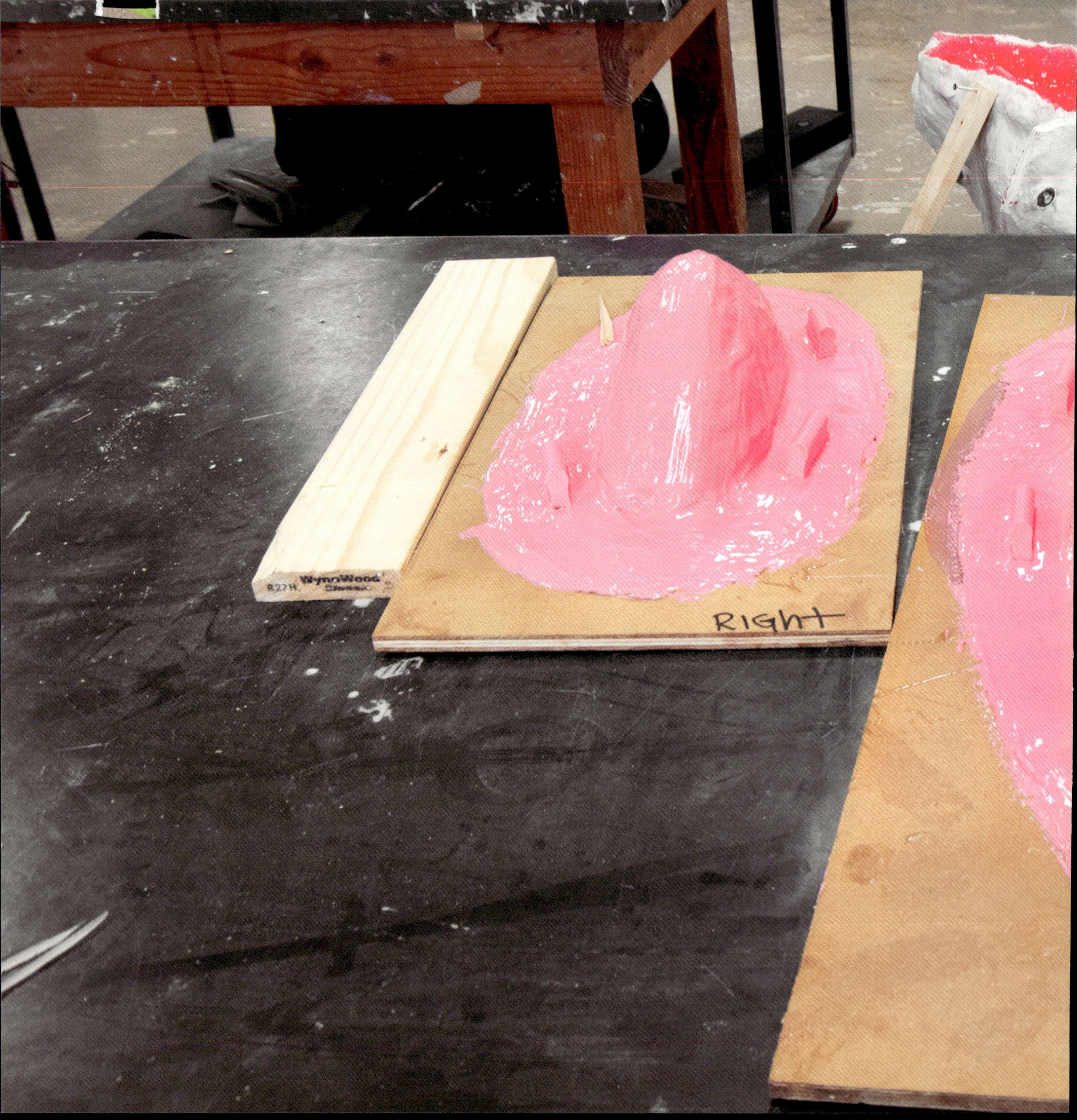

R27 H.
WynnWood
Classic
RIGHT

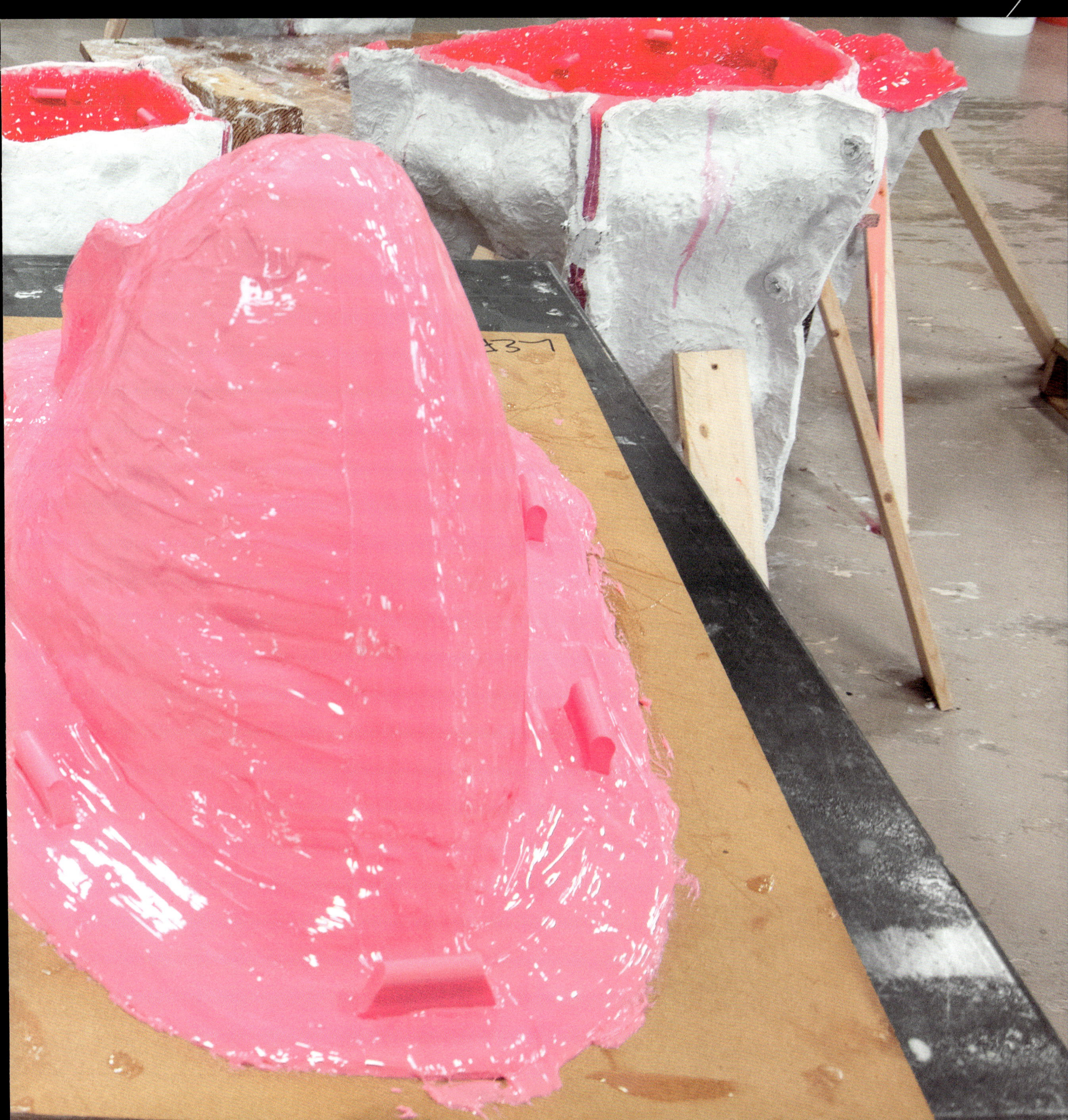

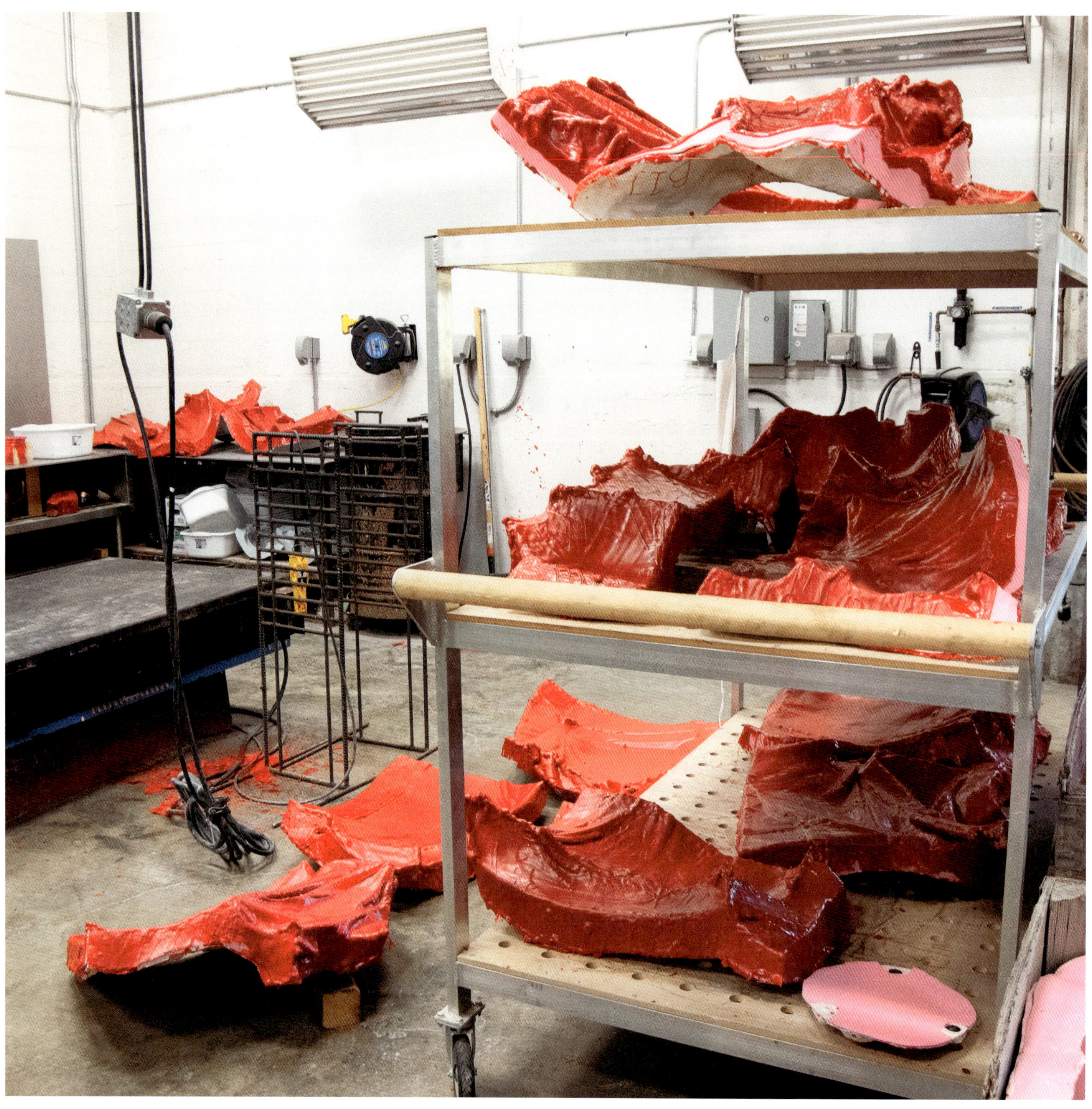

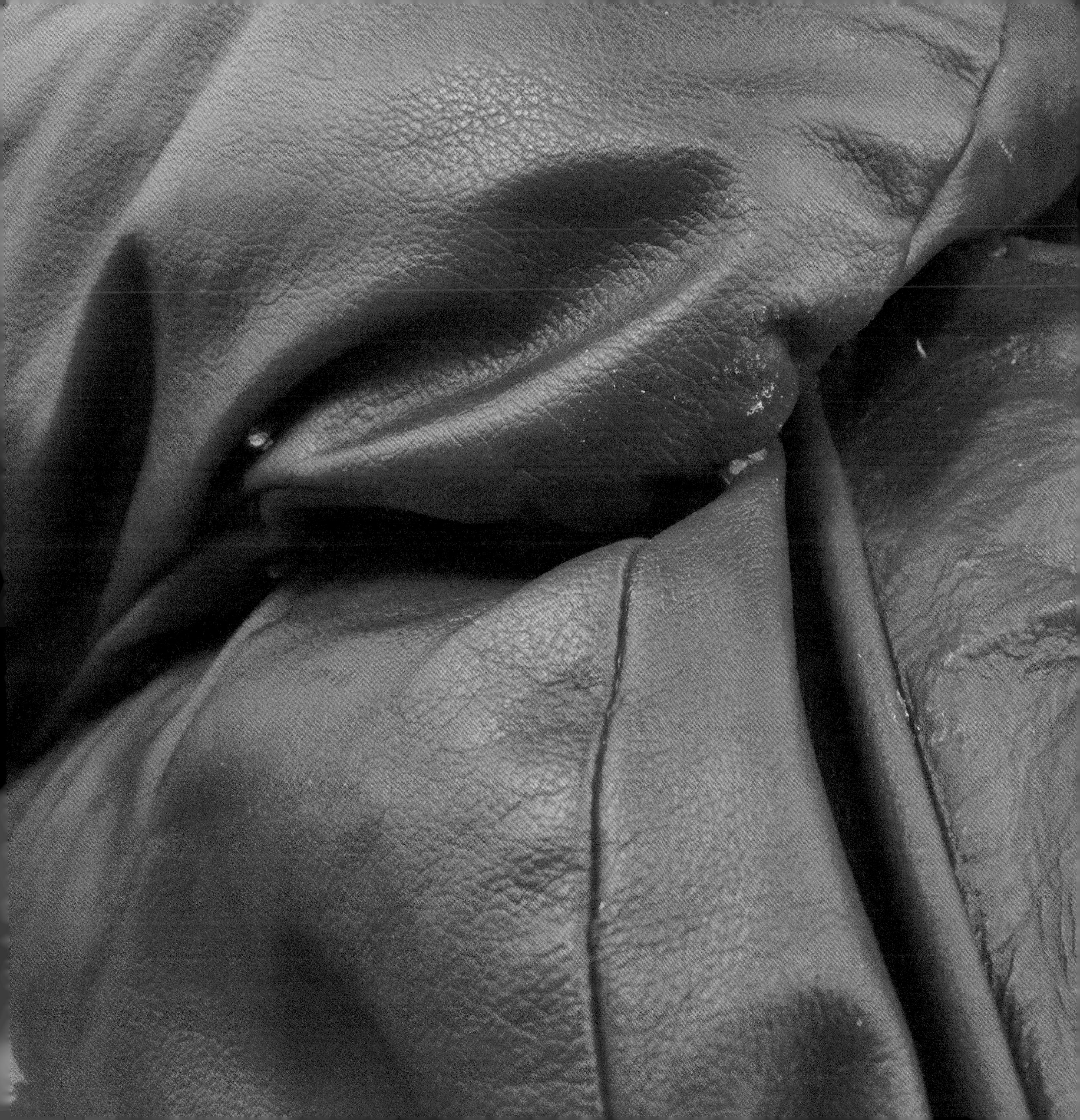

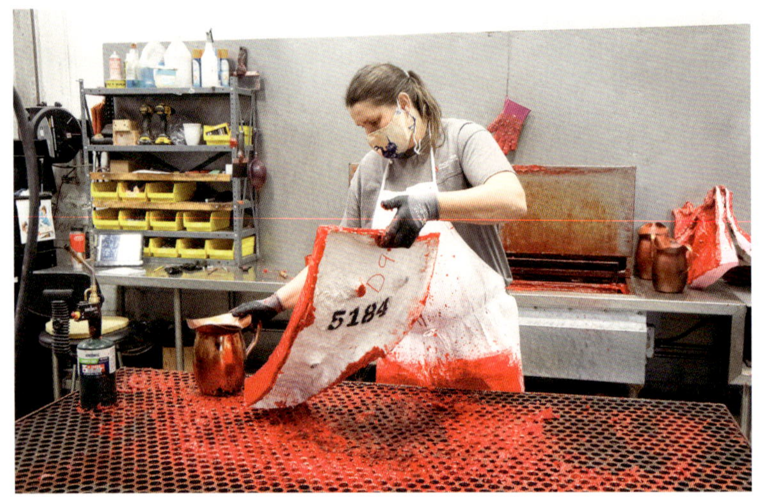
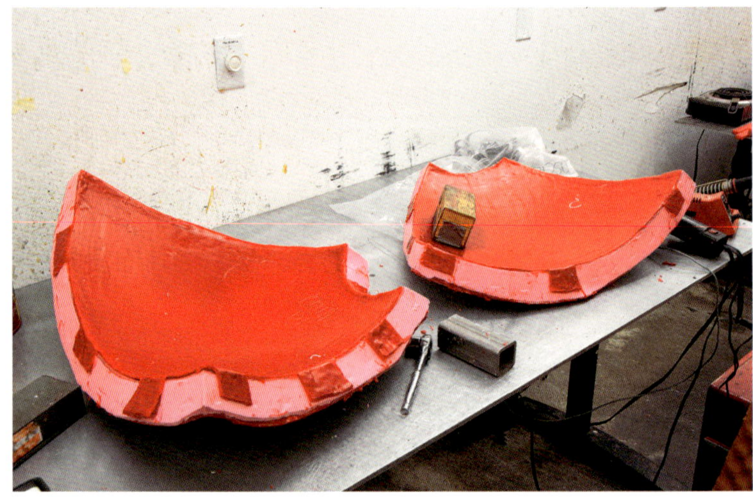
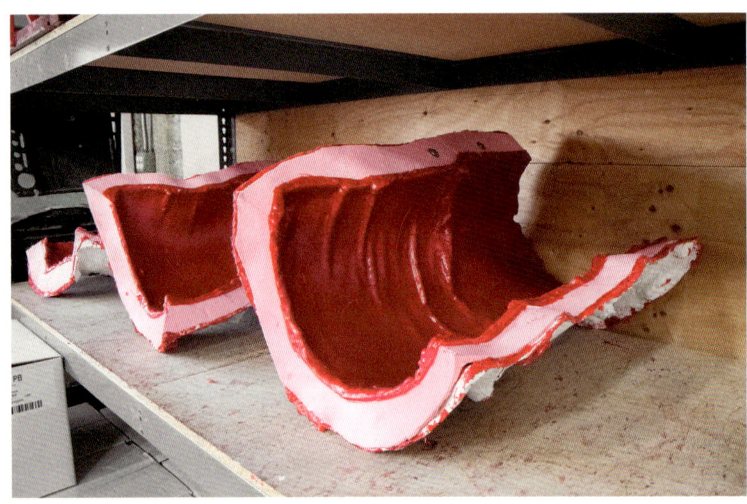
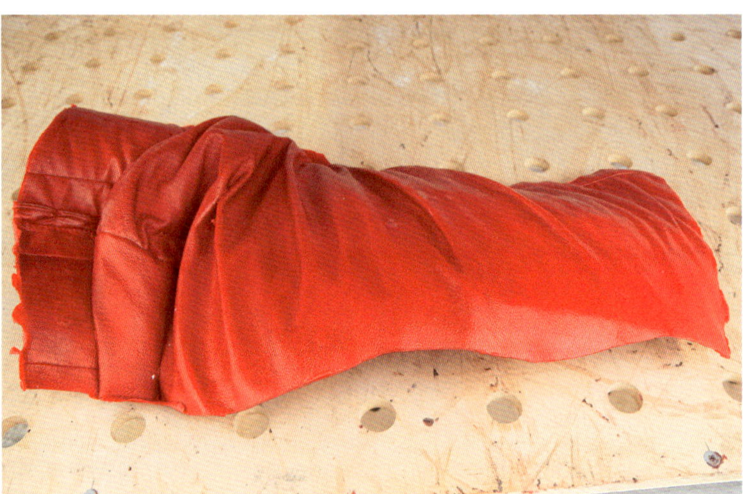
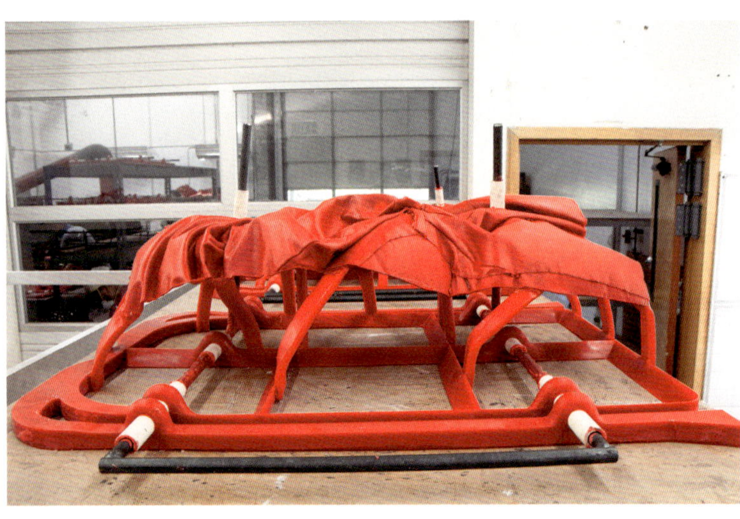
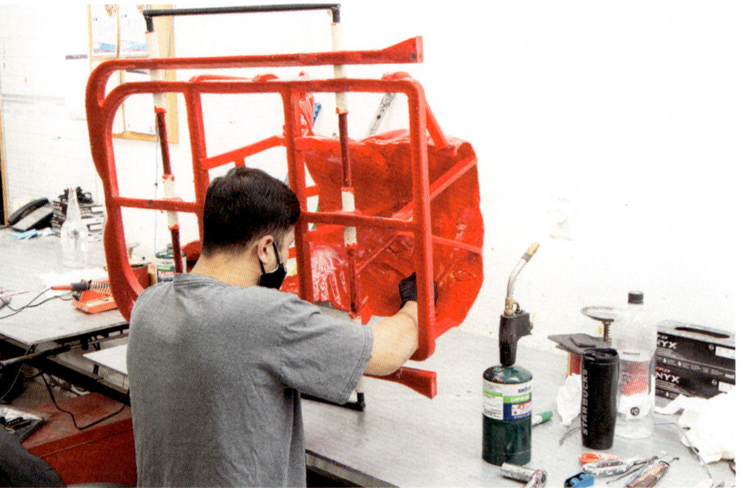

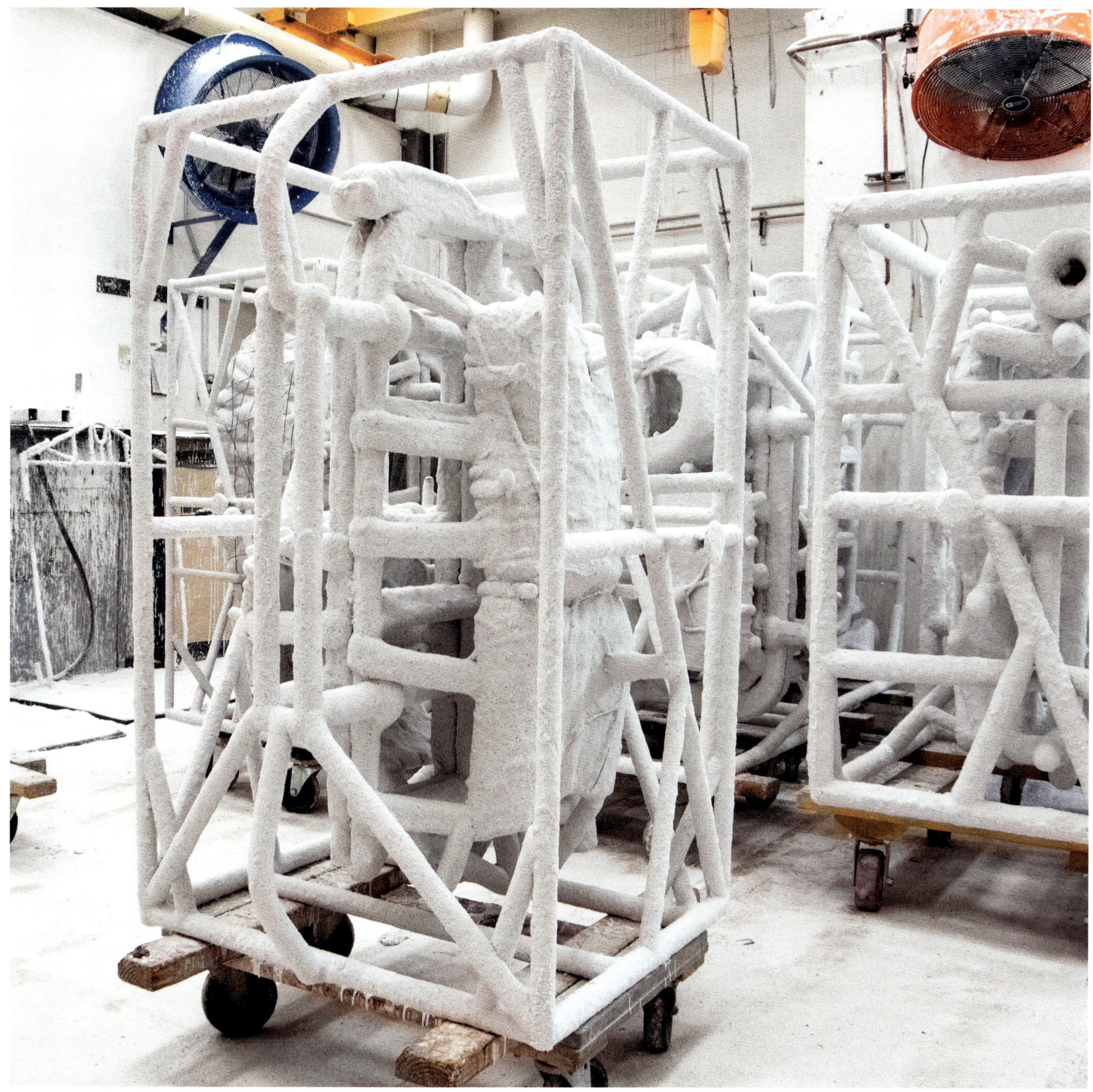

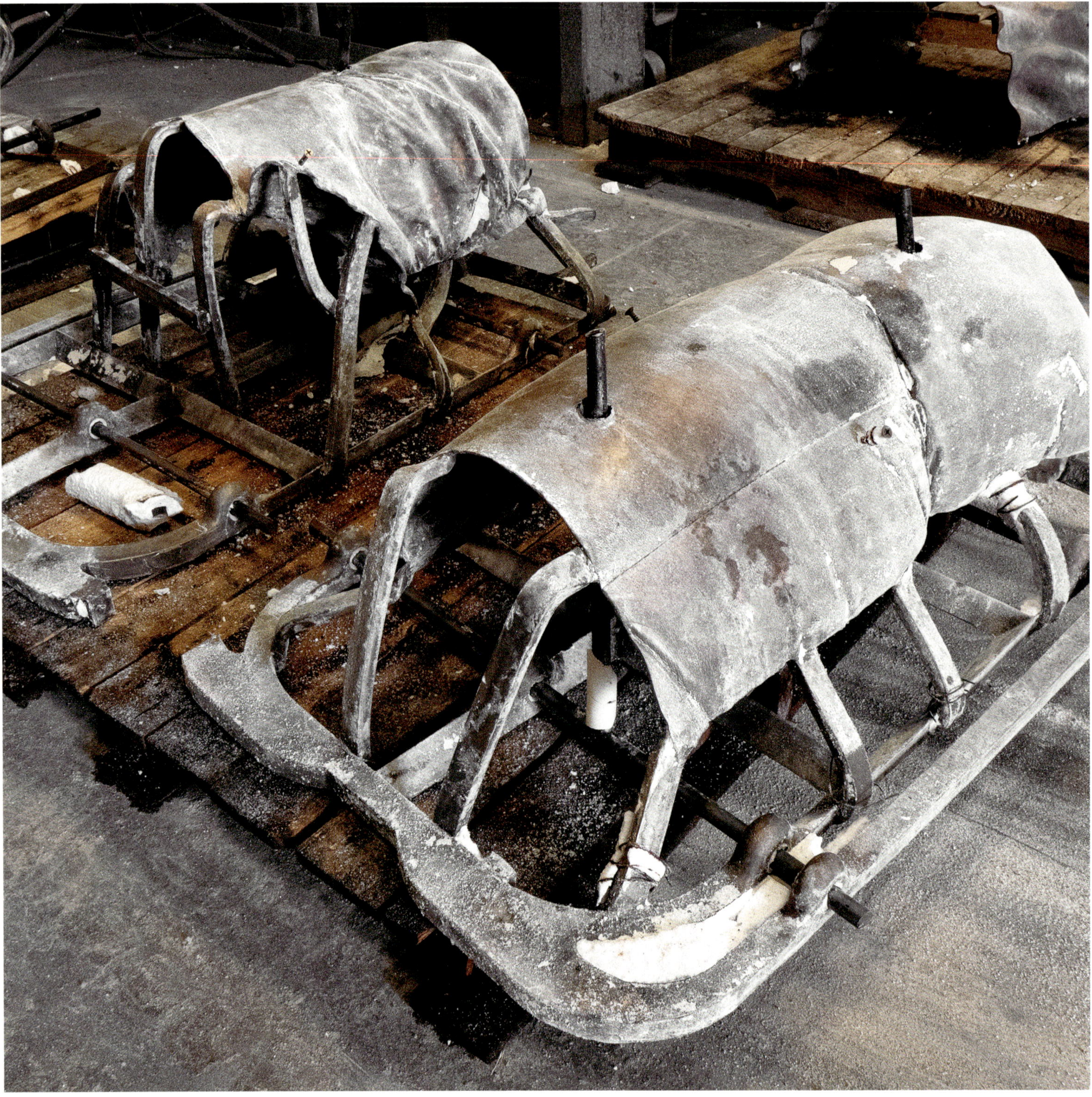

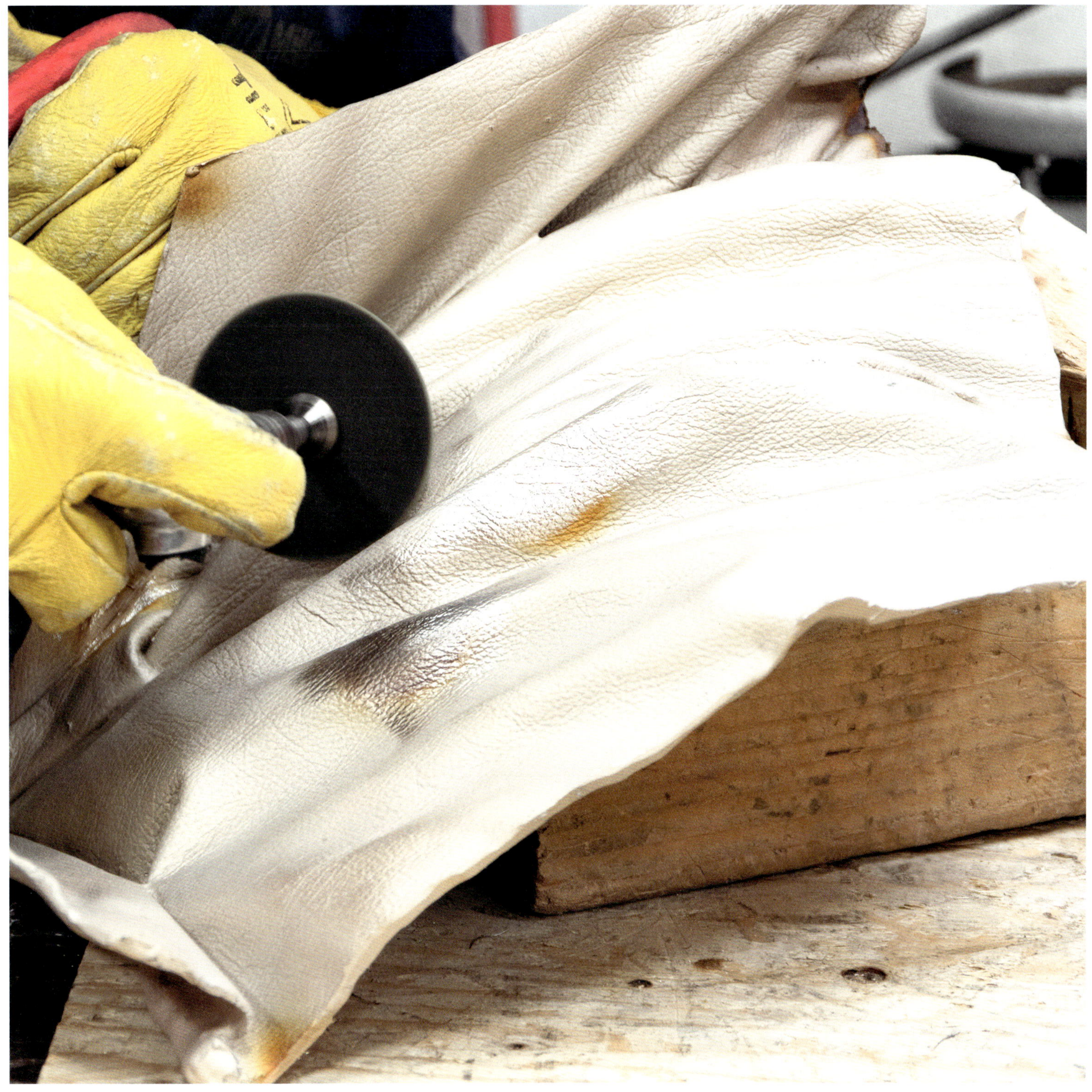

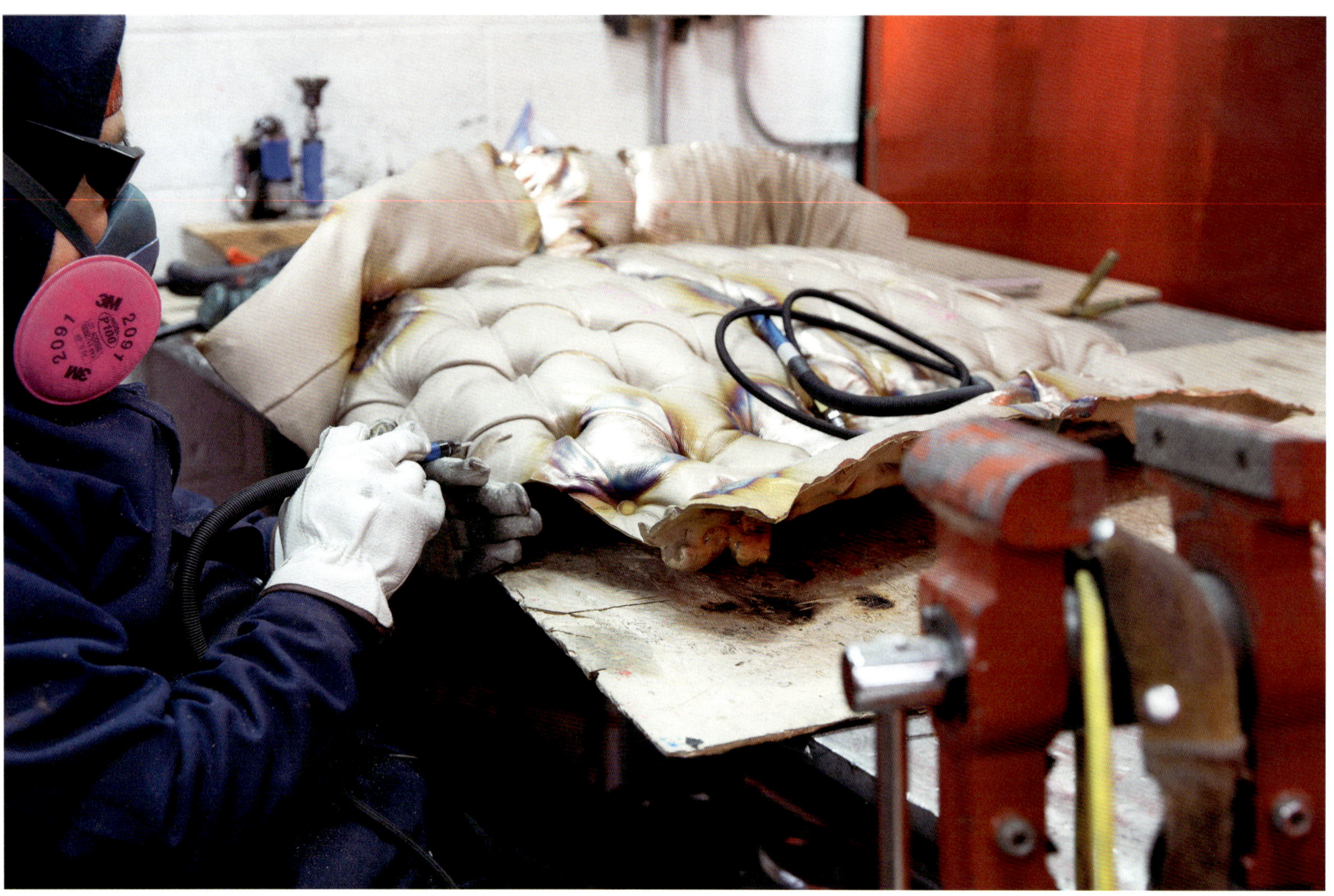

3M 2091
2091
3M 2091

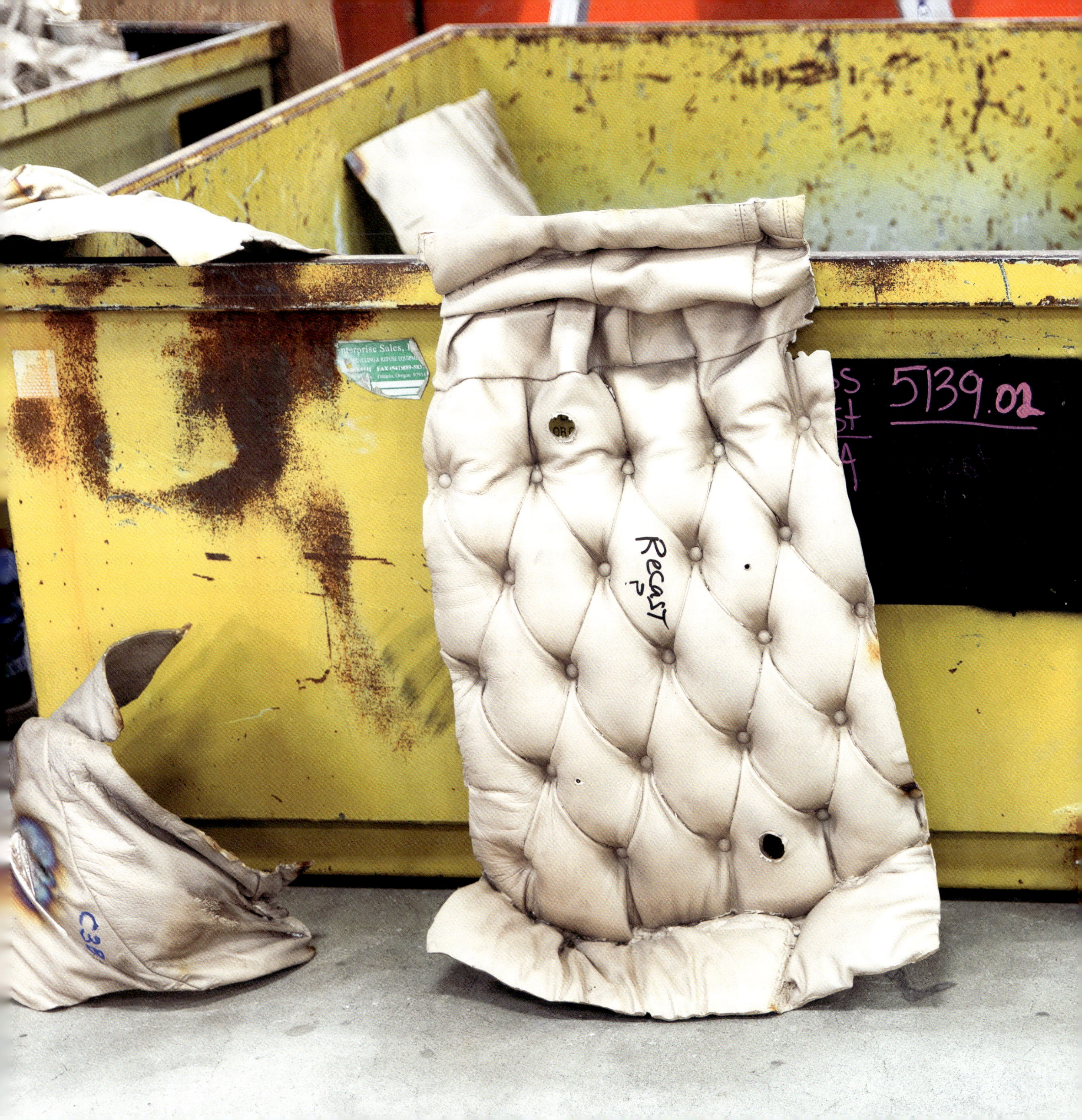
Recast
?
5139.02

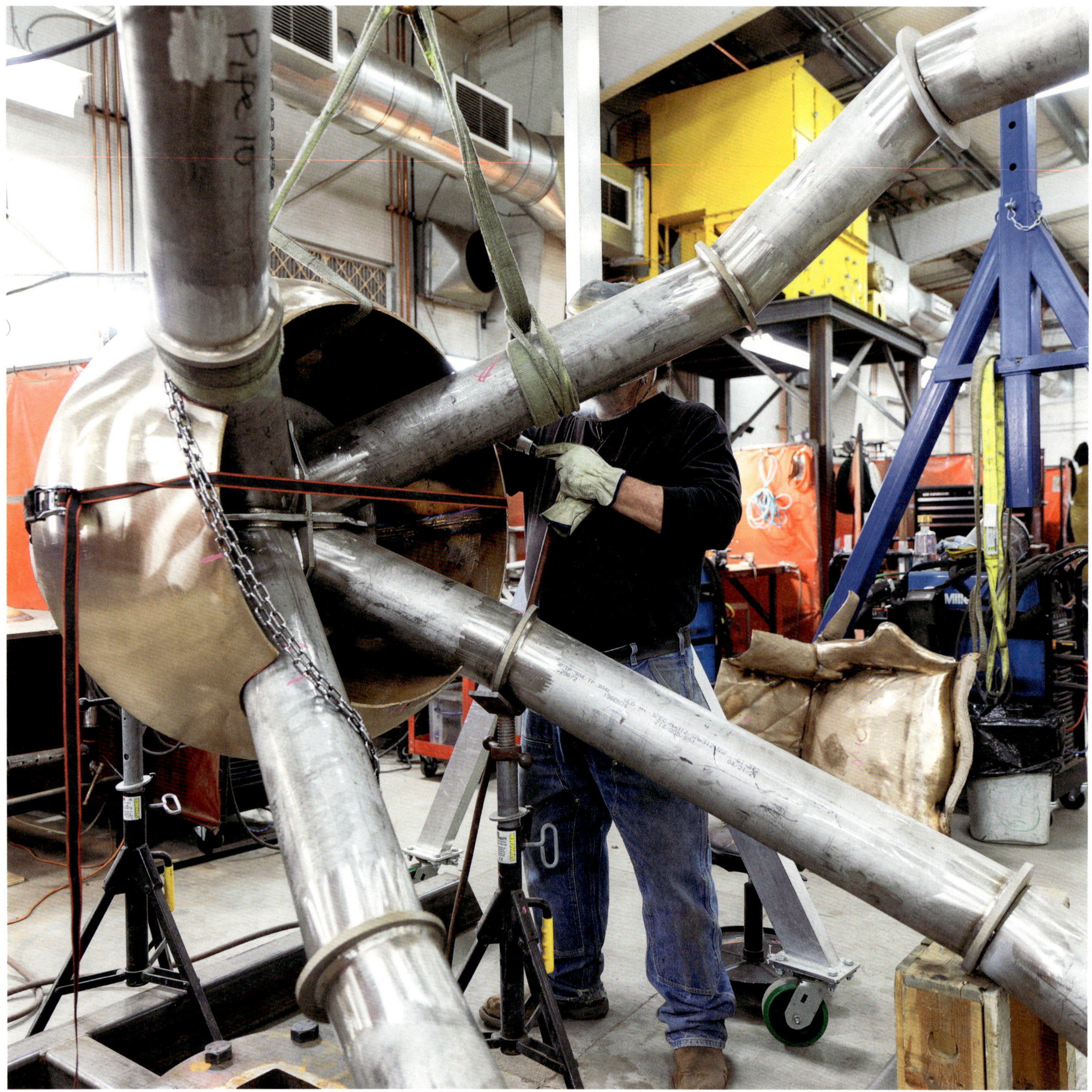

Pipe 10

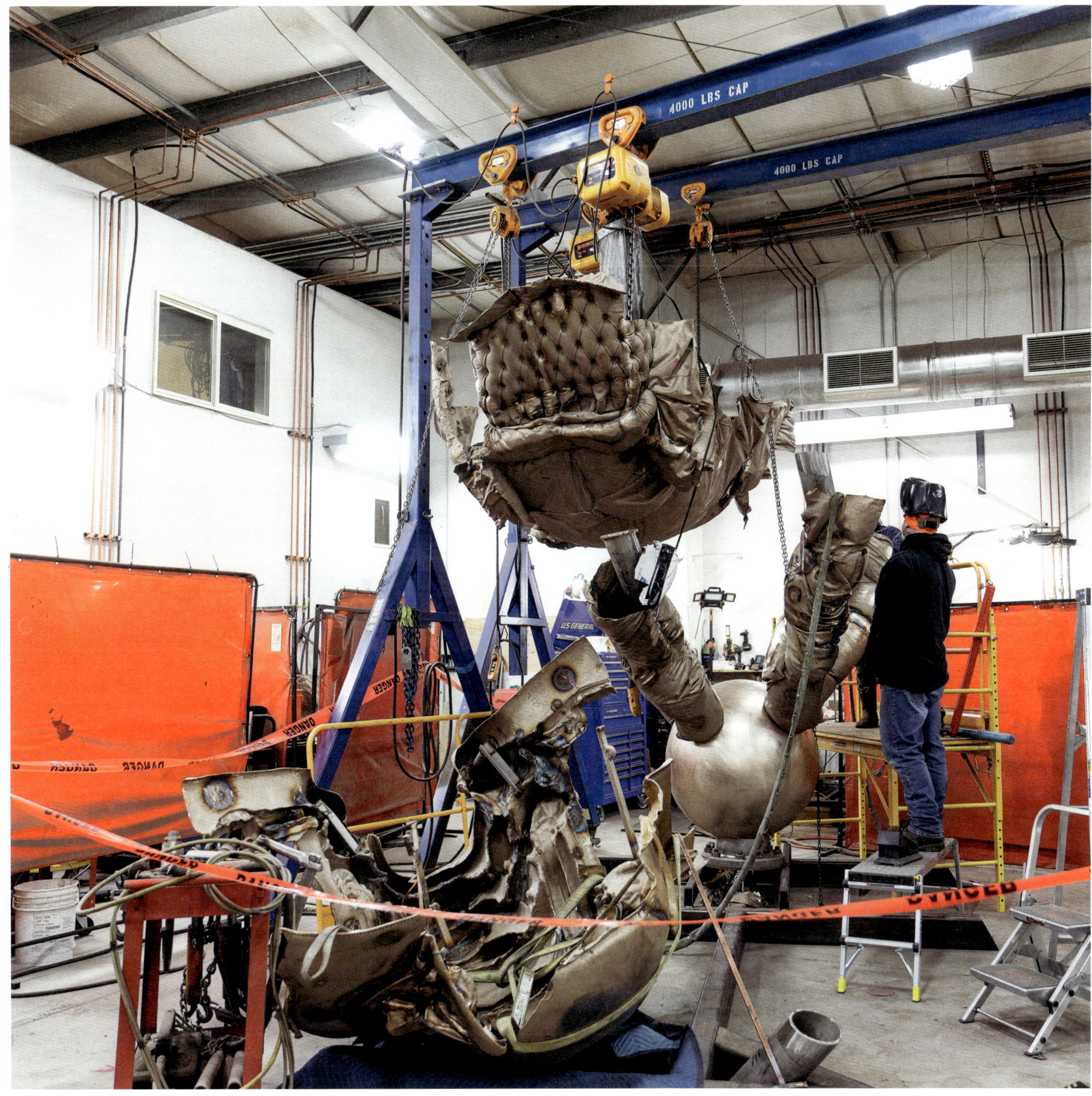
4000 LBS CAP
4000 LBS CAP
DANGER
DANGER
DANGER
US GENERAL

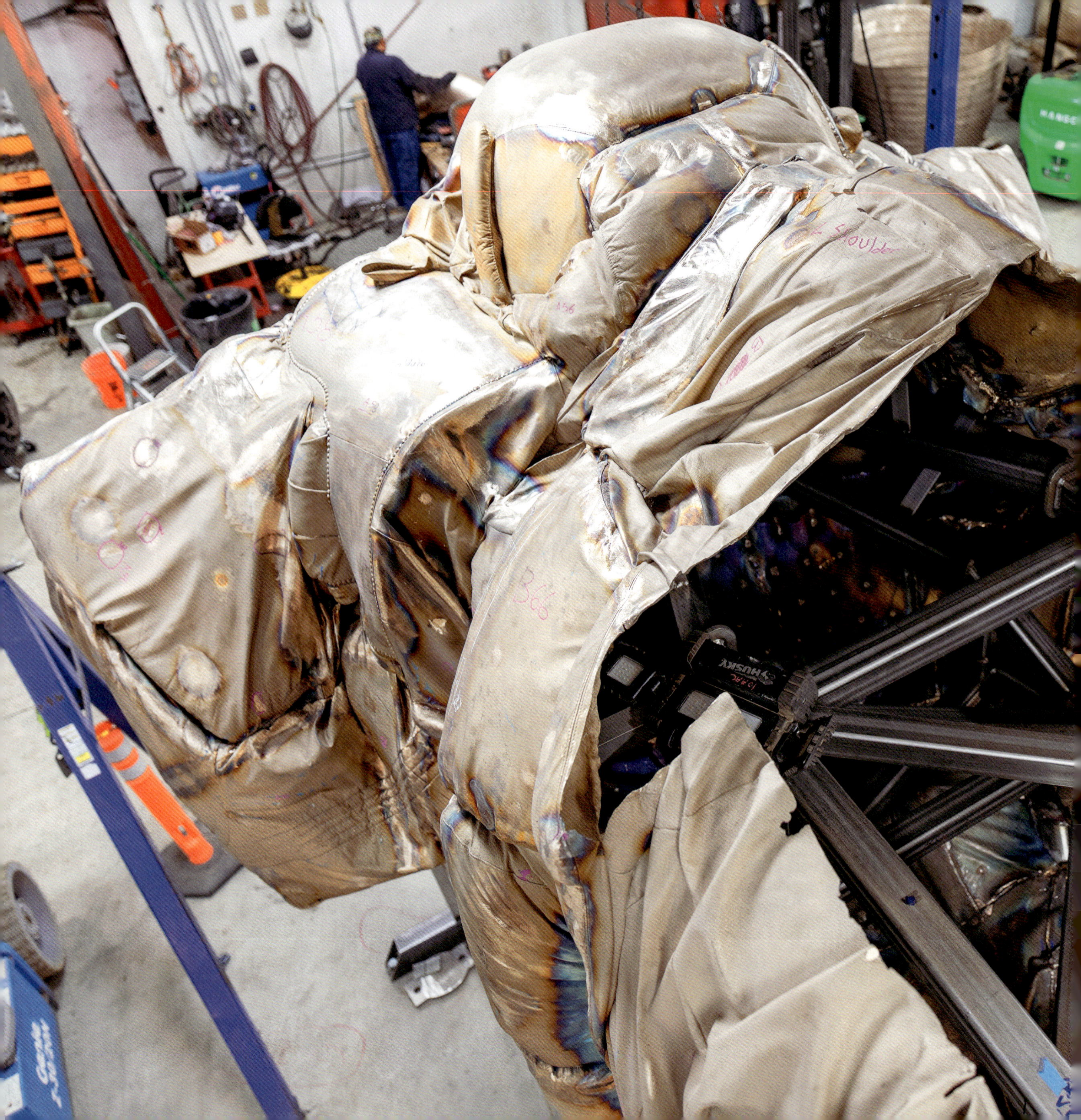

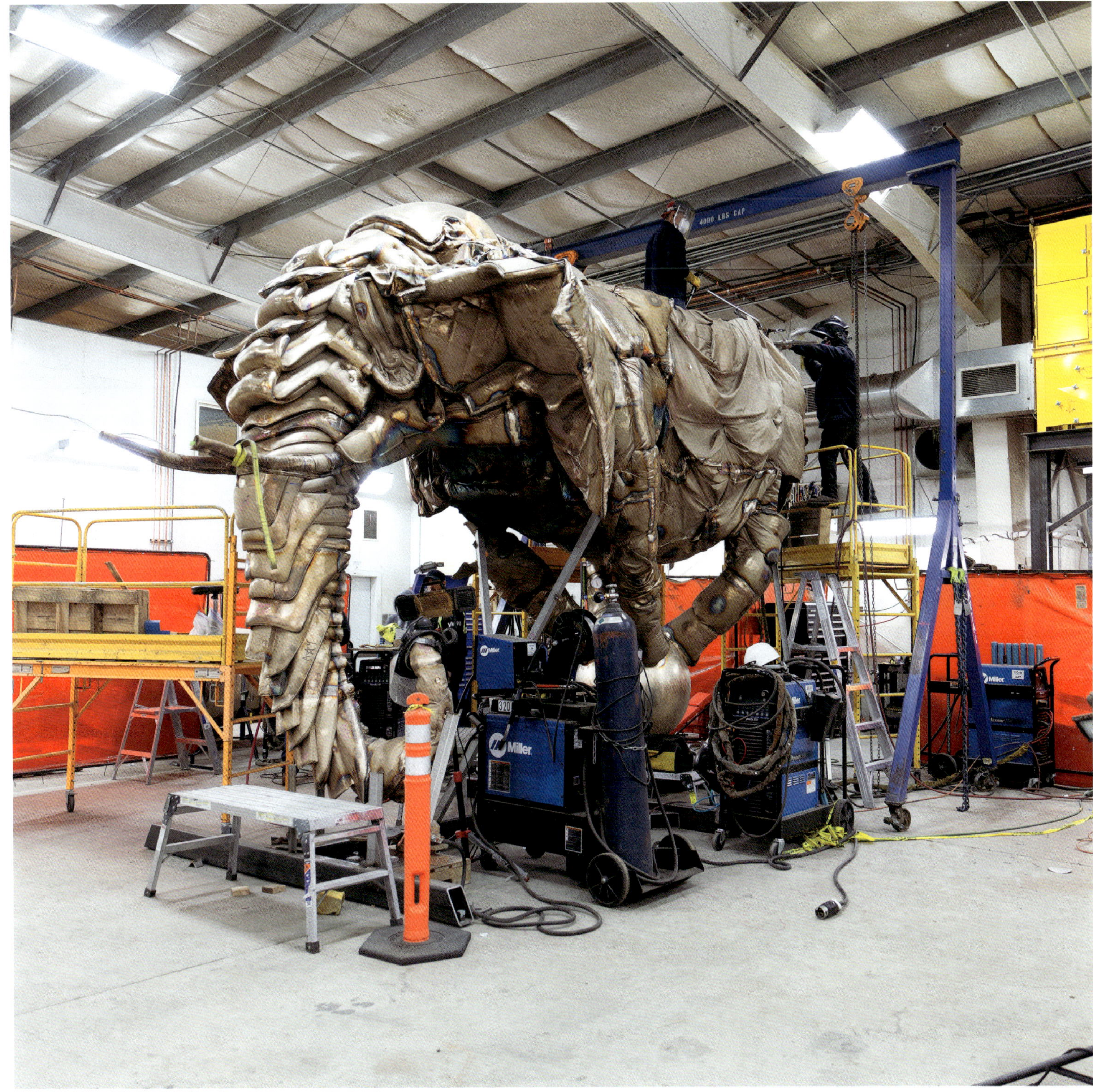

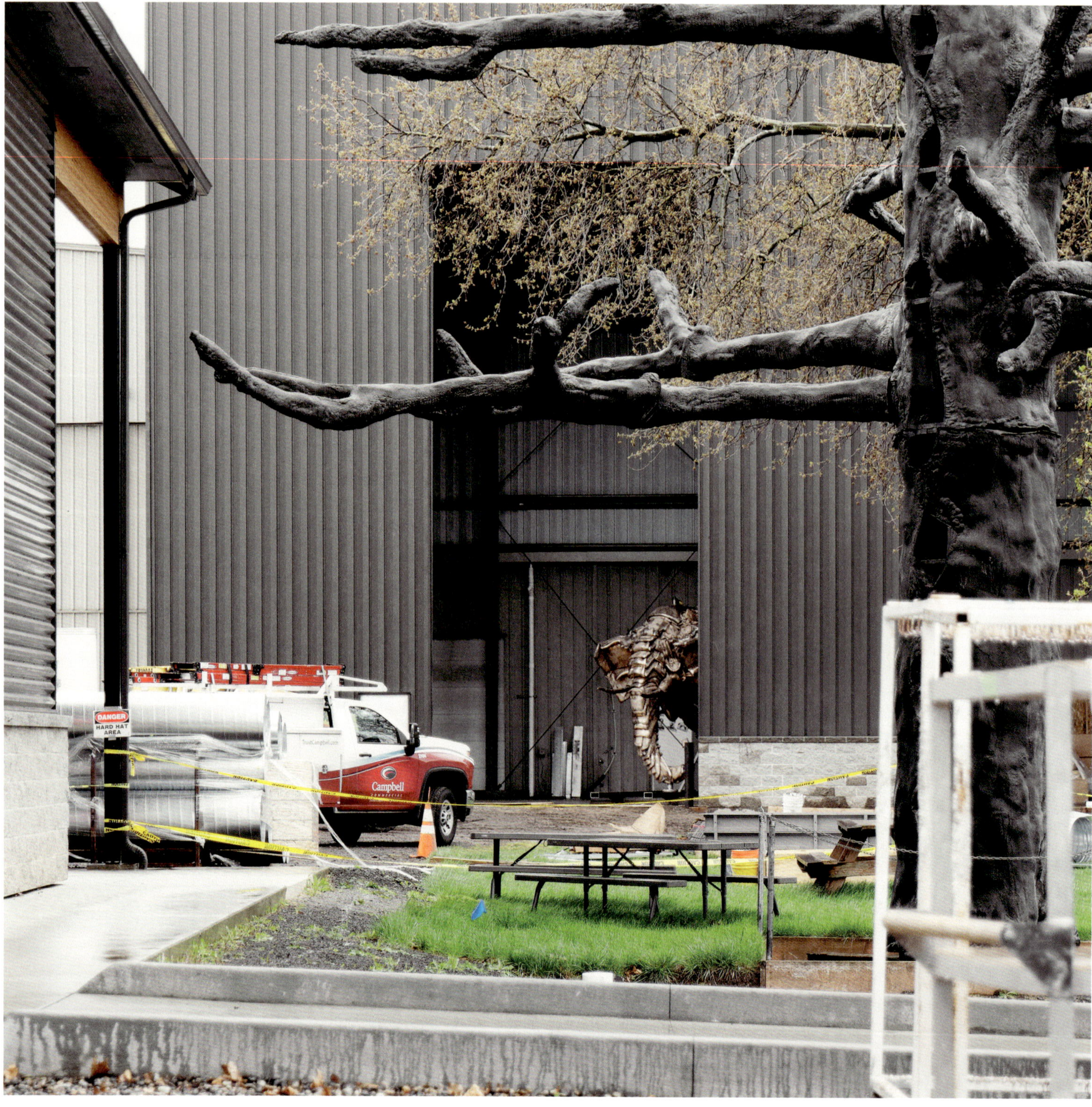

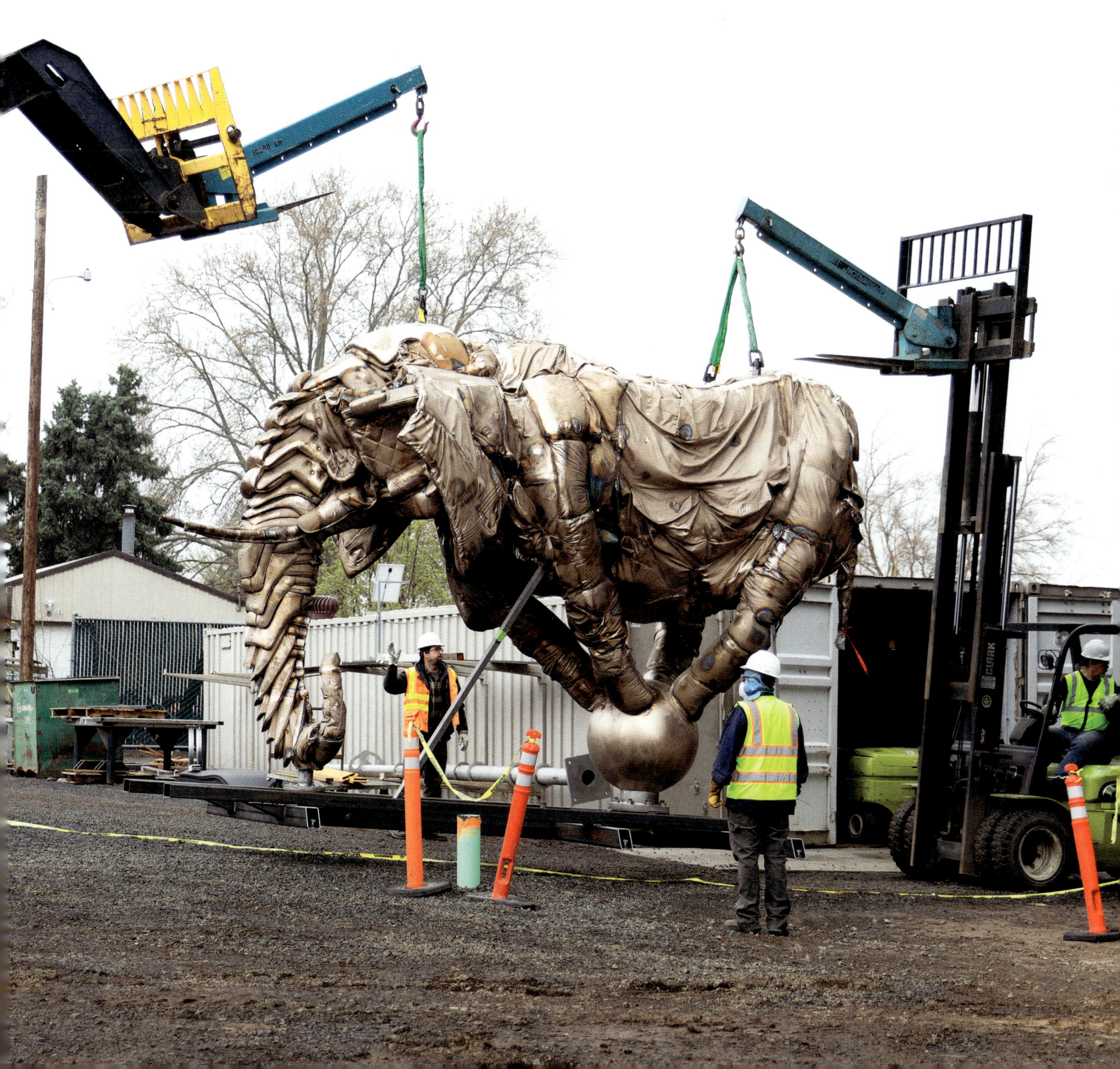

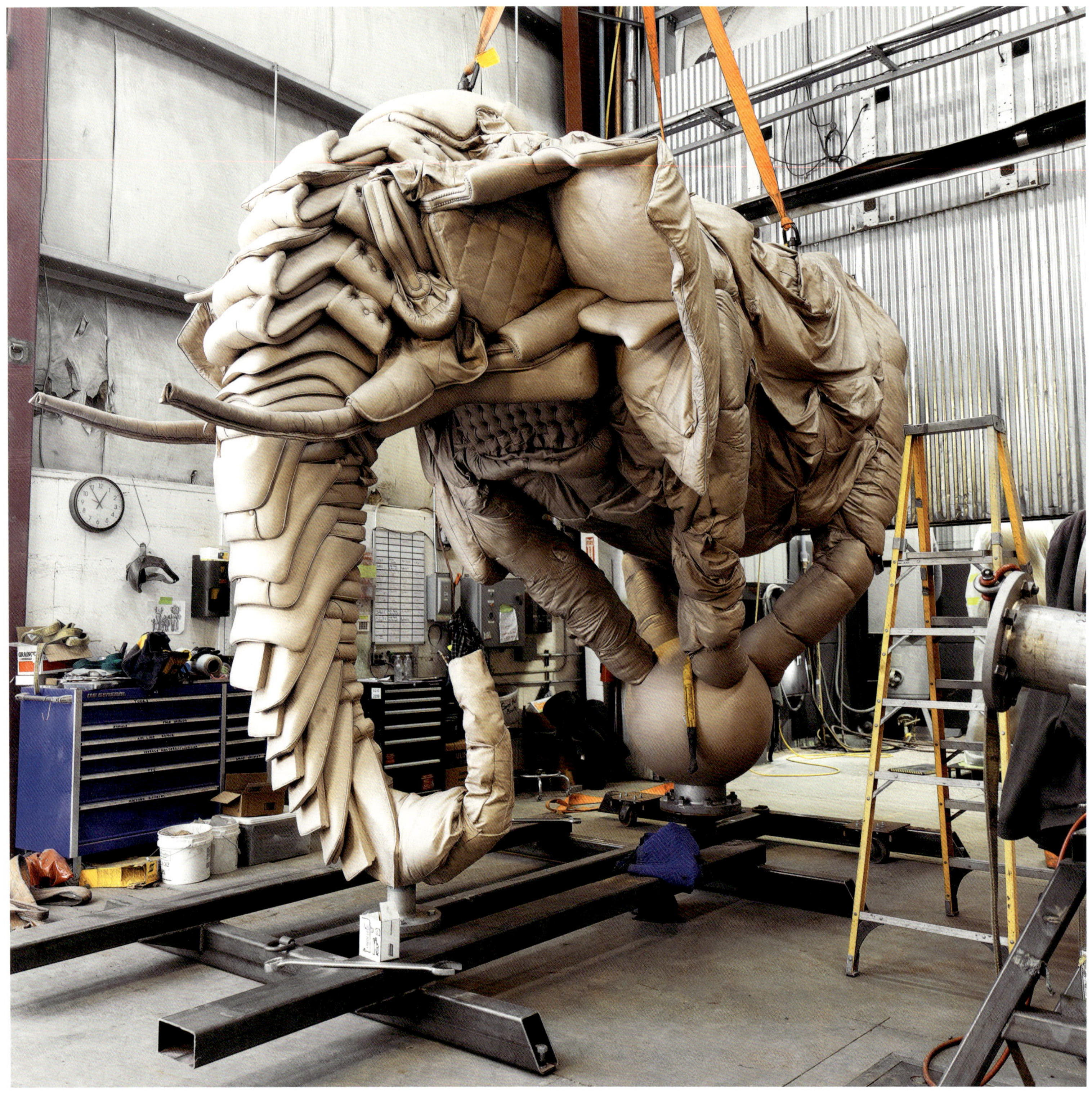

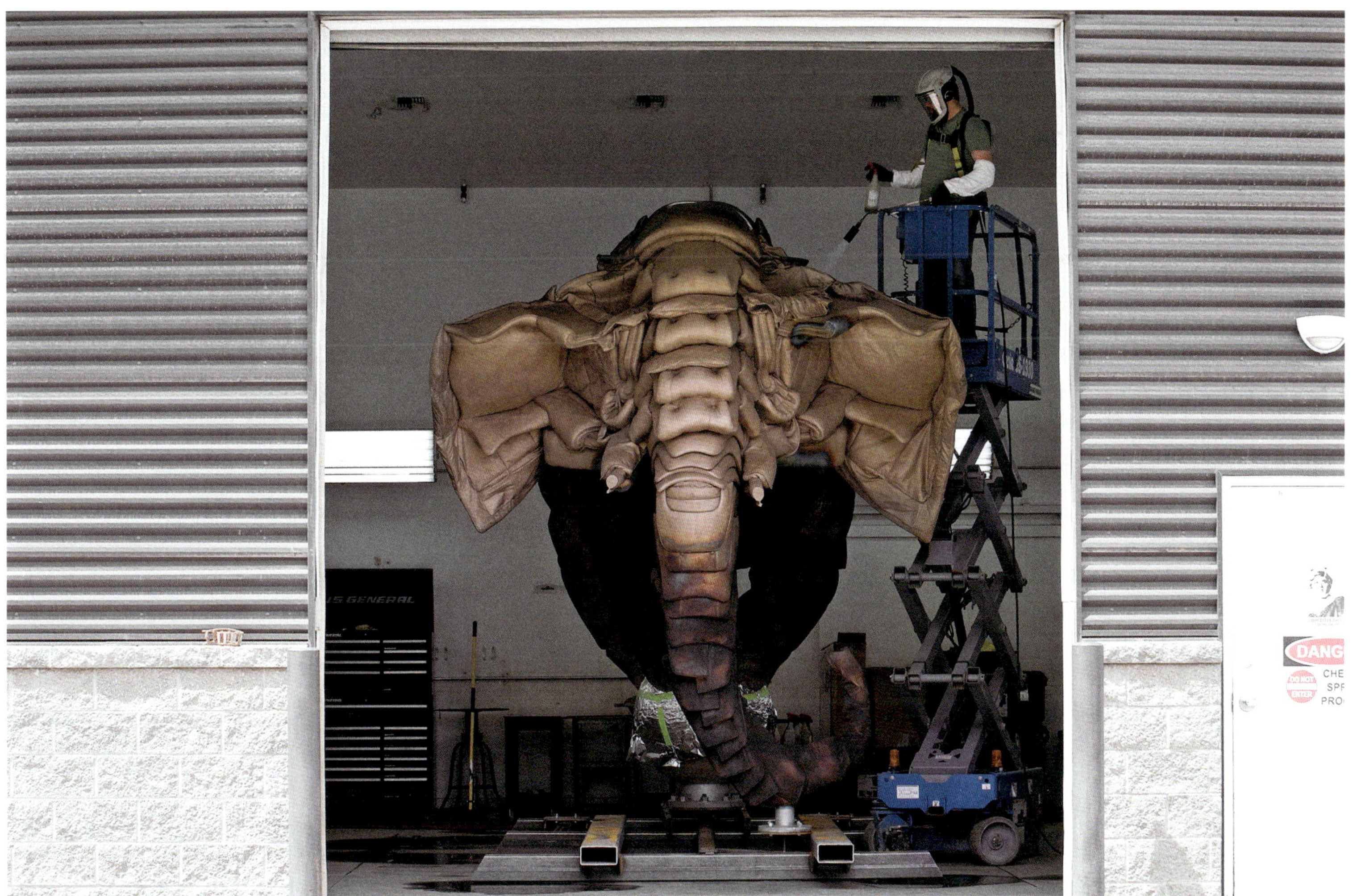

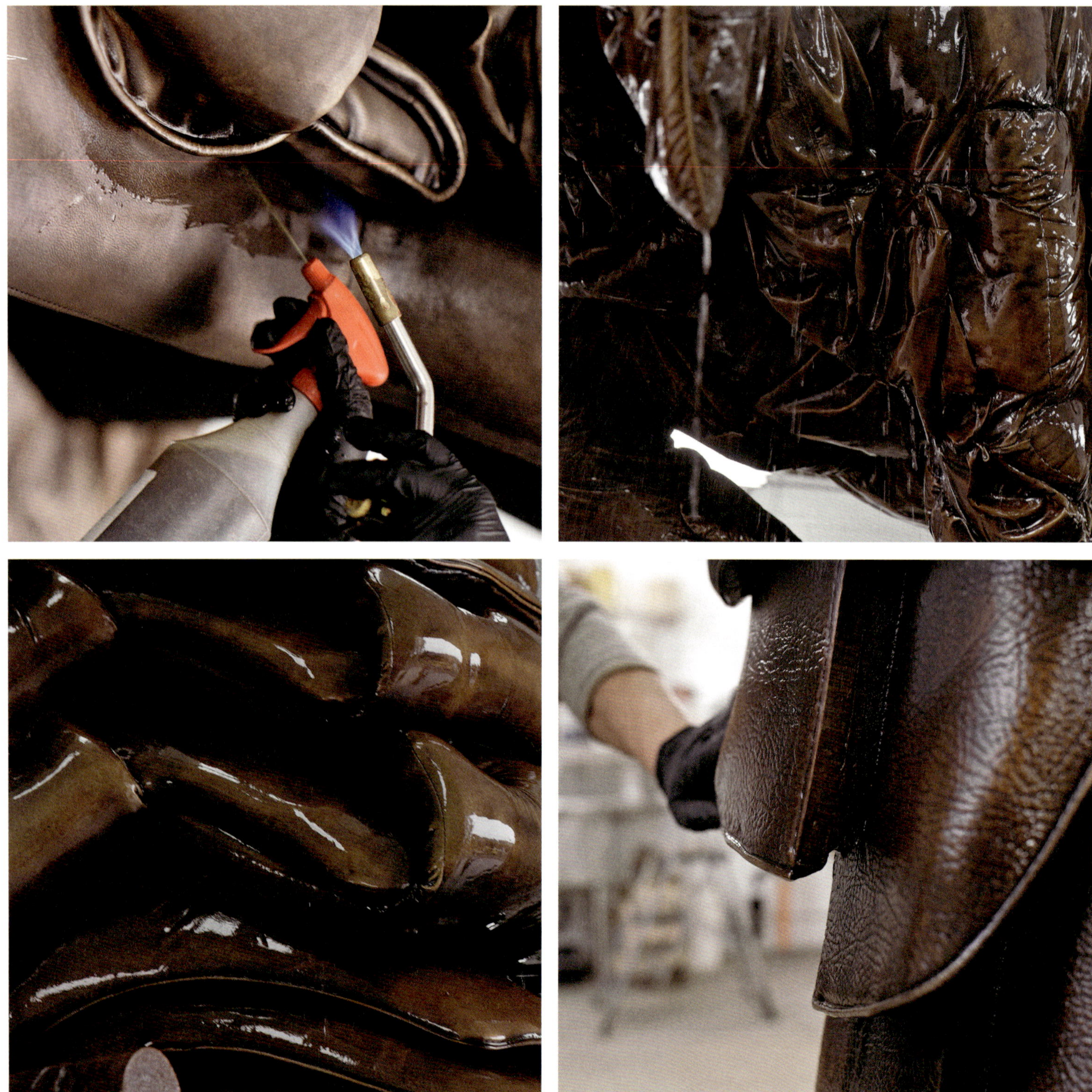

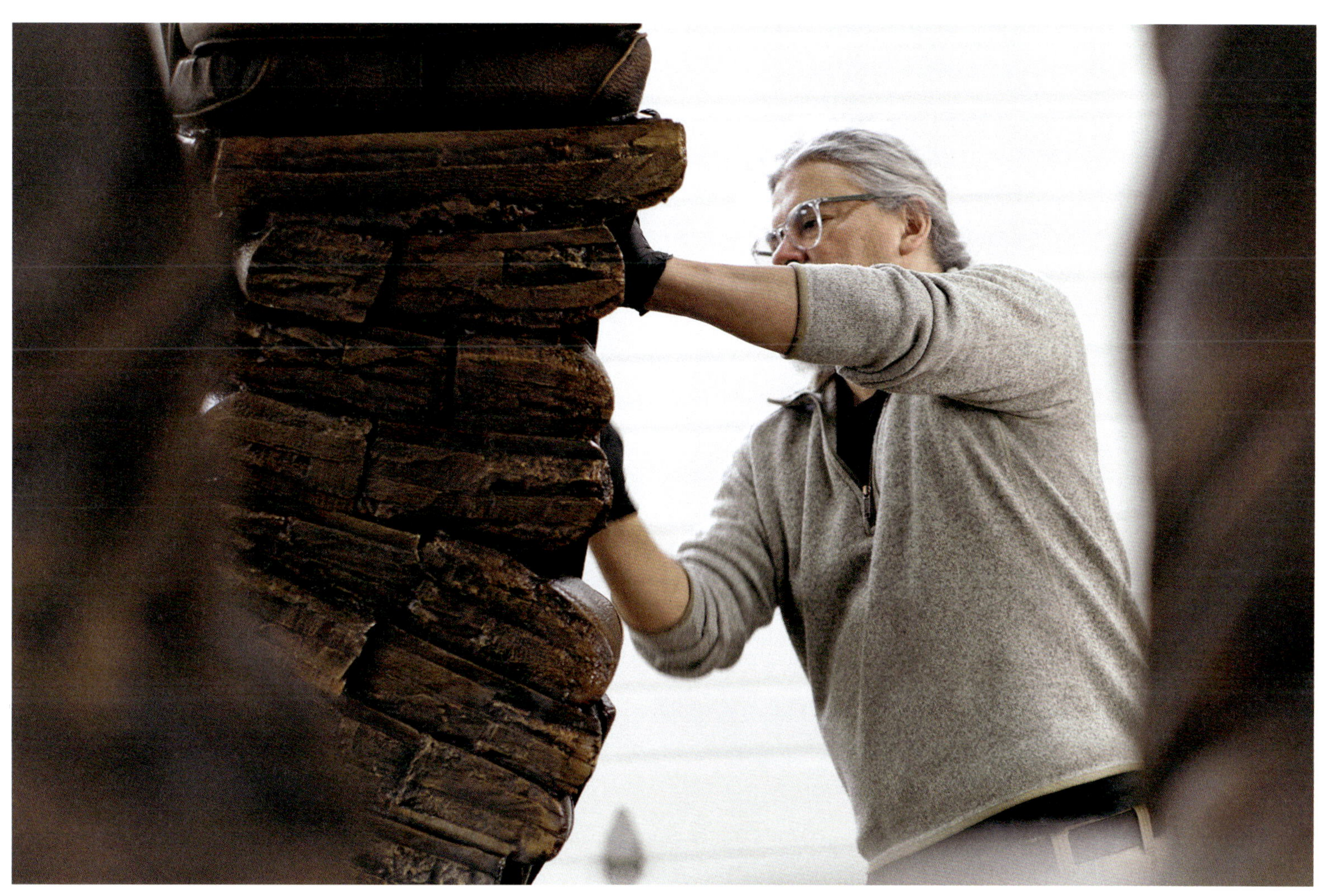

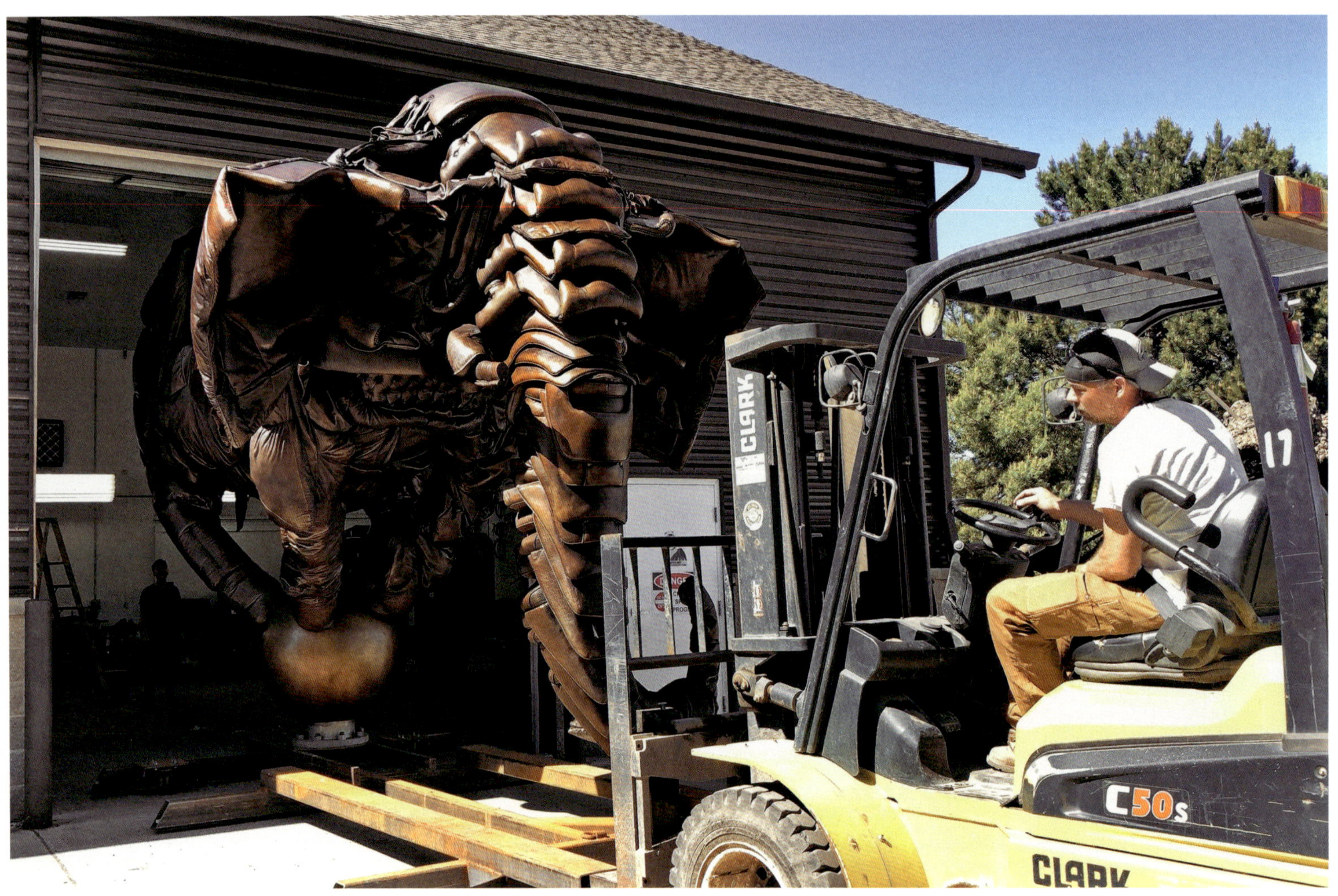

CLARK
C50s
CLARK

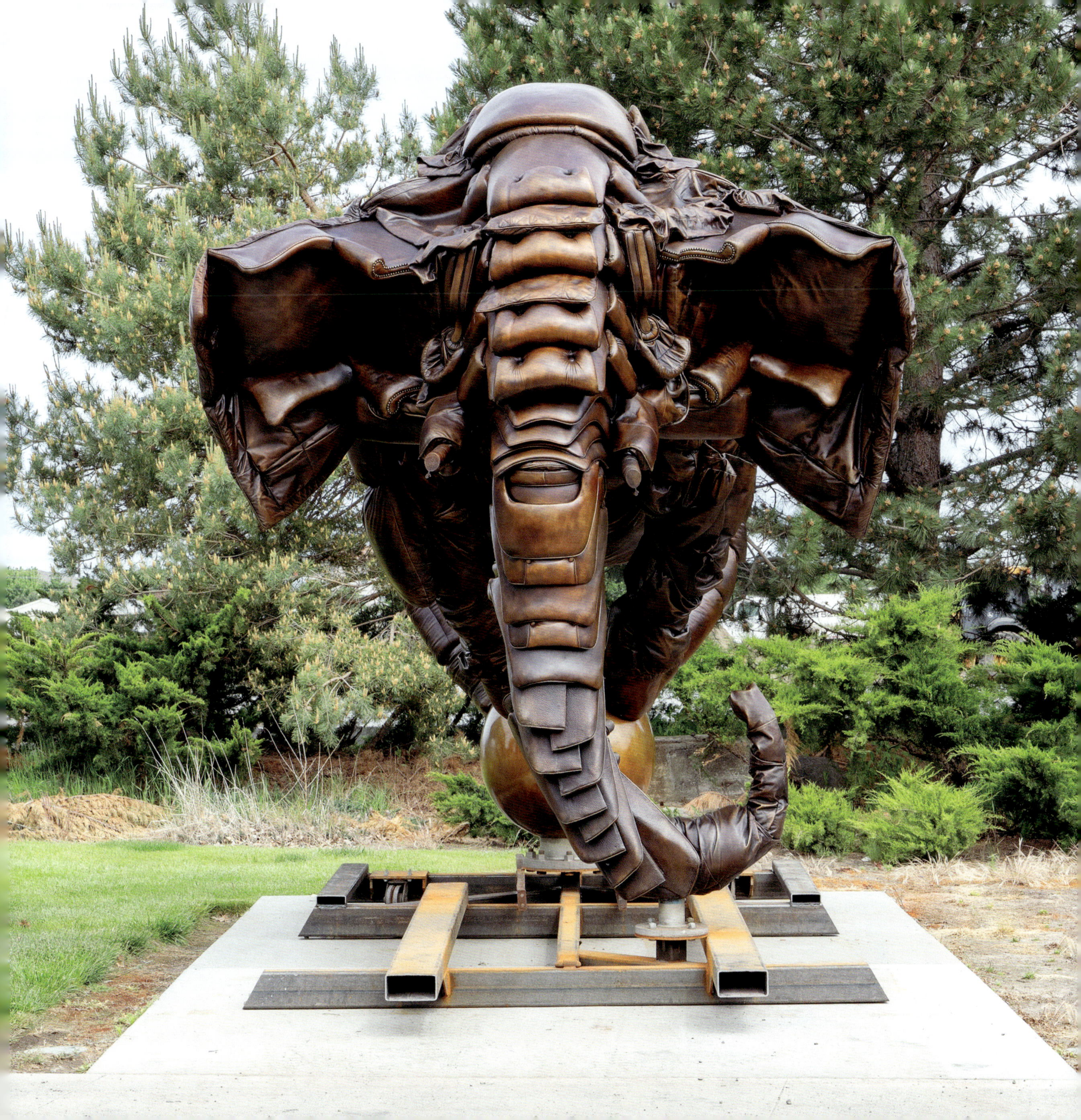

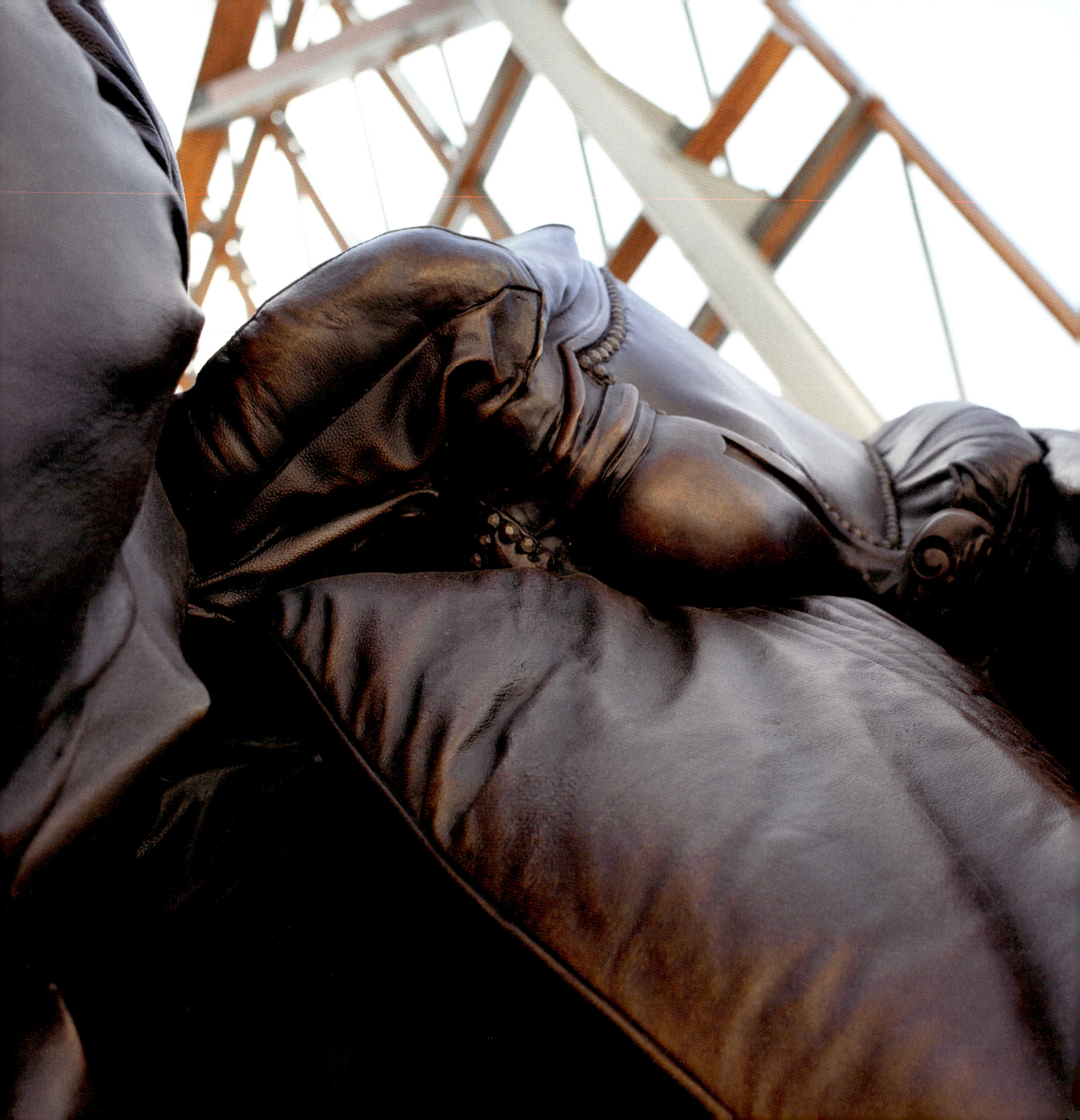

AGO

Couch Monster arrived at the AGO in June 2022. The sculpture, measuring five-and-a-half metres long and four metres wide and weighing more than 11,000 pounds, was crane-lifted by a crew of highly specialized movers and manoeuvred to its final destination. It now holds pride of place by the northeast corner of the AGO where Dundas and McCaul streets intersect, a bustling area populated by tourists, commuters, university students, and Chinatown residents. For the local community and beyond, the momentous arrival of *Couch Monster* signals the AGO's commitment to leading conversations about global contemporary art into the future.

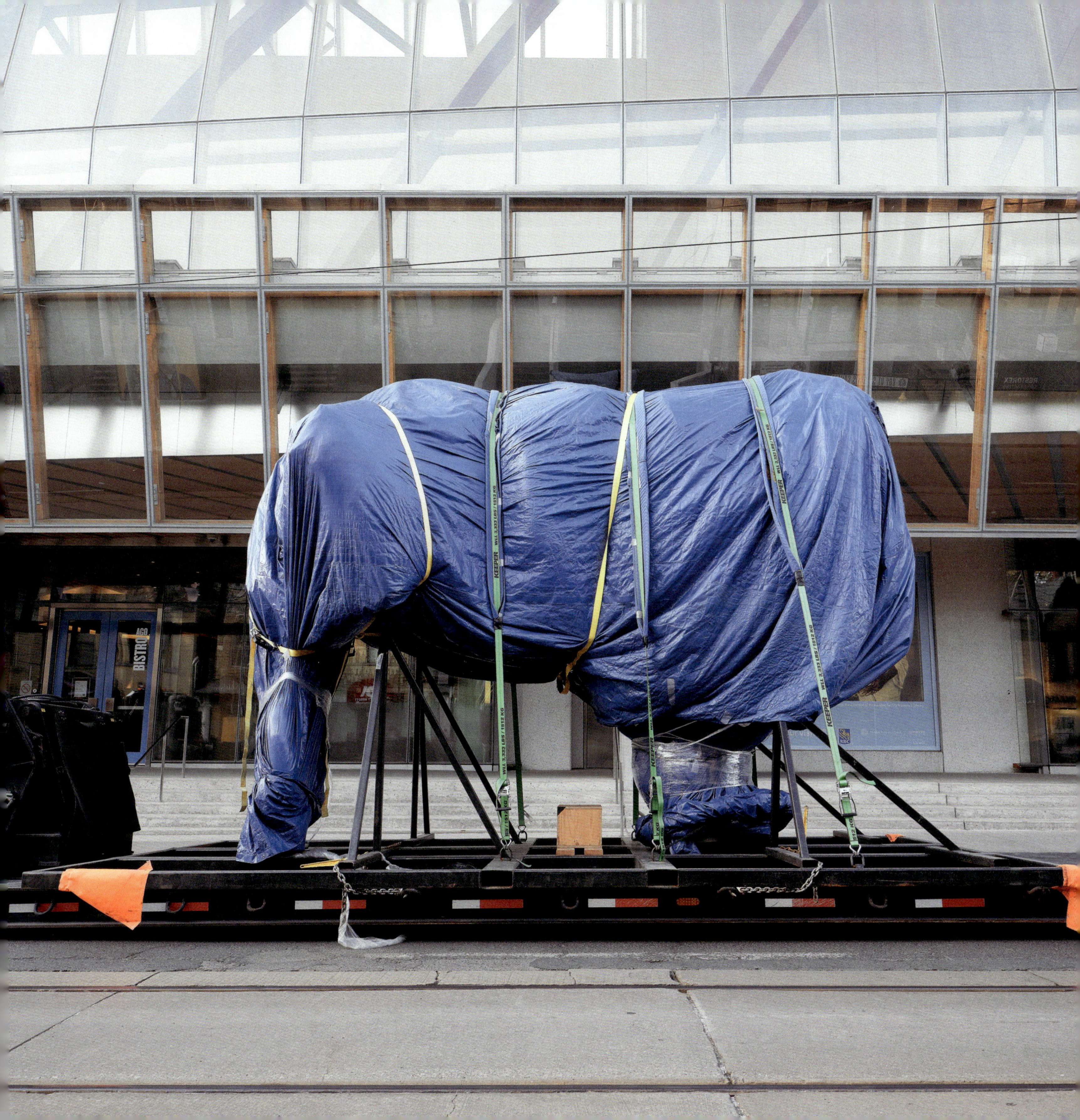

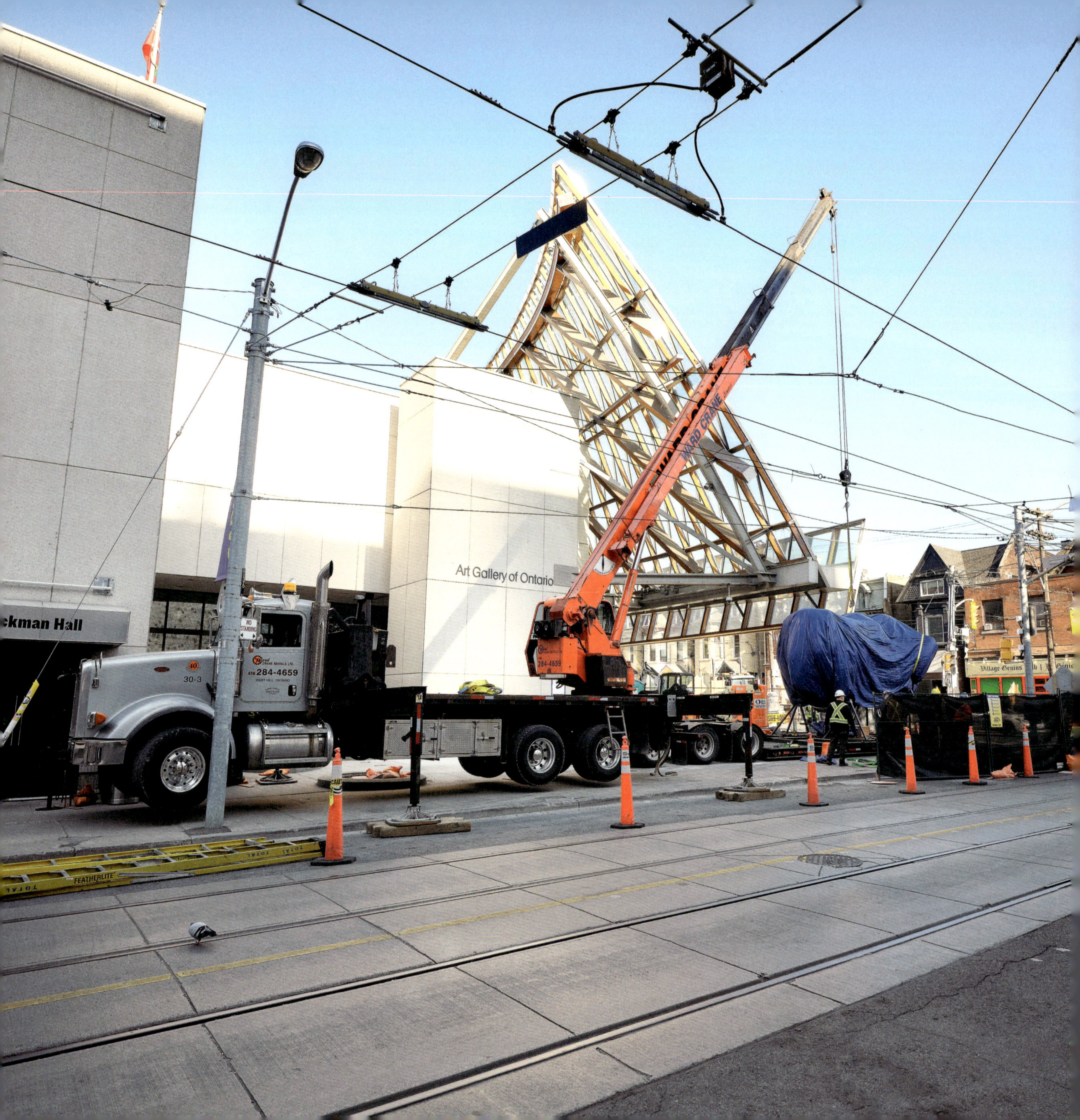

ckman Hall
Art Gallery of Ontario
WARD CRANE
416 284-4659
WEST HILL ONTARIO
30-3
FEATHERLITE
Village Genius

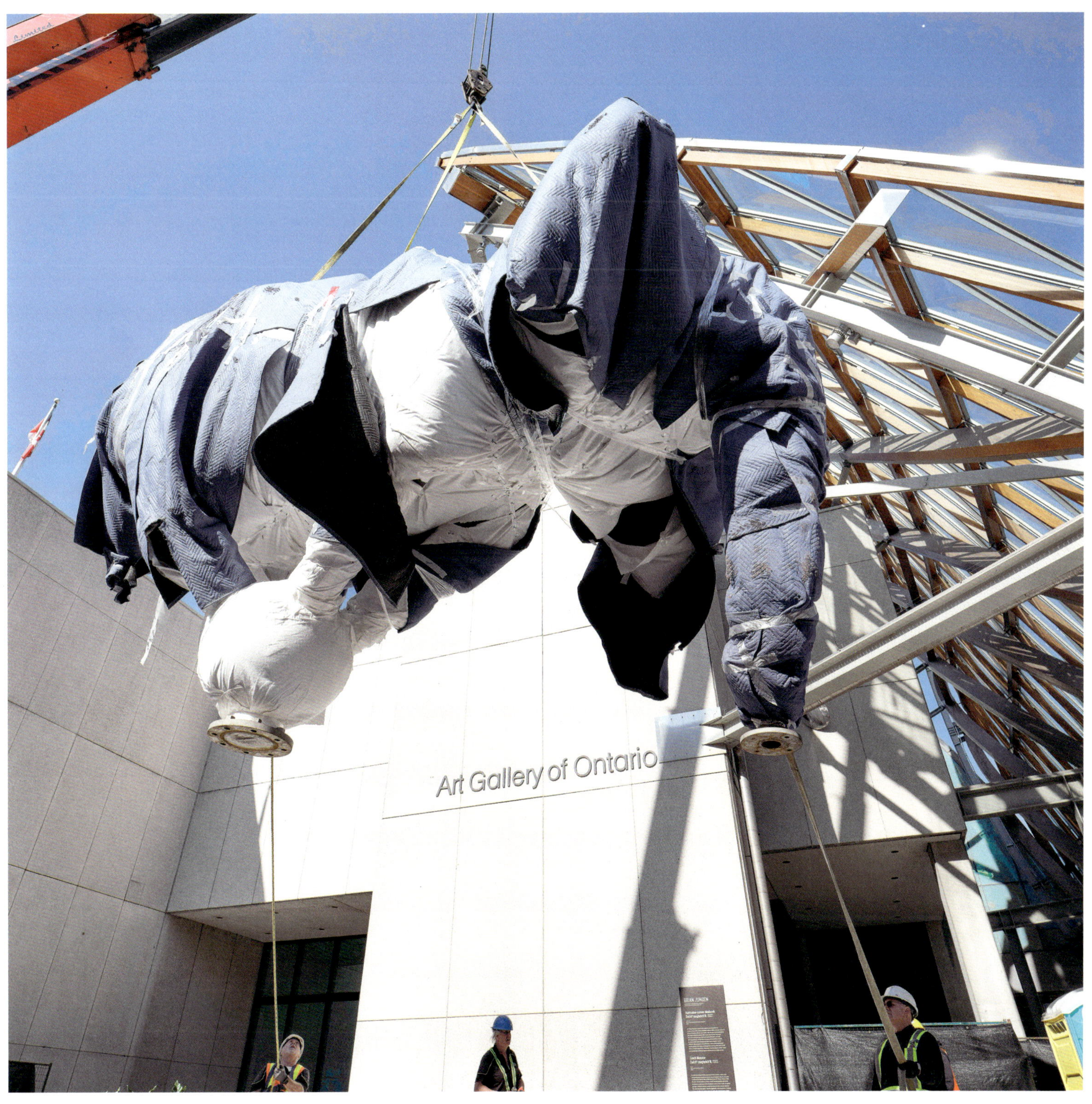

Art Gallery of Ontario

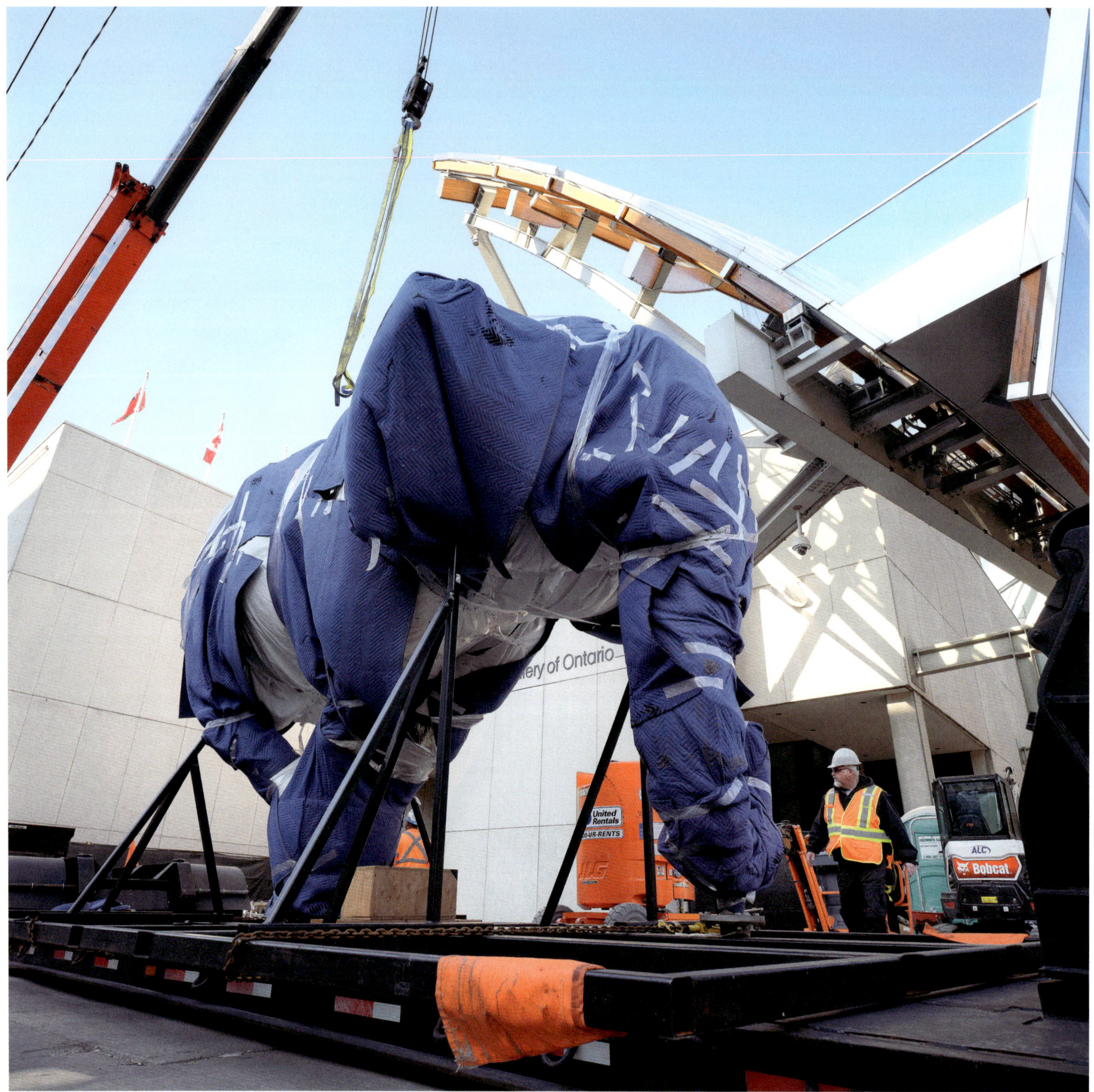
llery of Ontario
United Rentals
800-UR-RENTS
Bobcat
ALC
JLG

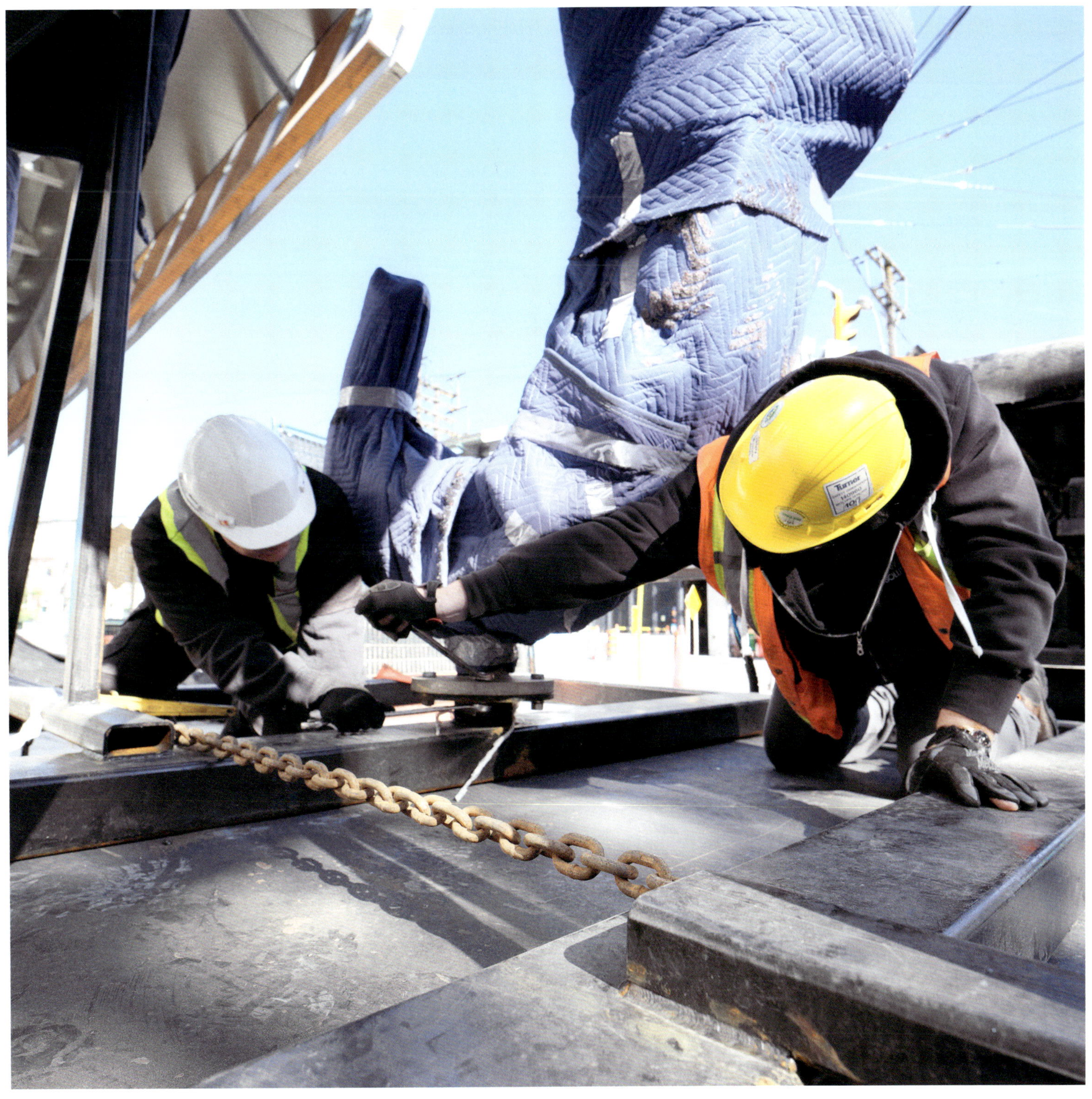

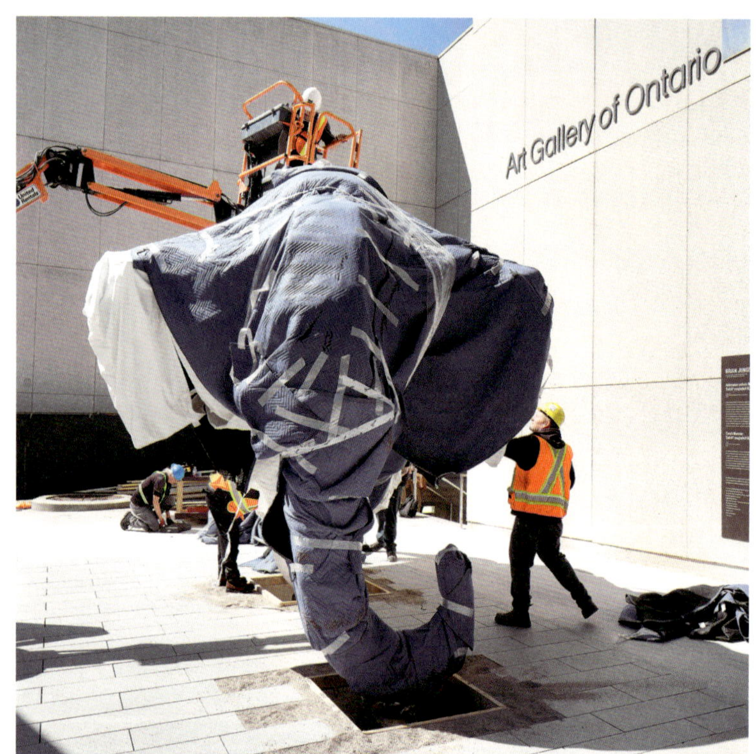
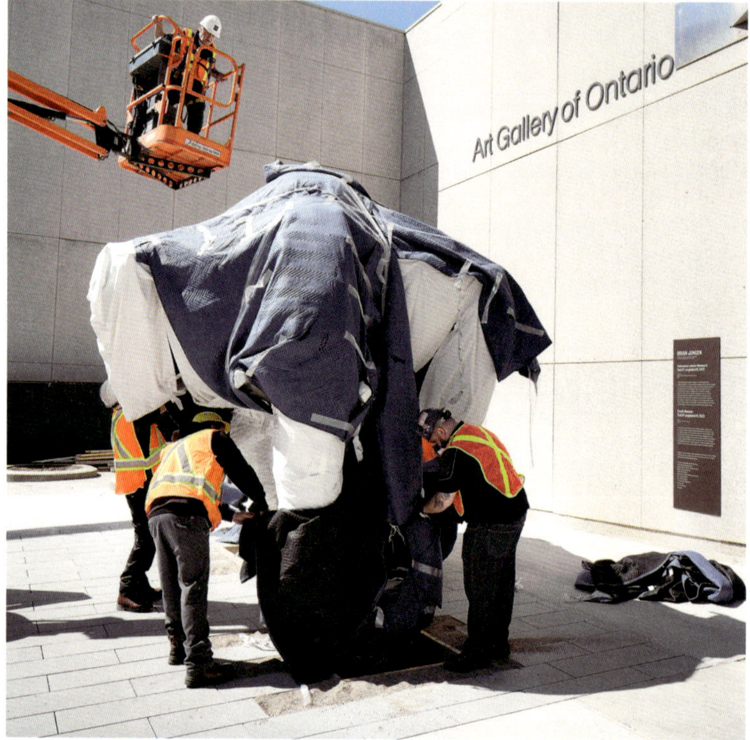
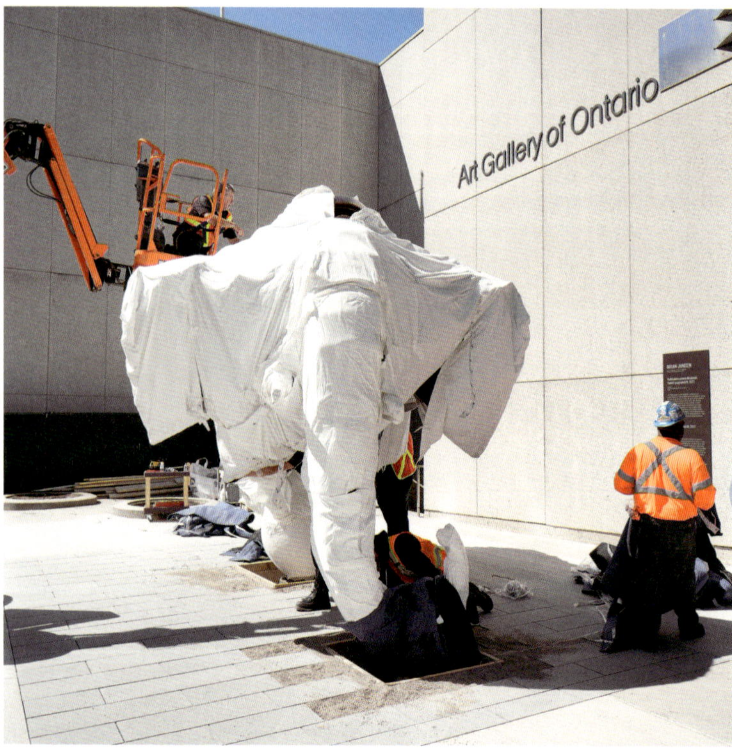
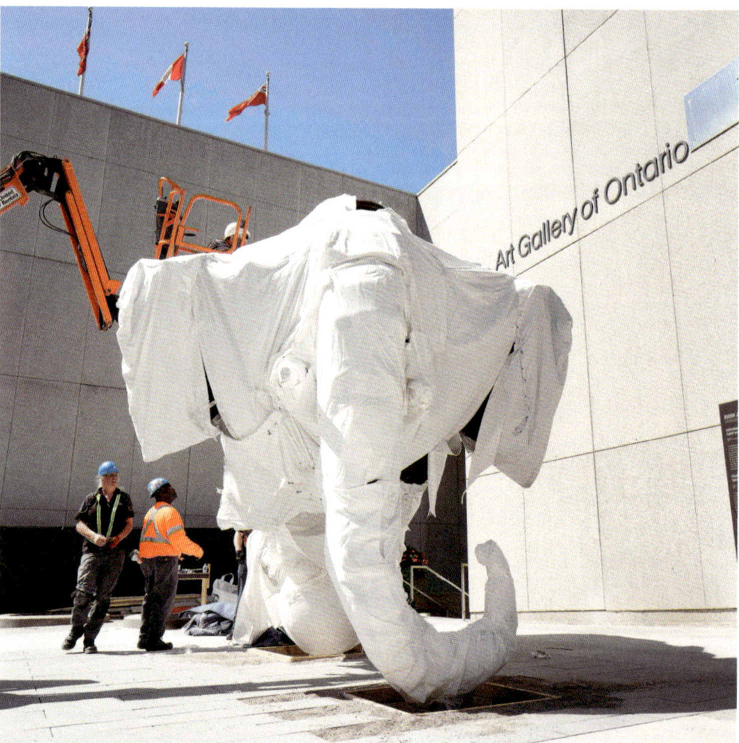

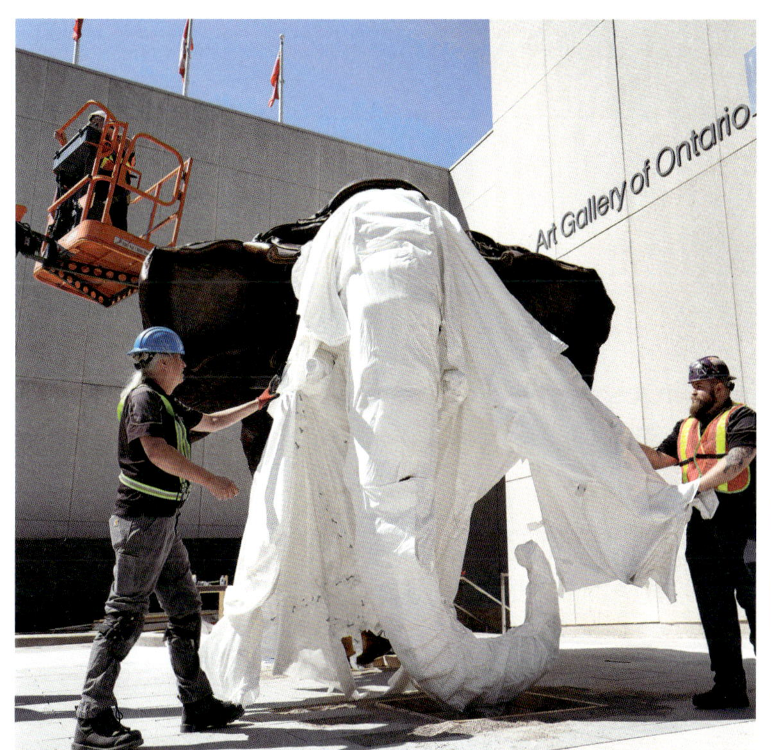
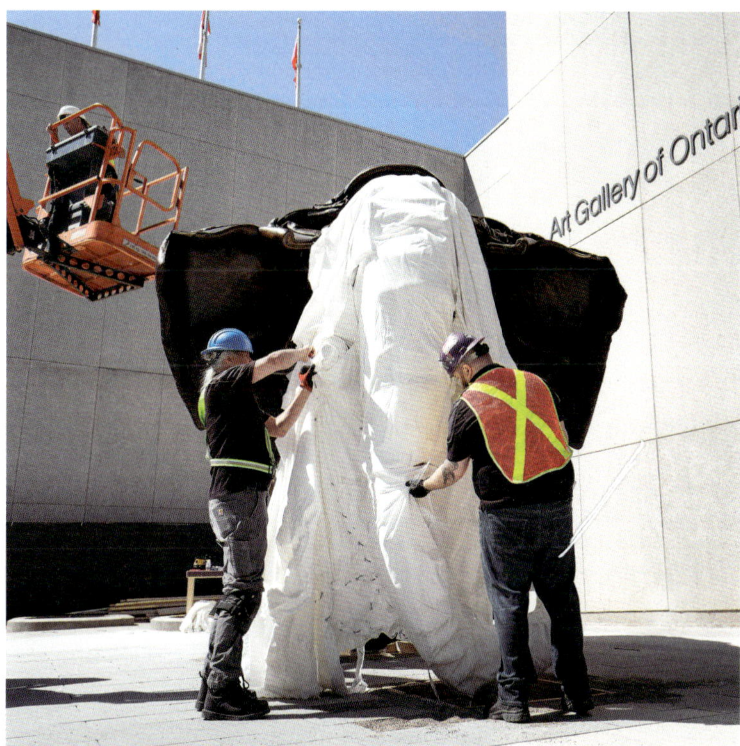
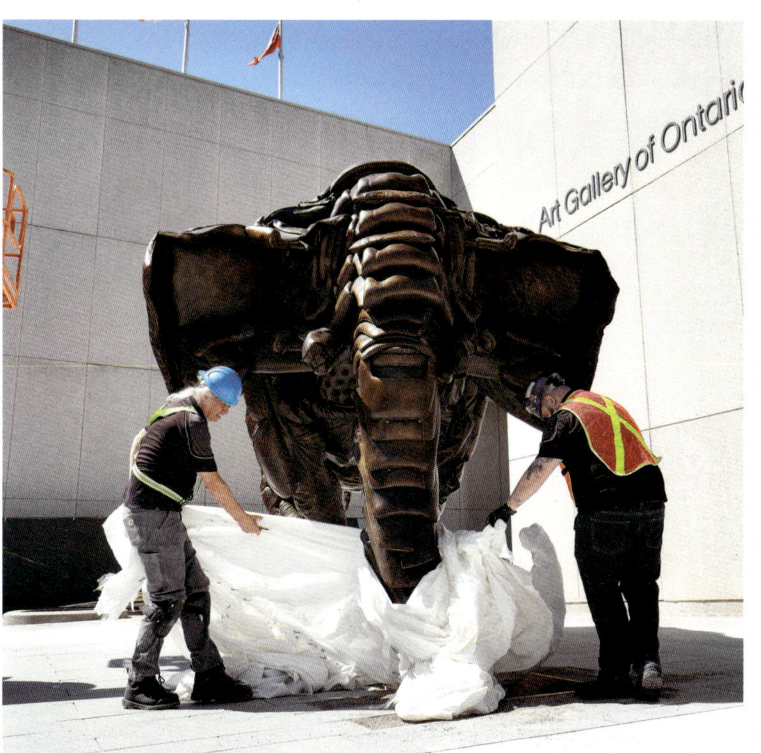
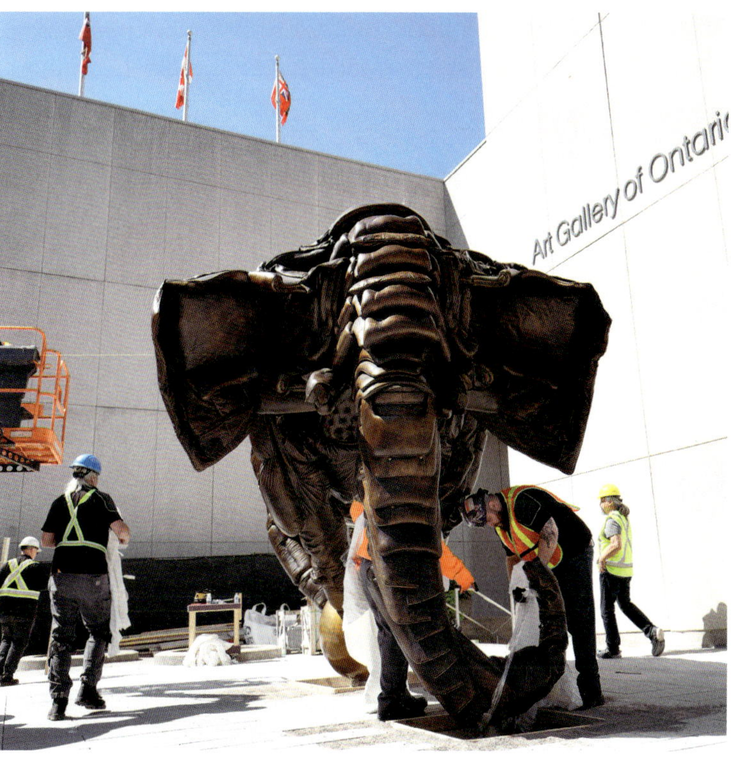

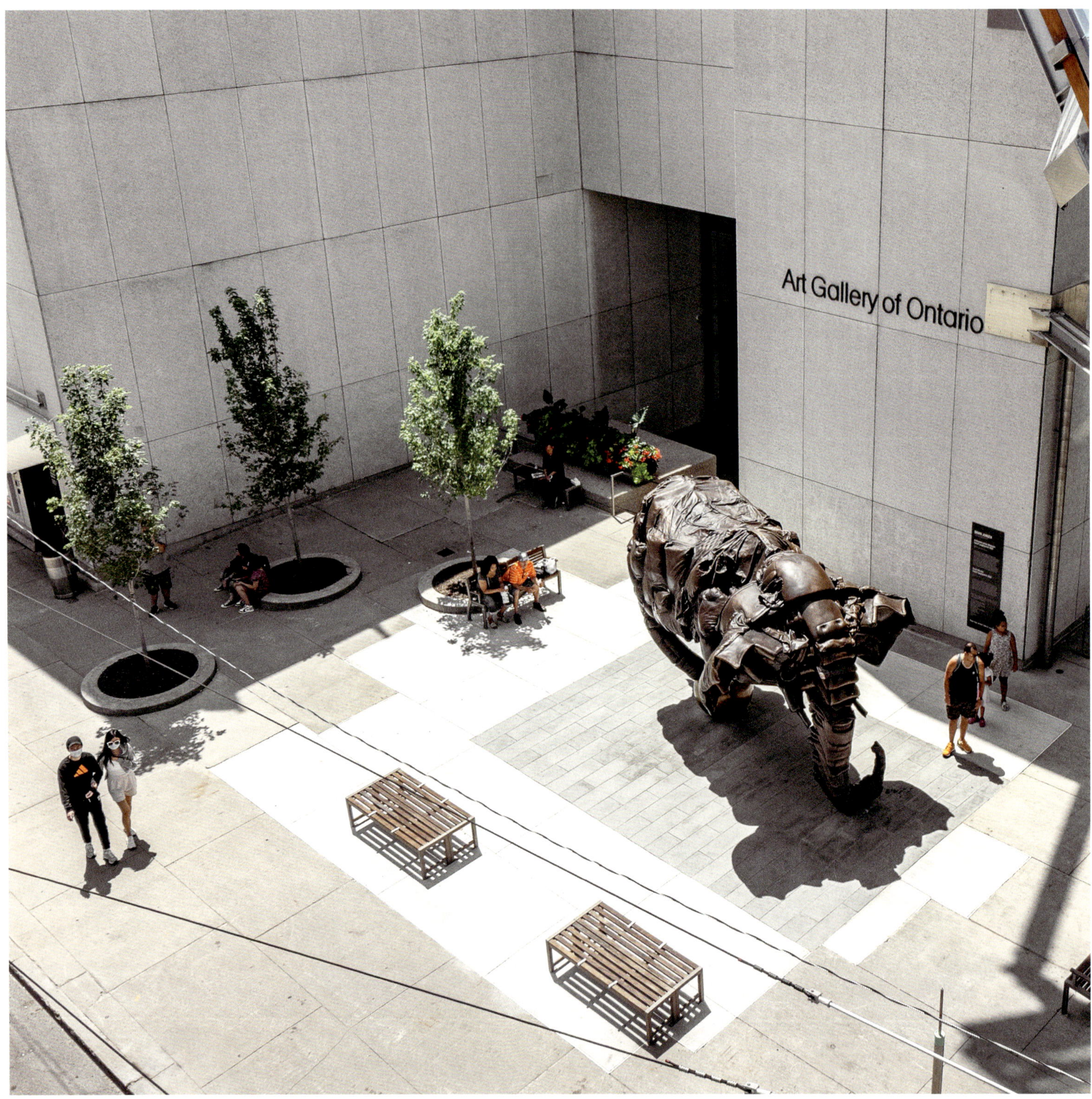
Art Gallery of Ontario

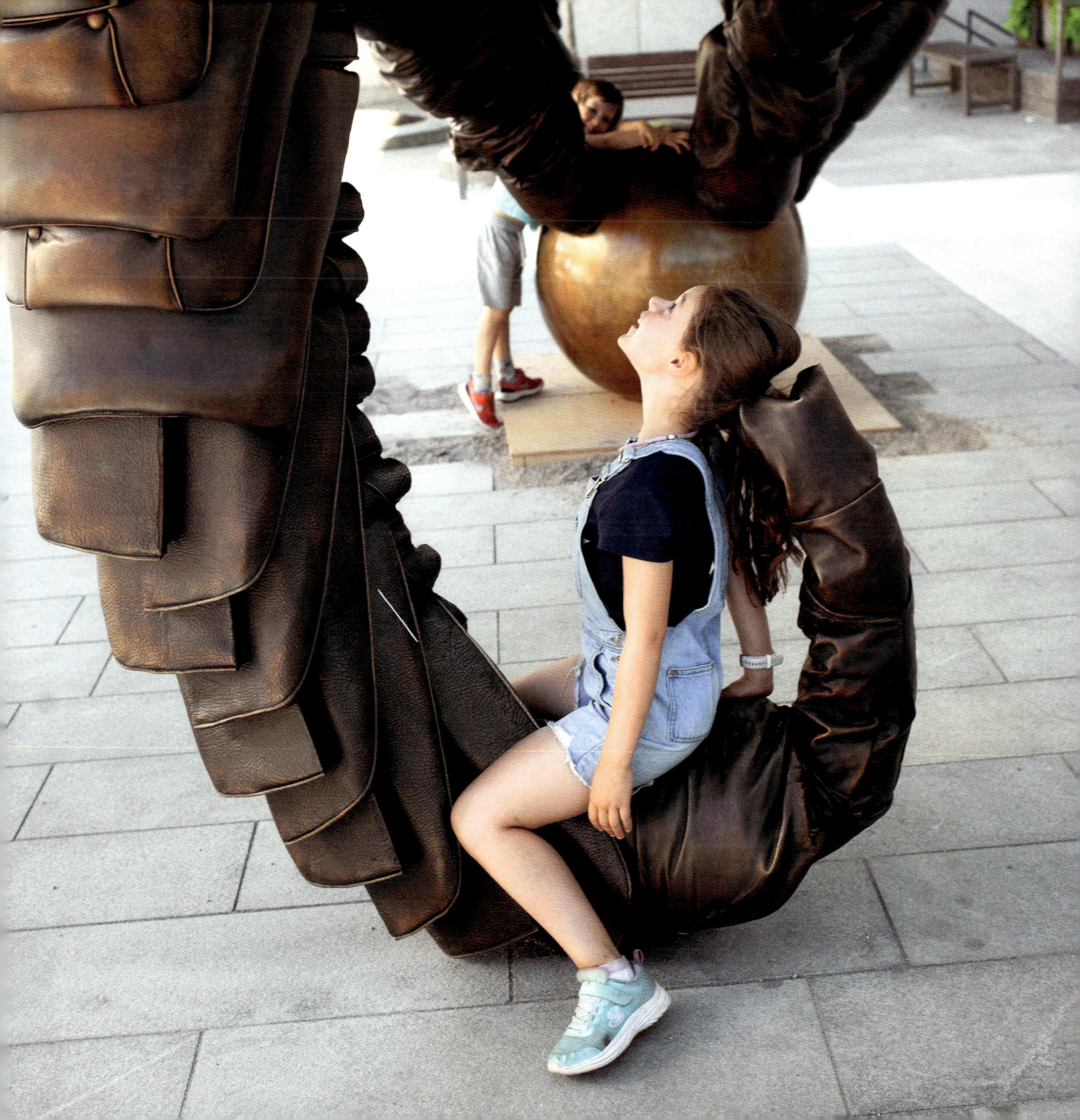

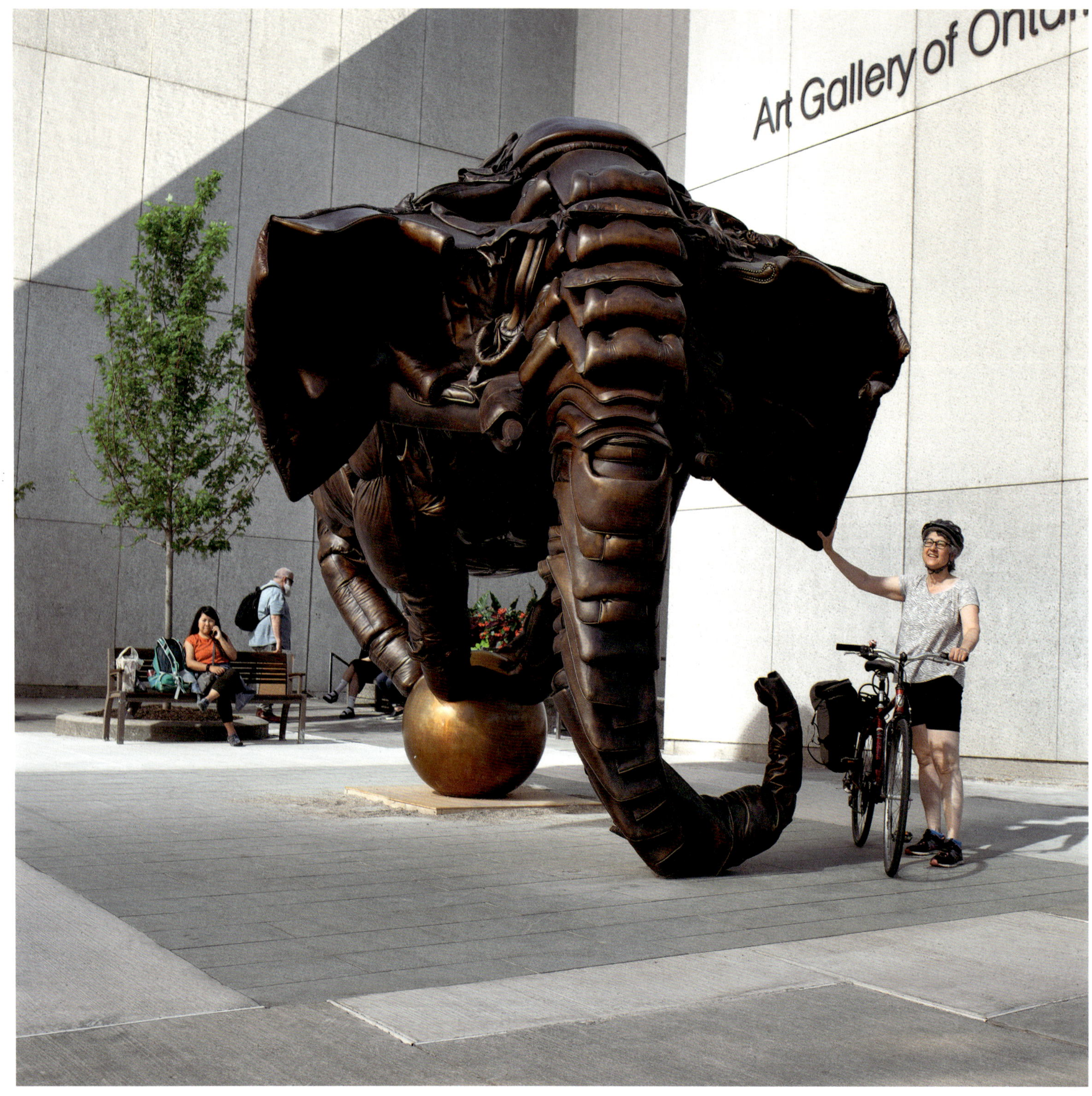
Art Gallery of Ontar

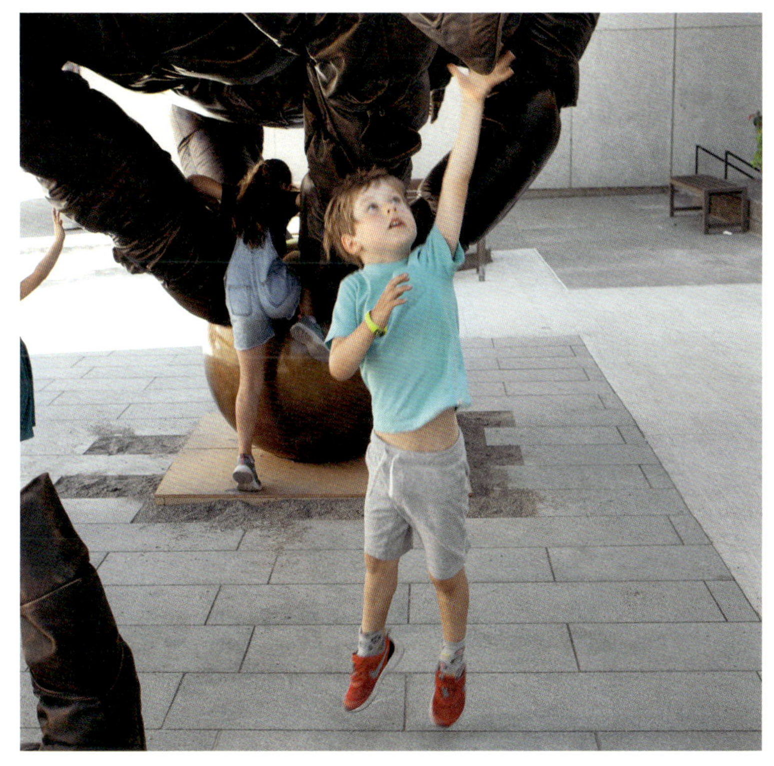
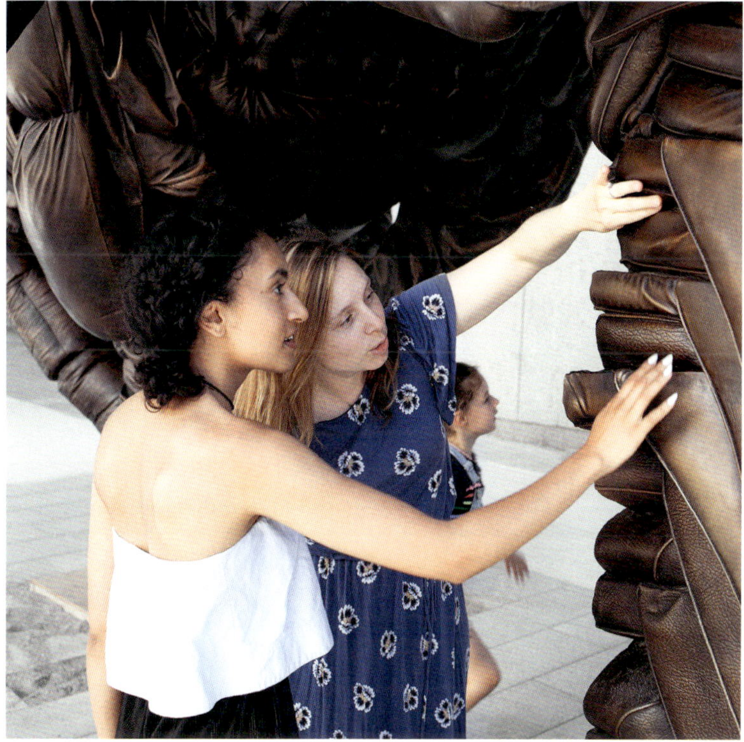
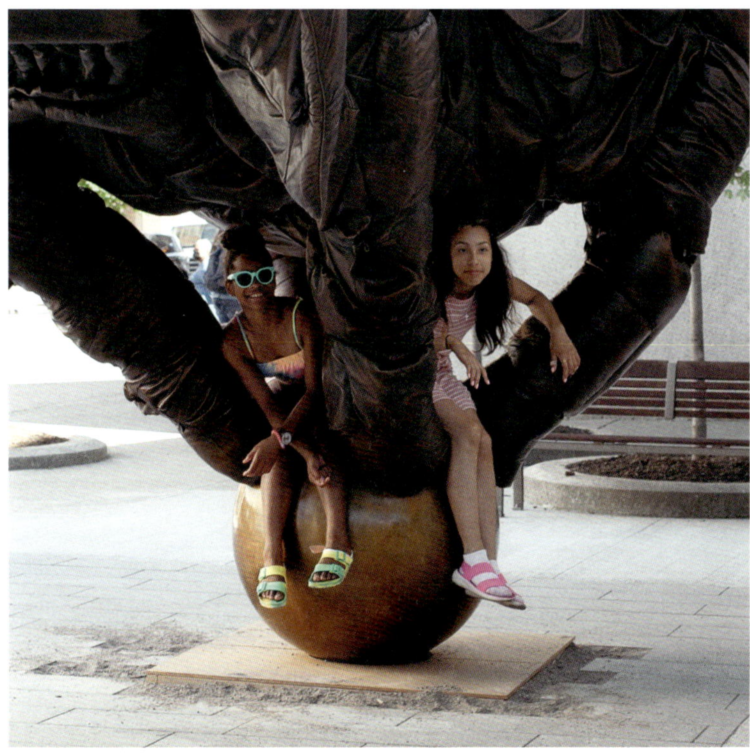
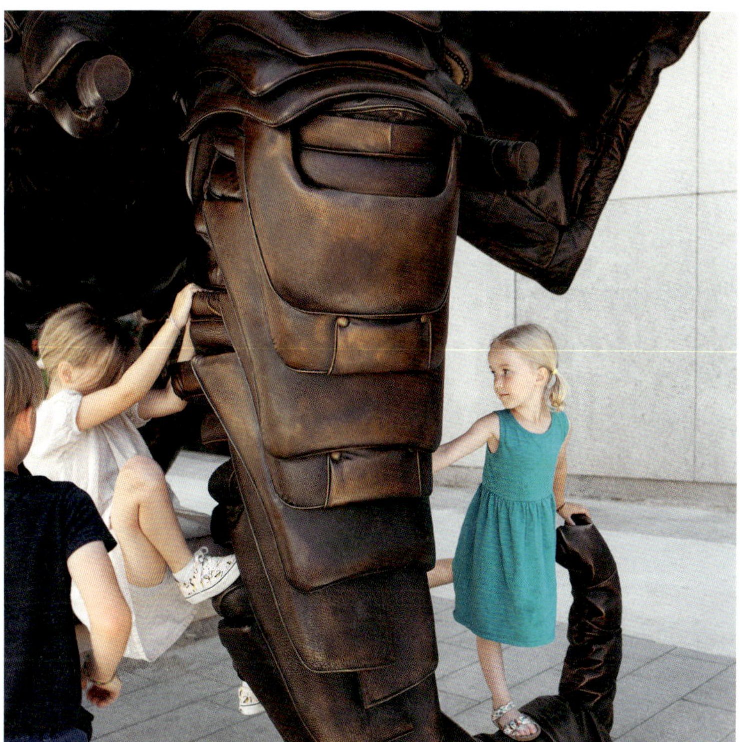

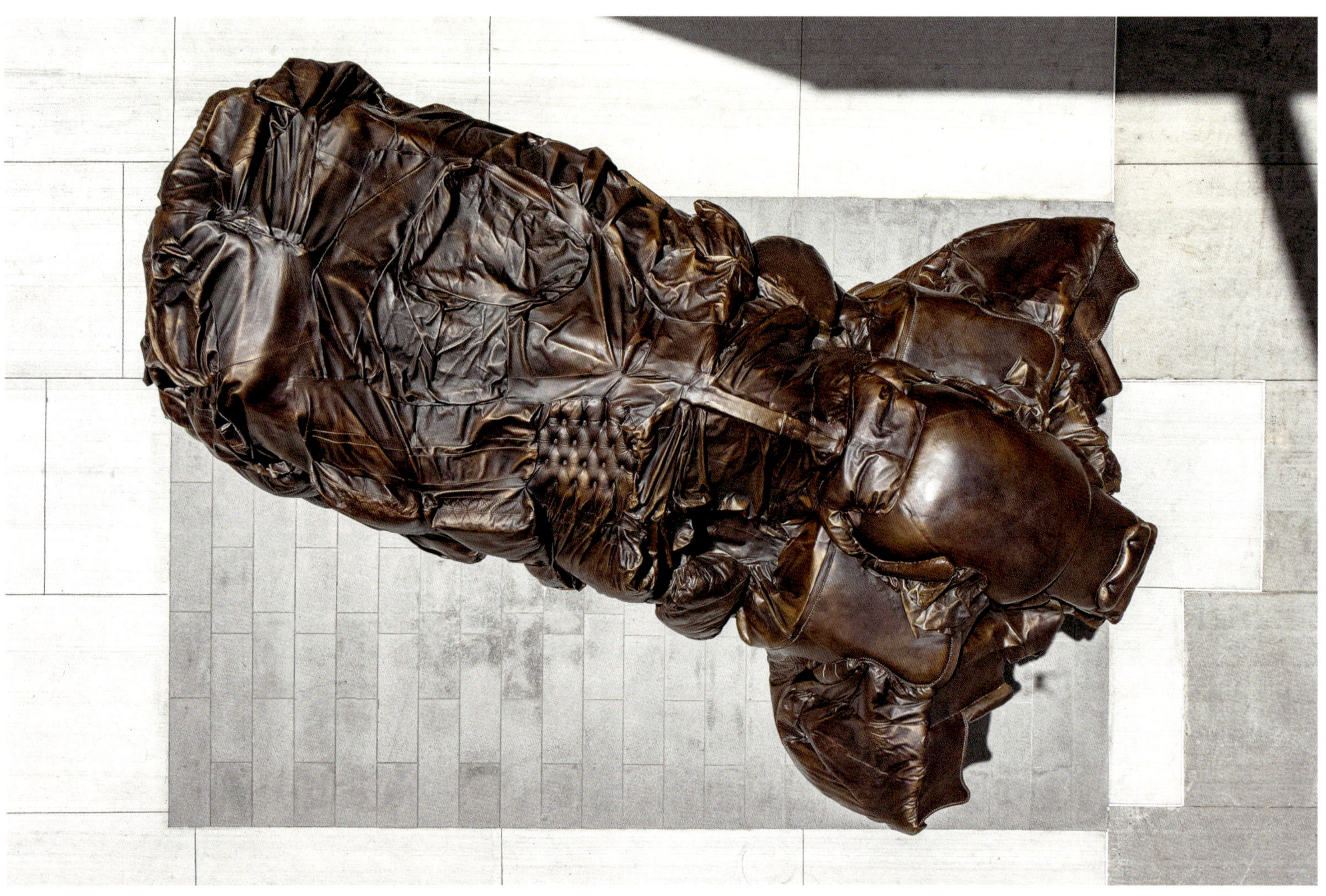

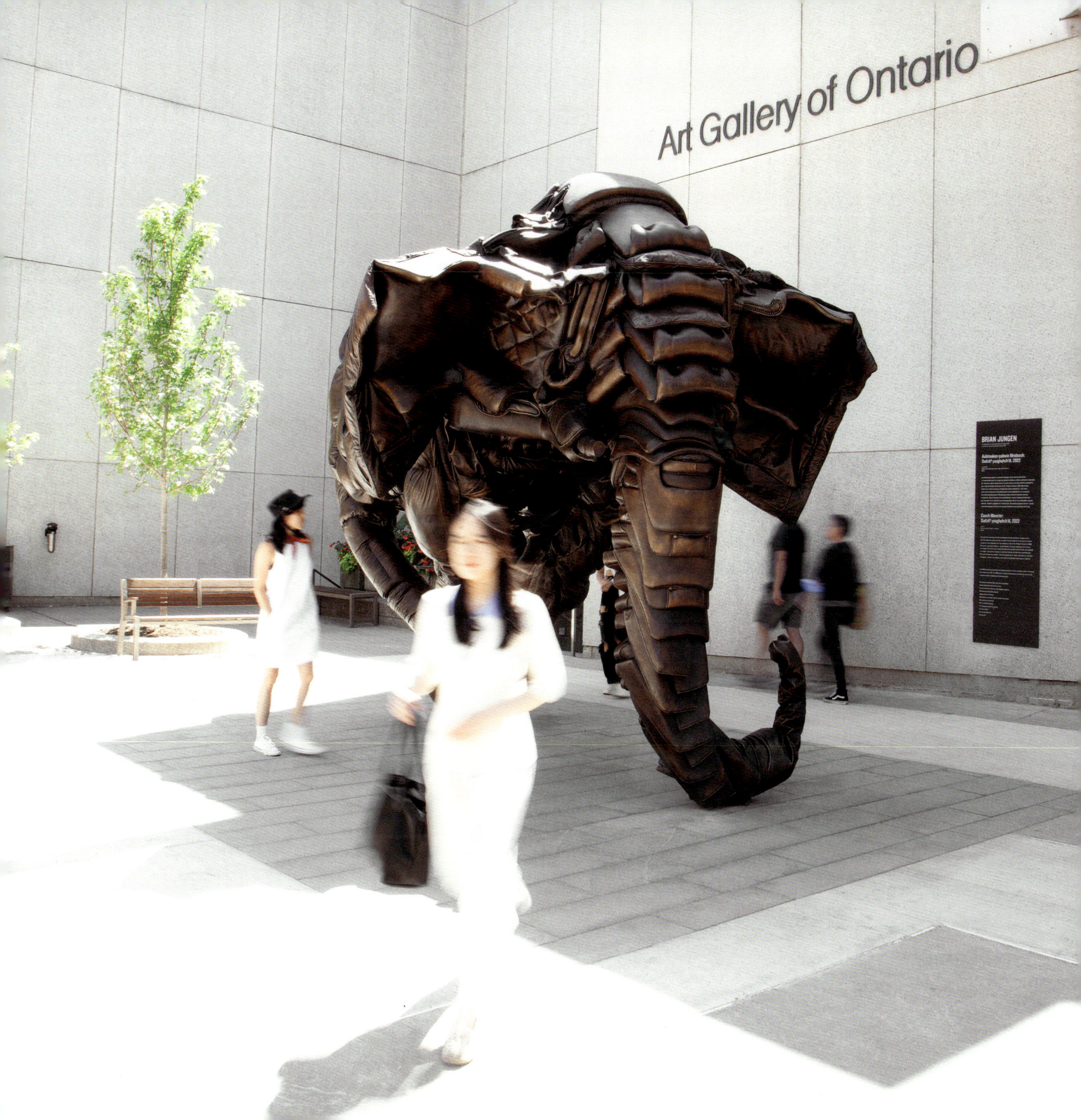

Art Gallery of Ontario
BRIAN JUNGEN
Couch Monster:

From *The Archer* to *Couch Monster*: A Journey Through Toronto's Bronze Age

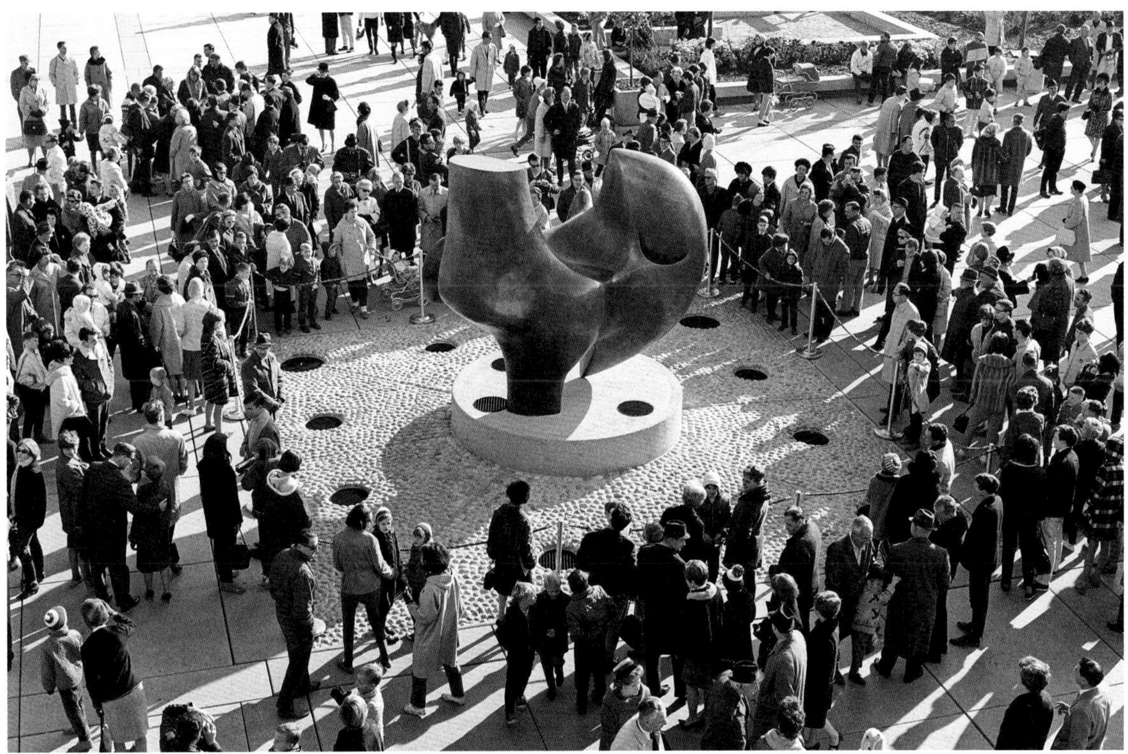

THE ARCHER

On October 27, 1966, Henry Moore's abstract sculpture *Three-Way Piece No. 2—*
more commonly referred to as *The Archer*—was unveiled in Nathan Phillips
Square, beside Toronto's newly erected City Hall. The now iconic building had
been designed by the Finnish modernist architect Viljo Revell (1910–1964),
who recruited Moore (1898–1986) to complement his vision through public art.
There was significant debate over the merits of *The Archer* (and of abstract
art in general), as representational forms were in vogue at the time; many also
viewed the costly sculpture as a waste of public money. Indeed, after City
Council refused to sign off on the required funding for the project, Toronto
mayor Philip Givens, who held office from 1963 to 1966, managed to generate
financial support through a private fundraising campaign. The installation of
The Archer signalled a turning point in the cultural life of a city that, in the years
following the Second World War, aspired to be seen as progressive, world-class,
and modern.

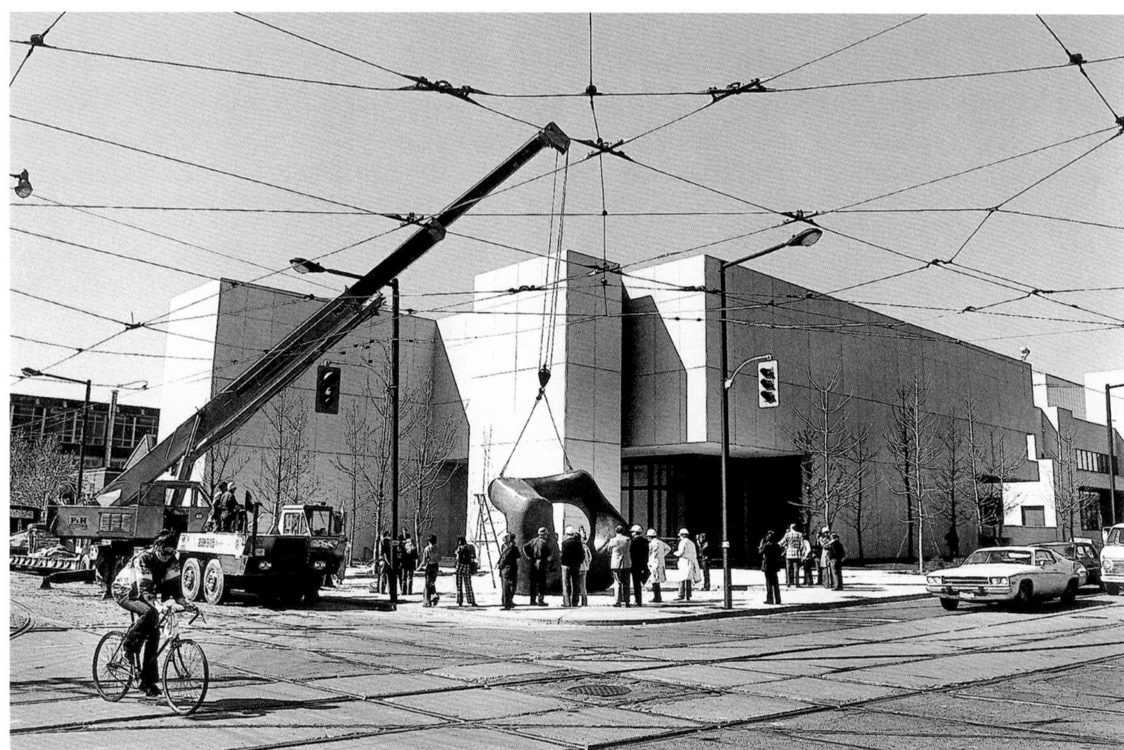

LARGE TWO FORMS

Moore visited Toronto for the first time to attend the unveiling of *The Archer*. While in the city, he was approached by Samuel Zacks, a patron of the Art Gallery of Ontario known for the modern art collection he and his wife Ayala built over decades; the two discussed, among other things, the prospect of the AGO purchasing Moore's sculpture *Large Two Forms* (1966–1969). In 1974, the monumental bronze found a home by the northeast corner of the gallery, at the intersection of Dundas Street West and McCaul Street, where it remained until 2016, when it was relocated to Grange Park, on the south side of the museum. *Large Two Forms* became an iconic part of Toronto's urban landscape: its impressive scale and its friendly shapes invited people to touch, climb, and explore the sculpture, which remains a popular backdrop for photographs.

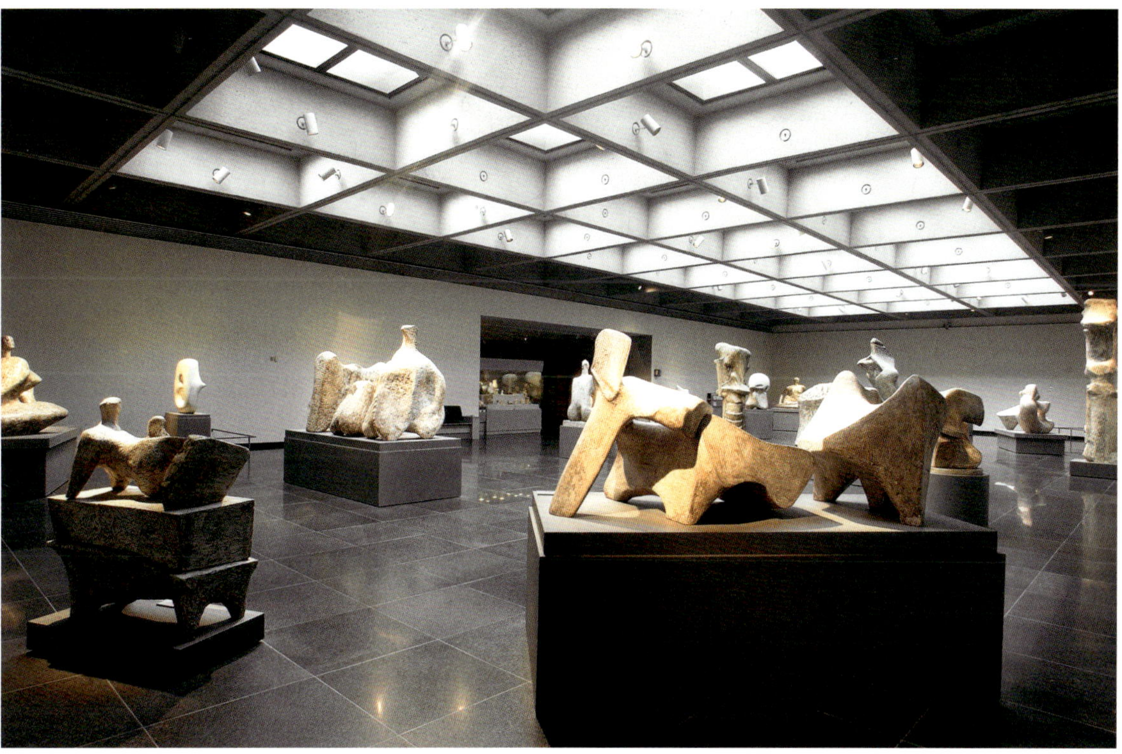

THE HENRY MOORE SCULPTURE CENTRE

In 1966, the year of Moore's visit, the Art Gallery of Toronto officially adopted its present name and became the Art Gallery of Ontario. At the time, the Gallery was in the process of planning a major expansion, led by revered Canadian architect John C. Parkin. This project happened in two stages, in 1974 and 1977, and included the Henry Moore Sculpture Centre, a mid-century modern space exclusively dedicated to the artist's work. While the Centre was criticized by those who felt that the Gallery should be showcasing Canadian work rather than devoting so much space to a British artist, the space cemented Moore's relationship to the city, attracted visitors, and became a source of inspiration for fans of modern art.

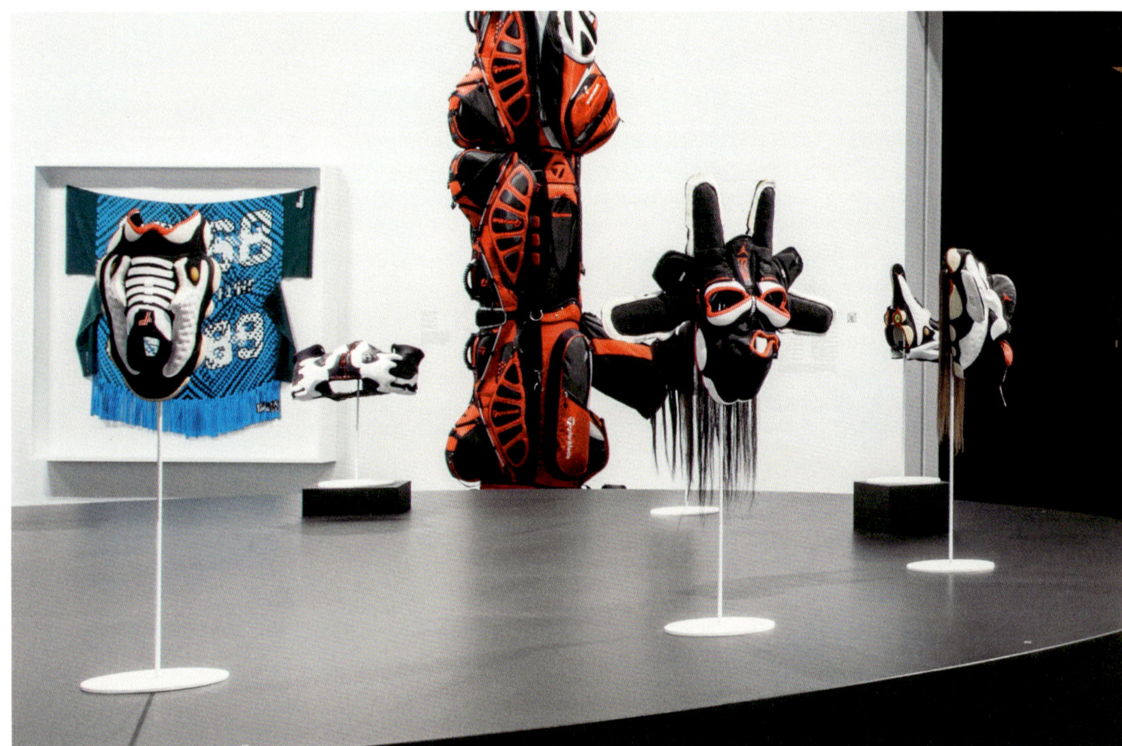

Installation view of *Prototype for New Understanding* series (1998–2005) in *Brian Jungen: Friendship Centre*, Art Gallery of Ontario, 2018.

PROTOTYPE FOR NEW UNDERSTANDING

In 2001, the Art Gallery of Ontario acquired its first piece by Brian Jungen. The work, part of the artist's *Prototype for New Understanding* series, was made by taking apart Nike Air Jordan sneakers and reassembling the pieces into soft sculptures that resemble Northwest Coast masks. These early works established the artist's strategy of drawing on Indigenous symbols and practices to repurpose objects from contemporary culture. Throughout his career, Jungen has conducted parallel explorations, reflecting on aspects of what his Indigenous identity means to him while also investigating unconventional materials and their potential to become new hybrid forms. These tandem paths are yoked together through larger ideas about sustainability and co-existence.

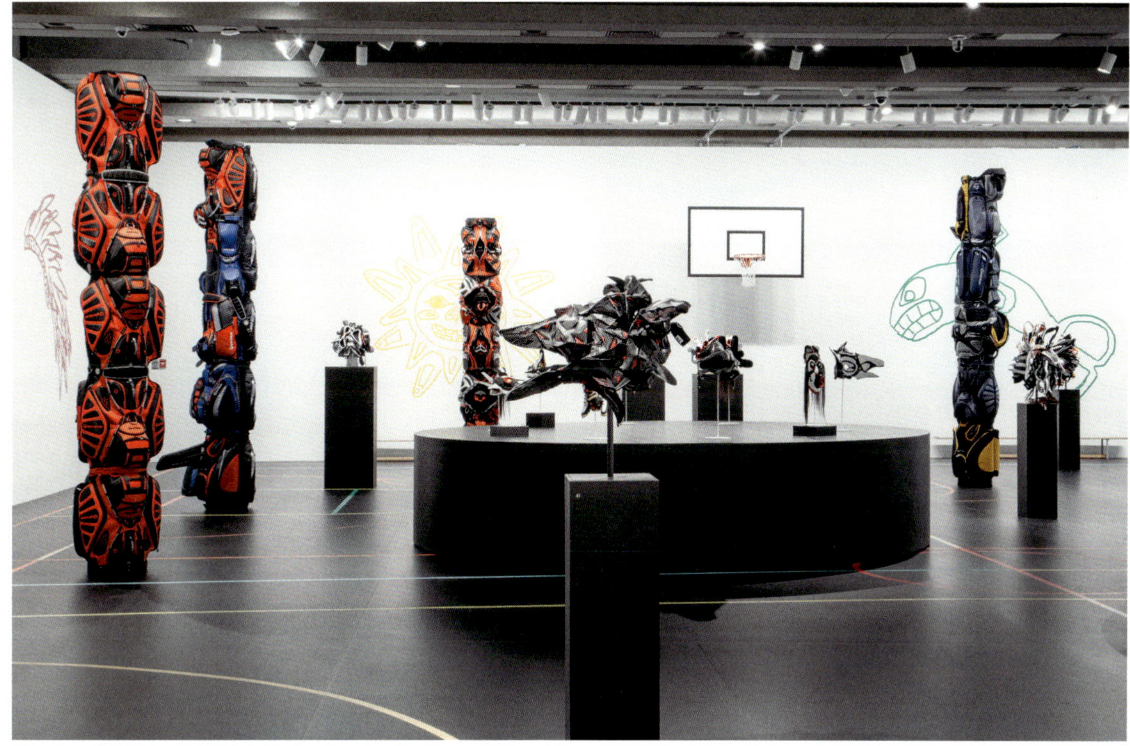

BRIAN JUNGEN, INDIGENEITY, AND ANTI-NATIONALISM

In 2007, Jungen produced a series of works resembling Haida totem poles, made from stacks of deconstructed TaylorMade golf bags. Each of these sculptures is named after the first year of a decade, starting with 1960, when Indigenous people were given the right to vote in Canada. Through this choice of material, Jungen provides a commentary on Indigenous claims to land (such as golf courses) that has been appropriated for recreational purposes; the familiar totem pole forms become markers of recent historical events that shaped Indigenous –Crown relations in Canada. The AGO quickly acquired *1960*, *1970*, and *1980* for its collection. Another notable acquisition was *Wieland* (2006), Jungen's wry tribute to Joyce Wieland (1930–1998), who in 1971 became the first living Canadian woman artist to receive a retrospective exhibition at the National Gallery of Canada. As a student in California, Jungen watched Wieland present some of her films, which, like her broader body of work, engaged with feminism, nationalism, and other timely social issues; he was saddened by her premature death. In *Wieland*, he cut up and machine-stitched red leather women's gloves into the form of a maple leaf, the symbol emblazoned on Canada's national flag since 1965. In Jungen's vision, this icon is intentionally inverted, and has a saggy, deflated look that undercuts its symbolic heft.

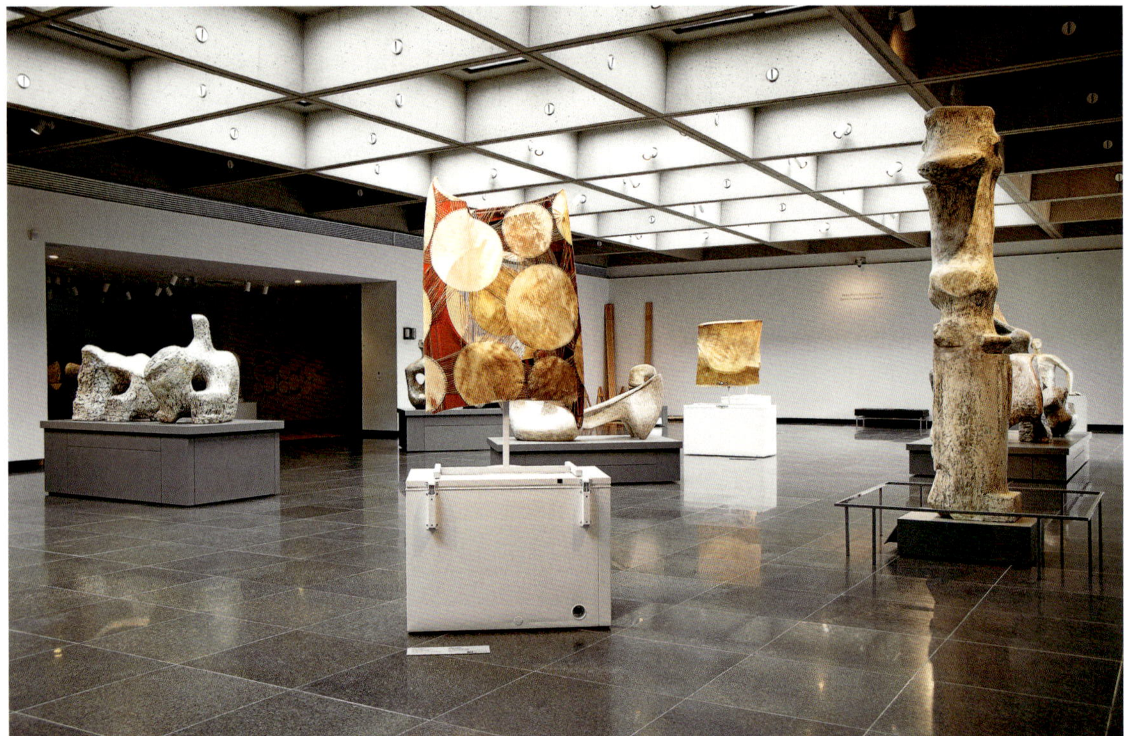

TOMORROW, REPEATED

When Brian Jungen won the Gershon Iskowitz Prize in 2010, he chose to display a new series of sculptures among the plaster casts in the Henry Moore Sculpture Centre. The exhibition, which was titled *Tomorrow, Repeated*, was a direct response to both the site and Moore's work; Jungen's sculptures co-inhabited the environment, creating a conversation that illuminated their shared affinities across time, including an interest in non-European sculptural traditions, a keen understanding of form, and an intimate relationship with materials. *Tomorrow, Repeated* featured works that expanded on Jungen's earlier sculptural shape-shifting: animal hides stretched over cut-up car parts and displayed on white chest freezers, police barricades built out of cedar and Douglas fir, and prints made using hide that was left over after he cut out circular drum skins. The raw texture of the animal hides visually echoed the "skin" of Moore's plaster figures, while Jungen's intervention introduced new narratives into the space—ones that challenged and complemented the colonialist history of both the Centre and the Gallery as a whole.

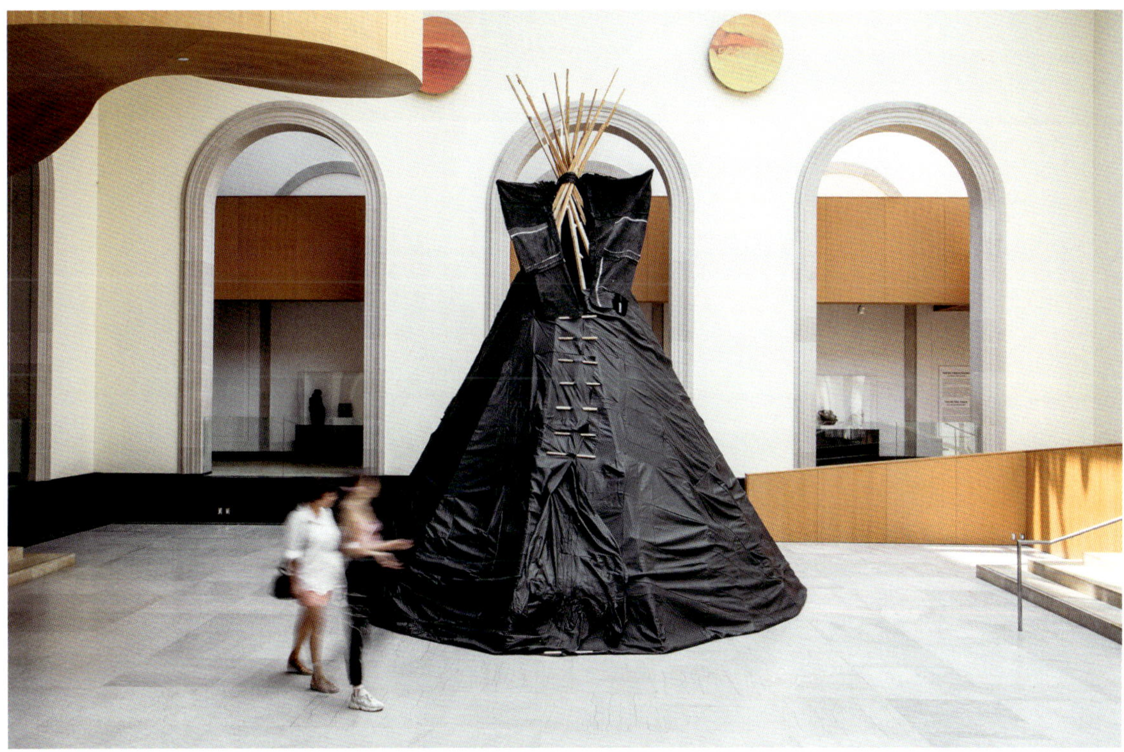

MODEST LIVELIHOOD AND *BRIAN JUNGEN: FRIENDSHIP CENTRE*

In 2012, Jungen collaborated with Duane Linklater, an Omaskêko Cree artist based in North Bay, Ontario, on the film *Modest Livelihood*. The title references a 1999 Supreme Court of Canada ruling that reasserted treaty rights for First Nations to hunt only for the purpose of a "moderate livelihood," and not for the accumulation of wealth; in the film, the two artists hunt for moose on Dane-zaa treaty lands in northern British Columbia. The following year, *Modest Livelihood* was featured in the AGO's Signy Eaton Gallery. It was shown again in the summer of 2019, when the AGO presented *Brian Jungen: Friendship Centre*, the largest exhibition of the artist's work to date. Among the highlights was *Furniture Sculpture* (2006), a monumental tipi made from eleven leather sofas, installed in Walker Court, the expansive "heart" of the main floor. Materials from Jungen's extensive archive were on view to the public for the first time as well, underscoring the fact that this was a landmark show for the artist and the Gallery.

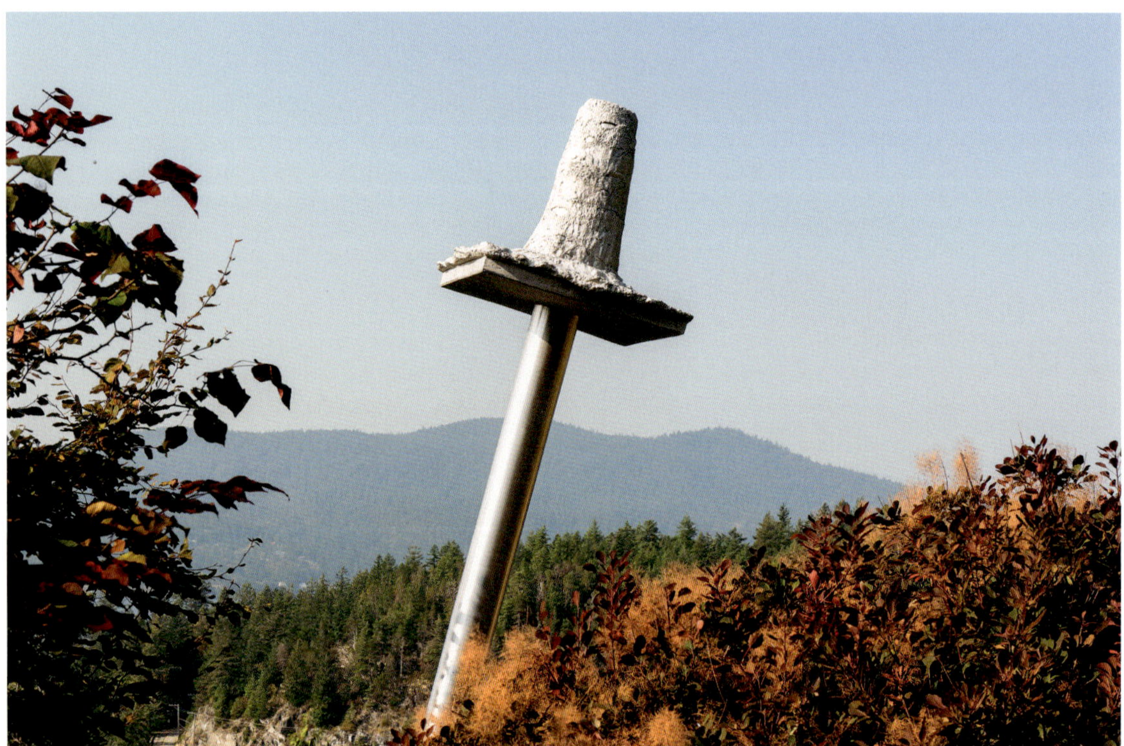

Brian Jungen, *Flagpole*, 2020.
Aluminum, 1019 × 140 × 152 cm.
Courtesy of Catriona Jeffries,
Vancouver. © Brian Jungen.

BRIAN JUNGEN AND PUBLIC ART

Public art has long been an important aspect of Jungen's practice. In 2011, the Banff Centre for Arts and Creativity commissioned *The ghosts on top of my head* (2011), three white steel benches that suggest antlers—caribou, elk, and moose—which were installed outside the institution's Canada Plaza. For dOCUMENTA 12 in Kassel, Germany, he created *Dog Run* (2012), a kind of interactive obstacle course, agility run, and amusement park for canines and their human companions. Between 2017 and 2020, Jungen developed *Upside Down Flagpole* which, as the title suggests, was modelled on an actual flagpole that Jungen removed from his property in the Okanagan. Intrigued by the concrete base that was uprooted along with the pole in the excavation process, the artist replicated and inverted the form as a critical commentary on land ownership and nationalism in the form of a large-scale commission for Vancouver's Polygon Gallery.

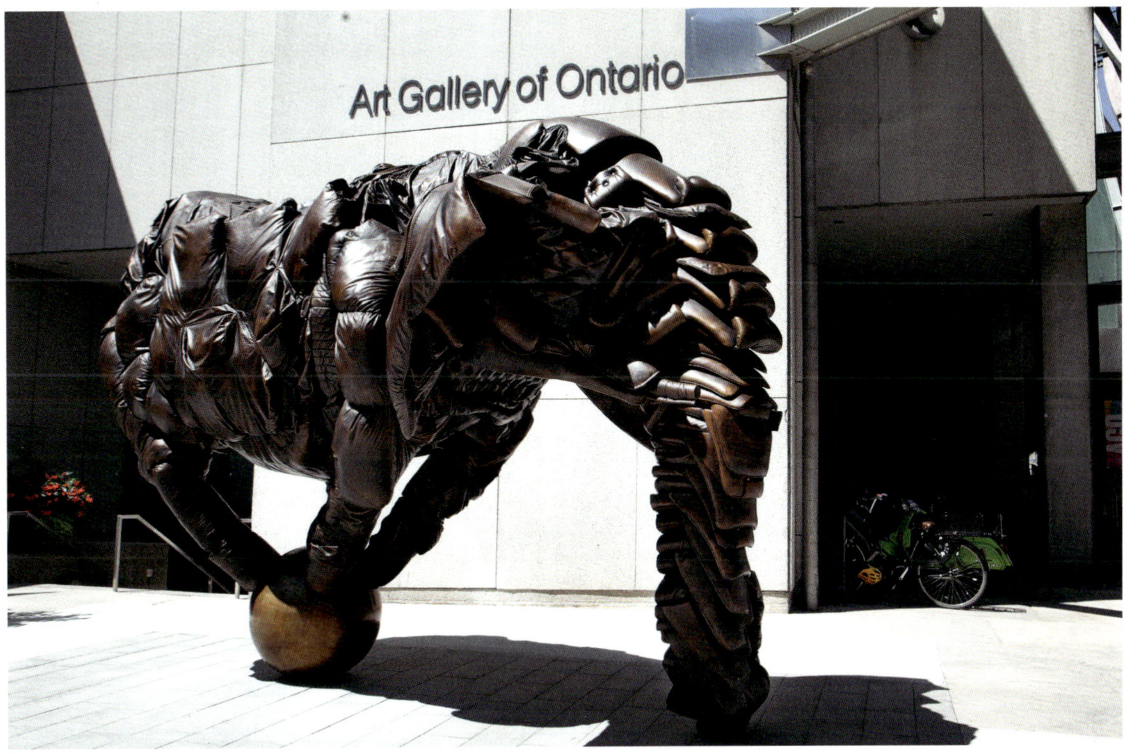

Installation view of *Couch Monster: Sadžĕ? yaaghęhch'ill*, Art Gallery of Ontario, 2022.

COUCH MONSTER

In 2016 the AGO began a conversation with Jungen about the possibility of producing a new large-scale sculptural work to take the place of Henry Moore's *Large Two Forms*. The artist built on the experience of his previous public-art endeavours to achieve his most ambitious work to date. After two years of complications and delays related to the COVID-19 pandemic and a technically and logistically complex transportation and installation process, the bronze elephant sculpture *Couch Monster: Sadžĕ? yaaghęhch'ill* finally settled into its new home in front of the AGO in June 2022—a vital landmark for a new era in the evolving history of the Gallery and the land that it occupies.

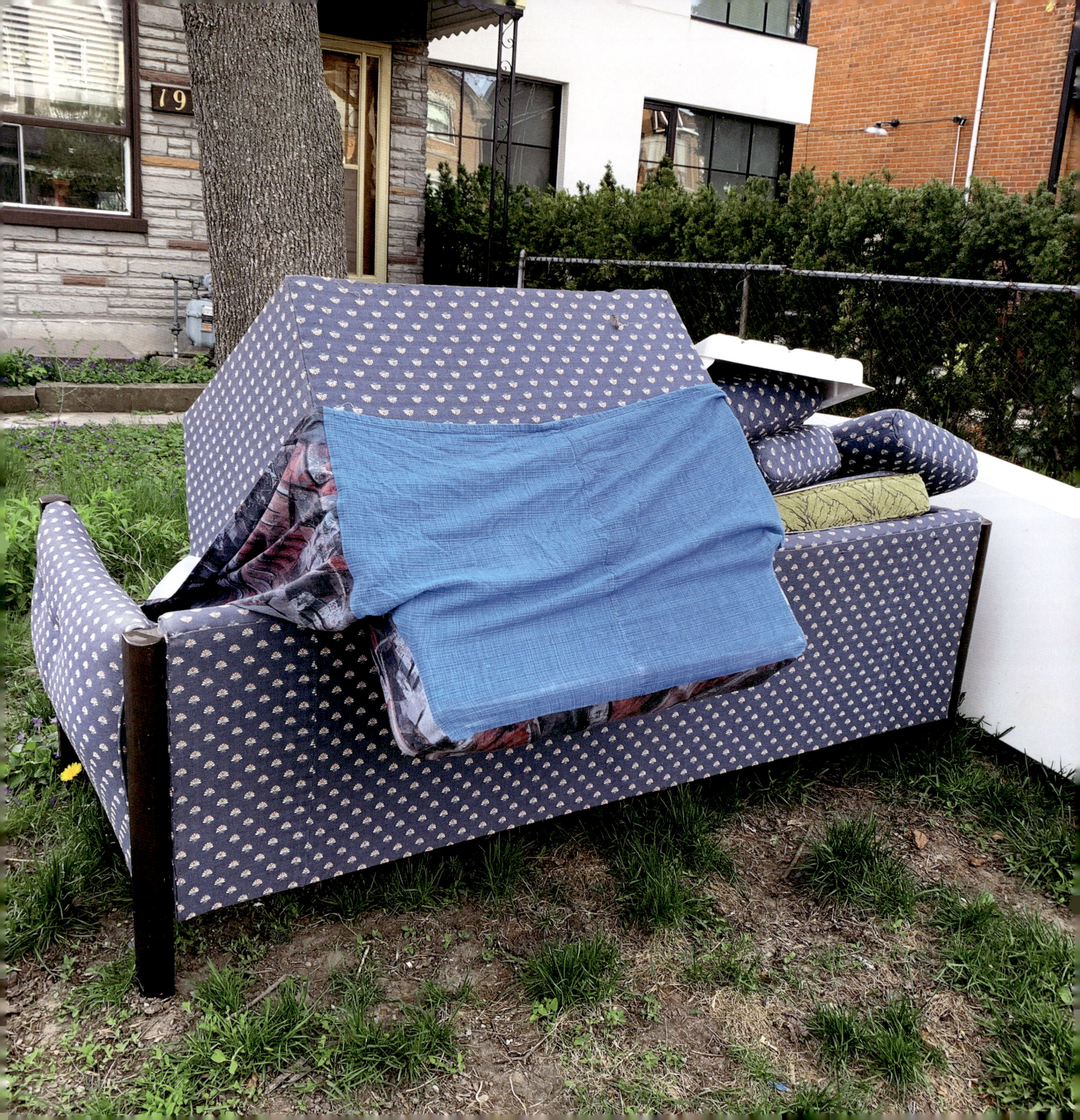

I want to thank the staff at the Art Gallery of Ontario,
all of our generous donors, and the team at the Walla Walla
Foundry. Special thanks as well to Kitty Scott, Garry Oker,
Madeline Oker, Dan Young, Risa Bissenden, Ray Bretzloff,
Brenda Draney, Kelly MacIntosh, Scott Moore, Cameron
Shook, Sean Waterhouse, and Matt Ryle.

—Brian Jungen

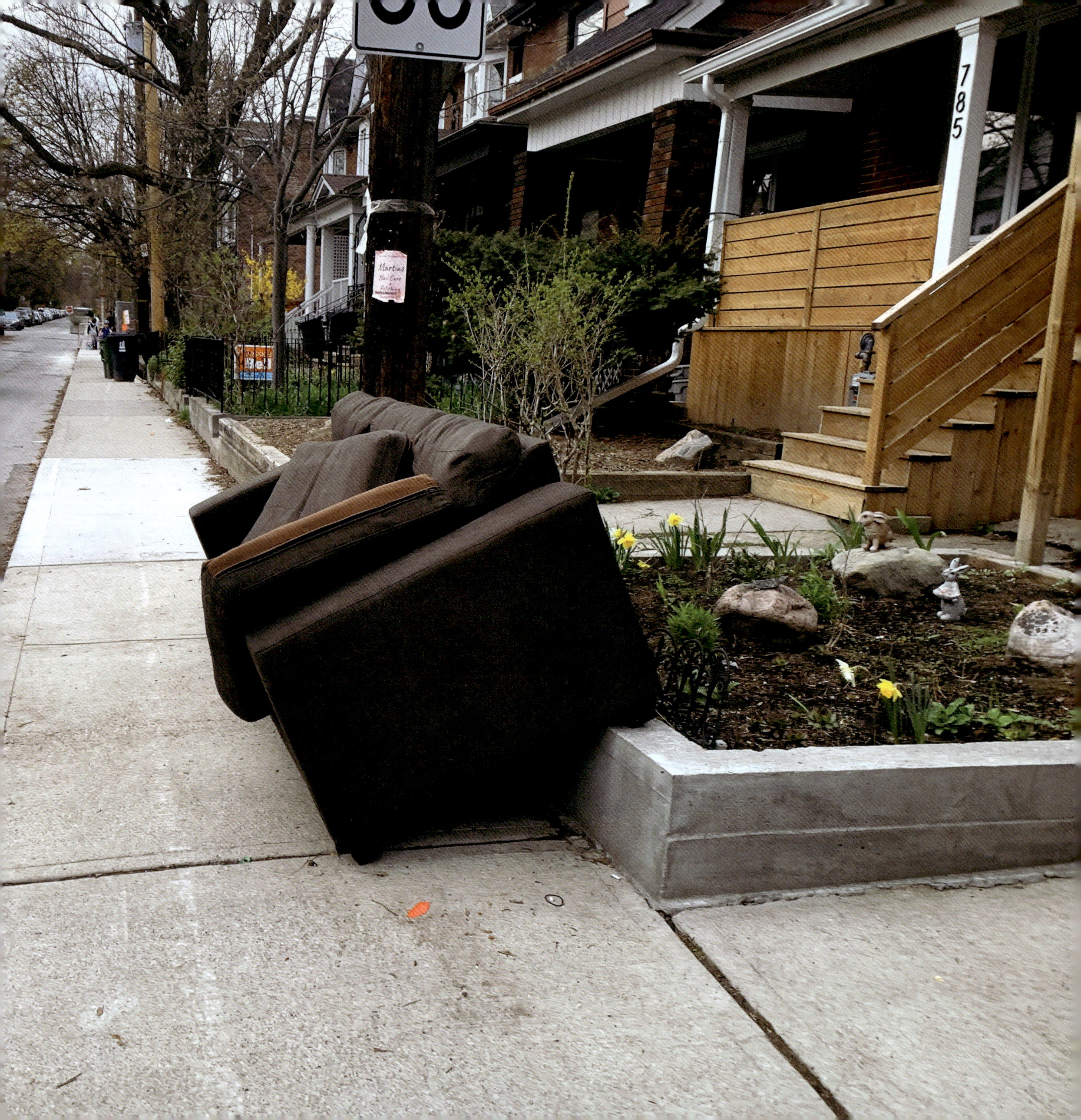

THANK YOU

The Renette and David Berman Family Foundation

Charles Brindamour & Josée Letarte

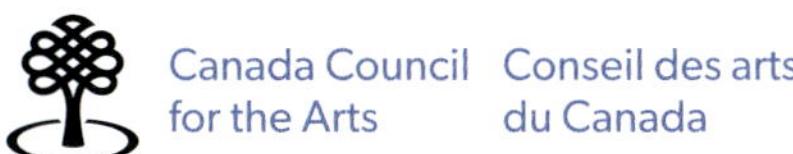

Bob Dorrance & Gail Drummond

Angela & David Feldman

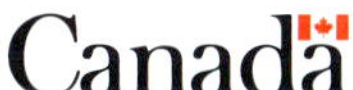

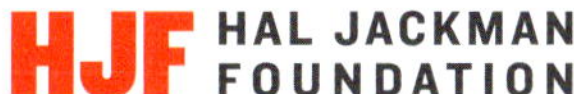

Phil Lind & Ellen Roland

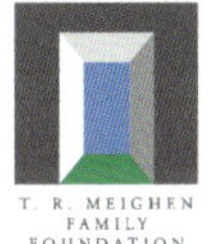

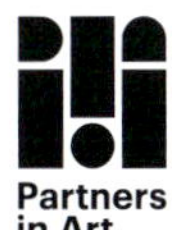

Paul & Jan Sabourin

Anonymous

ADDITIONAL SUPPORT PROVIDED BY

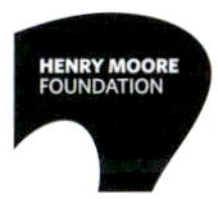

Public talks related to the commission
are presented as part of ArtworxTO.

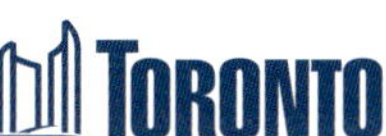

The Art Gallery of Ontario is partially funded by the Ontario Ministry of Culture. Additional operating support is received from the City of Toronto, the Department of Canadian Heritage, and the Canada Council for the Arts. This publication is supported by the Sorel Etrog Publication Fund.

Contemporary programming at the Art Gallery of Ontario is supported by

Canada Council   Conseil des arts
for the Arts   du Canada

Library and Archives Canada Cataloguing in Publication

Title: Brian Jungen : Couch monster : Sadzě? yaaghęhch'ill.
Other titles: Couch monster : Sadzě? yaaghęhch'ill | Sadzě? yaaghęhch'ill
Names: Cox, Julian, writer of added commentary, editor. | Container of (work): Jungen, Brian. Sculptures. Selections. | Art Gallery of Ontario, publisher, host institution.
Description: Text by Julian Cox and Brian Jungen; edited by Julian Cox. | This book is published to mark the unveiling of Brian Jungen's sculpture Couch Monster: Sadzě? yaaghęhch'ill, commissioned by the Art Gallery of Ontario and presented to the public on June 20, 2022.
Identifiers: Canadiana 20220286469 | ISBN 9781636810829 (hardcover)
Subjects: LCSH: Jungen, Brian— Exhibitions. | LCSH: Public sculpture, Canadian—Ontario—Toronto— 21st century—Exhibitions. | LCGFT: Exhibition catalogs.
Classification: LCC NB249.J86 A4 2022 | DDC 730.92—dc23

This book was published to mark the unveiling of Brian Jungen's sculpture *Couch Monster: Sadzě? yaaghęhch'ill*, commissioned by the Art Gallery of Ontario and presented to the public on June 20, 2022.

Published in 2022 by the Art Gallery of Ontario and DelMonico Books • D.A.P.

Copyright © 2022 by Art Gallery of Ontario.

Unless otherwise noted, all photography courtesy of the Art Gallery of Ontario.

Texts © 2022 Art Gallery of Ontario, Brian Jungen

Art Gallery of Ontario
317 Dundas Street West
Toronto, Ontario M5T 1G4
Canada
www.ago.ca

DelMonico Books
available through ARTBOOK | D.A.P.
75 Broad Street, Suite 630
New York, NY 10004
artbook.com
delmonicobooks.com

Every effort has been made to trace ownership of visual and written material used in this catalogue. Errors or omissions will be corrected in subsequent printings provided notification is sent to the publisher.

Printed and bound in Belgium

ISBN: 978-1-63681-082-9
10 9 8 7 6 5 4 3 2 1

Photography Credits
Art Gallery of Ontario: 15, 18, 20 (bottom right), 31, 96, 99–111, 114–119, 121; Brian Jungen Studio: 32, 35–59, 128; Debbie Johnsen: 4, 8; Robyn Lew: 2, 6, 10, 122, 124; Zachary Matchett-Smith: 106, 110; National Gallery of Canada: 23; One Production Place: 64–65, 91–94; The Paul Kaye Collection/Mary Evans Picture Library: 38 (top left); Toronto City Fire Department: 113; Walla Walla Foundry: 26, 60, 66–90, 95; Jason Wyche: 22.

front cover image: Brian Jungen, *Couch Monster: Sadzě? yaaghęhch'ill*, 2022. Bronze, stainless steel, 378.5 × 332.7 × 557.5 cm, 4032.5 kg. Collection of the Art Gallery of Ontario. Commission, with funds from the Government of Canada through the Federal Economic Development Agency for Southern Ontario (FedDev Ontario), Canada Council for the Arts' New Chapter program, The Renette and David Berman Family Foundation, Charles Brindamour & Josée Letarte, Bob Dorrance & Gail Drummond, Angela & David Feldman, Hal Jackman Foundation, Phil Lind & Ellen Roland, T. R. Meighen Family Foundation, Partners in Art, Paul & Jan Sabourin, an anonymous donor, and with funds by exchange from Morey and Jennifer Chaplick, 2022. © Brian Jungen.

back cover and endpaper images: Brian Jungen, *Couch Monster: Sadzě? yaaghęhch'ill* (detail), 2022.

PUBLICATION

ART GALLERY OF ONTARIO

Editor
Julian Cox

Managing Editor
Jim Shedden

Publishing Coordinators
Robyn Lew
Kathryn Yuen

Production and
Content Editors
Nives Hajdin
Sarah Liss

Researchers
Clint Enns
Debbie Johnsen

Designer
Lauren Wickware

Photographers
Paul Ayers
Sean Weaver
One Production Place
Brianna Wray

Pre-Press
Paul Jerinkitsch

Printing
Type A Print Inc.

WALLA WALLA FOUNDRY

President
Jonathan Follett

Project Manager
Matt Ryle

Project Coordinator
Hannah Bartman

BRIAN JUNGEN STUDIO

Studio Manager
Scott Moore

INSTALLATION

Deputy Director
and Chief Curator
Julian Cox

Curators
Kitty Scott
Adelina Vlas

Project Manager
Laura Comerford
Sarah Yaffe

Research Assistant
Yasmin Nurming-Por

Curatorial Coordinator
Debbie Johnsen

Editors
Nives Hajdin
Sarah Liss

Graphic Design
Aleksandra Grzywaczewska

Production
Malene Hjørngaard
Evelyn Quinn

EXHIBITIONS
AND COLLECTIONS

Chief, Exhibitions,
Collections, & Conservation
Jessica Bright

Associate Director,
Exhibitions
Laura Comerford

Registration
Alison Beckett
Cindy Brouse
Jerry Drozdowsky
Joel Herman
Dale Mahar
Sabine Schaefer
Curtis Strilchuk

Collection Information
Alexandra Cousins
Tracy Mallon-Jensen
Liana Radvak
Joe Venturella
Olga Zotova

Conservation
Sherry Phillips
Sjoukje van der Laan
Lisa Ellis
John Williams
Curtis Amisich

LOGISTICS AND
ART SERVICES

Iain Hoadley
Craig Whiteside

EDUCATION
& PROGRAMMING

Richard & Elizabeth Currie
Chief, Education & Programming
Audrey Hudson

Director, Engagement
& Learning
Paola Poletto

Director, Strategic Projects
& Operations
Deborah Nolan

Education & Programming
Danah Abusido
Elizabeth Adams
Lesley Ashton
Madelyne Beckles
Samantha Benjamin
Erica Chan
Maureen DaSilva
Sarah Febbraro
Nathan Huisman
Natalie Lam
Idalette Martins
Kathleen McLean
Zavette Quadros-Evangelista
Annie Roper
Melissa Smith

MEDIA PRODUCTION

Catherine Thomson
Danny Winchester
Matthew Scott

DEVELOPMENT

Chief Development Officer
Kate Halpenny

Philanthropy
Norah Farrell
Jane Hopgood
Andrea Orr
Christie Parker

Donor Relations
Michelle Greenspoon
Aneesa Guerra-Khan
Matt Semansky

Programming & Events
David Yu

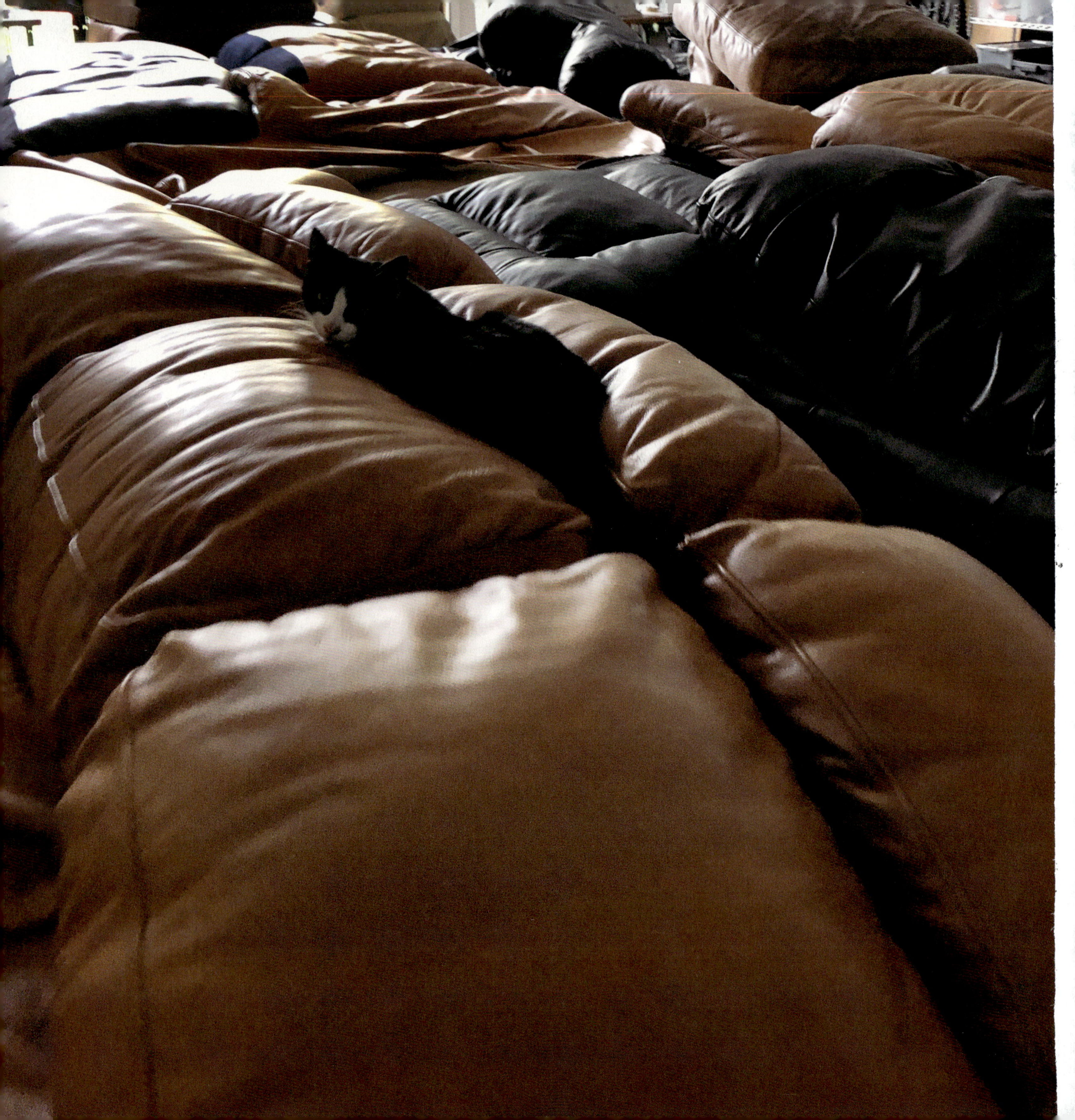

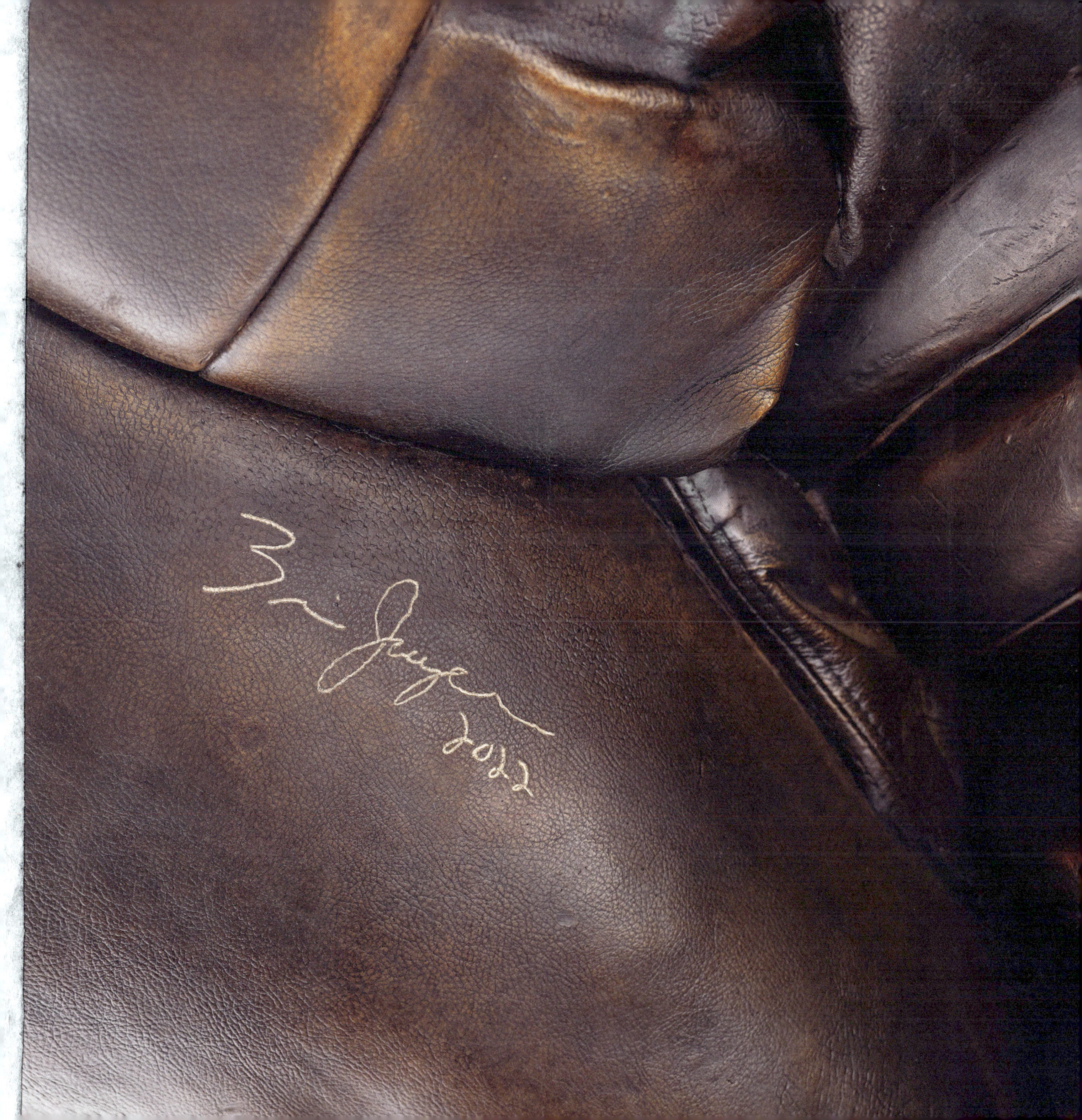

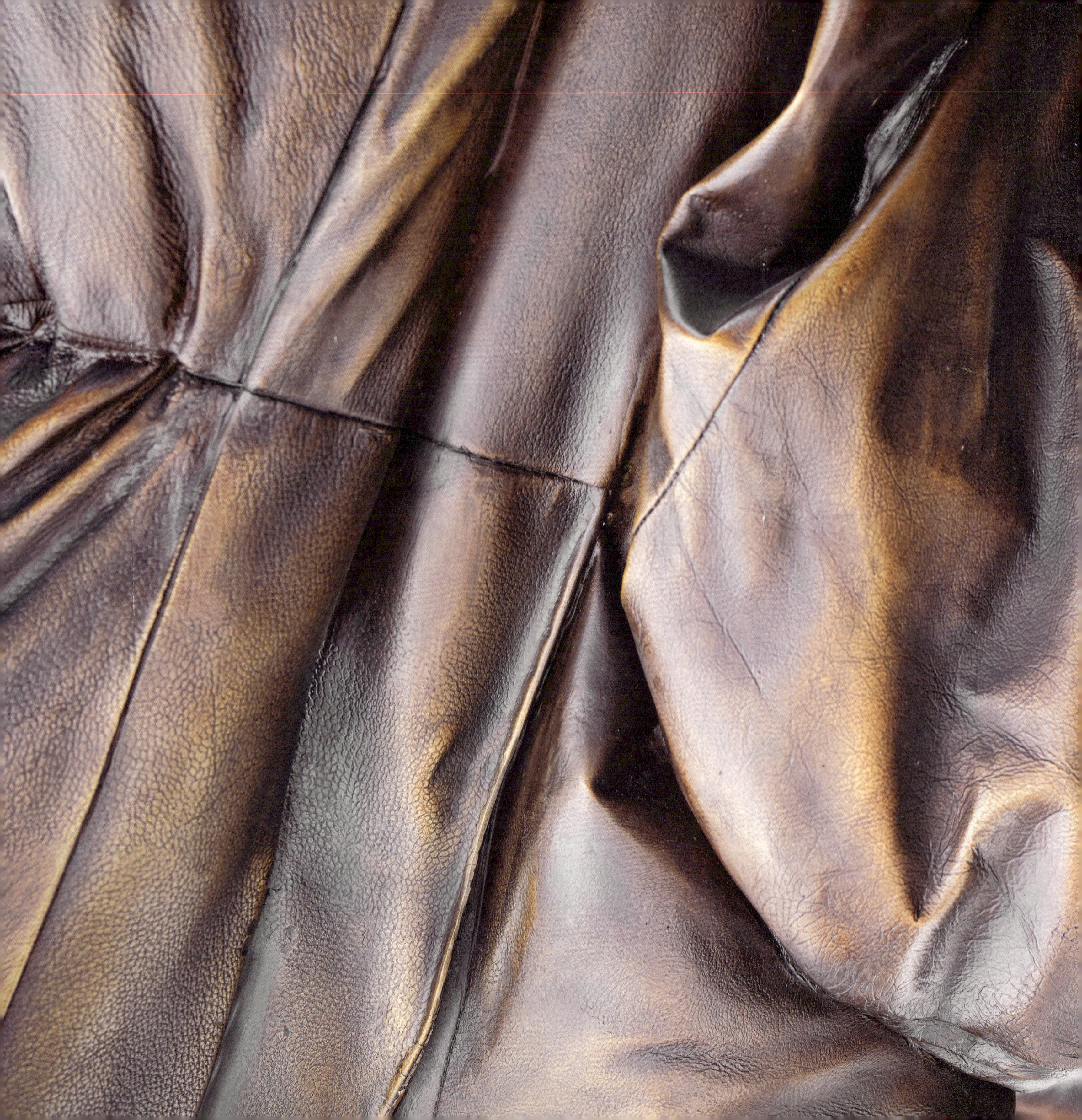